THE SEA

Photographs by

D.P. Wilson
Peter Stackpole
Kurt Severin
Douglas Faulkner
Ron Church
Steve McCutcheon
Ray Atkeson
Al Giddings
Keith Gillett
and others

Color map by Ken Thompson

A CHANTICLEER PRESS EDITION

THE SEA

The Random House Illustrated Science Library

by Robert C. Miller

Photographs by

D. P. Wilson
Peter Stackpole
Kurt Severin
Douglas Faulkner
Ron Church
Steve McCutcheon
Roy Atkeson
Al Giddings
Keith Gillett
and others

Color map by Ken Thompson

A Chanticleer Press Edition

Random House, New York

To the Memory of
THOMAS GORDON THOMPSON
Distinguished Oceanographer
Good Companion and Esteemed Friend
With Whom I Have Sailed on Many Seas
In Calm and Storm

Preface to the Second Edition

Recent advances in sea research, including a change of thrust concerning the Mohole project, an increasing acceptance of the Wegener hypothesis of continental drift, and the revolutionary development of plate tectonics made me welcome the opportunity to make revisions in the original text.

All the evidence suggests that oceanography will continue to be an exciting subject in the years to come—as exciting as the sea itself. We are only on the threshold of discovery.

Robert C. Miller
January, 1975

Contents

Introduction:
The Call of the Sea

Man is a creature of the land who finds within himself an irresistible urge toward the sea.

The reasons for this are perhaps beyond all finding out. It would be easy to say that it is an atavistic urge, an inner remembering. For we know almost beyond a doubt that man is descended from a long line of marine organisms, and that the greater part of his evolution, up to and including development of the vertebrate form, took place within the sea. And it is a simple fact of body chemistry that man carries salt water in his veins.

Even so, it has not been and never can be proved that man's turning toward the sea is an innate recollection of his ancestral home. Perhaps it is merely the universal human urge to know, to explore, to pit one's ingenuity against a difficult and often hostile environment. Suffice it to say that man has conducted himself throughout recorded history as though he regarded the ocean as his proper sphere, to which he must go back at every opportunity and at whatever cost.

Man's love of the sea is an unrequited love. However he may personalize the sea, however he may apostrophize it in poetry or prose, it does not love him in return. Always beautiful, whether serene or raging in the wildest tempest, the sea is ruthless, implacable, indifferent to man. She is an inconstant mistress, and he loves her at his peril.

Yet there is a call to the sea that will not be denied. It is recorded in the earliest poetry. Nearly three thousand years ago the long voyage of Odysseus amid unknown dangers on uncharted seas, and his safe return home, were the subject of Homeric ballads. Likewise David the Psalmist, who was quite possibly a contemporary of Homer, wrote: "They who go down to the sea in ships—they who do business in great waters—they behold the works of the Lord and his wonders on the deep." Anyone who has ever helped to man a small ship such as a fishing boat, sailing yacht, schooner in inter-island trade, so-called tramp steamer, or even oceanographic vessel knows what it is to be cold and wet for days and nights on end, to sleep fitfully in wet clothing in a wet bunk, to eat what food he can find while standing in a galley holding on to any convenient support, to hear the relentless pounding of the sea against creaking timbers that afford uncertain protection from disaster, to be pressed to the limit of human endurance. And if and when he gets to shore, does he kiss the good earth and vow never to go to sea again? He does not. Whether skipper, fisherman, seaman, or scientist, he is ready the next day for the next voyage.

It is man's indomitable love of the sea that has led him to explore its farthest reaches, to discover every continent and every island; to study the winds and currents; to probe the depths over which he sailed, and to devise ways to study the curious creatures that inhabit them. Thus was born the science of oceanography.

Yet oceanography as a special field of scientific inquiry is little more than a century old. Edward Forbes, who died in 1854, and Matthew Fontaine Maury, who died in 1873, have each been called "the founder of oceanography." Forbes was a British biologist who studied starfish, mollusks, and other marine animals, and who did some dredging in the ocean at very moderate depths. Maury was a United States naval officer who devoted himself to the study of currents, tides, and wind systems, and to charting the oceans for the information of mariners. Forbes might be called a biological oceanographer, and Maury a hydrographer or a physical oceanographer. Each gave a strong stimulus to further studies. But no man can be called the founder of oceanography. It is a many-faceted science to which contributions have been made by a multitude of workers.

The first major expedition that attempted to investigate the oceans on a world-wide scale was the *Challenger* expedition in the years 1872 to 1876. This was a British expedition under the command of Sir Wyville Thomson, a Scottish biologist who unfortunately died a few years after the conclusion of the voyage. The work of organizing and supervising the publication of fifty quarto volumes of the scientific results fell to his assistant, Sir John Murray, who carried out this long and arduous assignment with such diligence and success that he came to be regarded throughout the world as the grand old man of oceanography.

It appears to have been Murray who introduced the word oceanography as a comprehensive term for the science of the sea. Purists attacked it as being a "hybrid" derived partly from Latin, partly from Greek, and they wanted to substitute "thalassography," derived entirely from the Greek. Murray defended his word, pointing out that *thalassa* meant to the Greeks an inland sea like the Mediterranean, not the open ocean. Since the *Challenger* expedition, almost every advanced maritime nation has become involved in oceanographic research, and there has been a large and growing measure of international cooperation; the job is too large for any one nation to do alone.

International congresses of oceanographers have been held at frequent intervals, the first one at Stockholm in 1899. The International Council for the Study of the Sea, with headquarters in Copenhagen, was established in 1902 to serve as a clearing house of oceanographic information. More recently the International Geophysical Year was a magnificent example of the international cooperation that can be achieved. From July 1, 1957, to December 31, 1958, coordinated studies in all phases of the sciences relating to the earth, the oceans, and the atmosphere were carried on simultaneously all over the world.

Such large-scale international cooperation is still continuing—in Antarctica and in the long-range program for investigation of the Indian Ocean begun in 1961. The latter project has involved a fleet of forty research ships from thirteen nations. One of the least-studied oceanic areas of the world may soon become one of the most thoroughly known.

Thus we progress toward ever-increasing knowledge of man's last frontier on earth—the ocean that covers so great a portion of it.

1

Origin of Earth and Sea

However great his interest in the sea, and however compelling his desire to sail upon and to explore it, man is, and has been through the last one hundred million years of his evolution, a land-based creature. It is on land that he fabricates his ships, from land that he puts out to sea, and to land that he must return.

This gives him an exaggerated idea of the importance of the land. It comes to him with a start to learn that seven-tenths of the world is under water. (A recent calculation is 70.8 per cent, but absolute accuracy is obviously impossible.) Considerably less than a third of the surface of the earth is above sea level; and of this—when we consider high mountains, burning deserts, and frozen polar regions—not all is available for human habitation. These continents, which seemed so vast to early travelers and which are still impressive even when we are whisked across them in jet planes half into the stratosphere, are hardly more than modest islands in a great world ocean.

The immense Johns Hopkins Glacier, augmented by several tributary glaciers, enters the sea at Glacier Bay, Alaska.
(William Bacon)

Their distribution is, moreover, curiously uneven, and no one is quite sure how it came about. A glance at a globe or any map of the world shows immediately that the greater part of the land is in the Northern Hemisphere. When we compare the polar regions, we find that the north polar area is occupied by the Arctic Ocean, while the south polar area is occupied by the Antarctic Continent. Notwithstanding this odd antipodal imbalance of a southern polar continent and a northern polar sea, we still find that about two-thirds of the land area of the world (38.8 million out of a total of 57.5 million square miles) is north of the equator.

There is still a further inequality in the distribution of land and water when we consider the Pacific area. If we take a globe and turn it until we are looking as nearly as possible at the middle of the Pacific Ocean, we find that we are gazing at almost an entire hemisphere of water. We can see just the edges of North America, South America, Asia, and Australia making a thin border, which we call, for both geographical and geopolitical purposes, the Pacific rim. The Pacific, widest and deepest of the oceans, constitutes about three-sevenths of the oceanic area of the world, and is itself a little more extensive than all of the land areas combined.

Some have asked such questions as why there is more sea than land, why there is a continent at the South Pole and a sea at the North Pole, and why most of the land is in the Northern Hemisphere. These are questions

A hundred-foot ice cliff near Wilkes Station, Antarctica. The Antarctic continental ice is mostly a mile or more in thickness, and contains by far the greater part of all the glacial ice on earth.
(J. R. T. Molholm)

which oceanographers and geophysicists are constantly trying to answer.

The circumference of the earth at the equator is about 25,000 miles. This figure was arrived at by the Greek philosopher and mathematician Eratosthenes around 300 B.C. This knowledge was forgotten for a long time, and Columbus' belief that he had discovered the Indies was based on the assumption of a considerably smaller earth. But the calculations of Eratosthenes have been borne out, and if the earth is 25,000 miles in circumference, it is about 7,900 miles in diameter. The greatest vertical distance on earth, from the top of Mt. Everest to the bottom of the Mindanao Deep, is around thirteen miles. Thus an eight-inch globe would, if molded in true relief, have a surface inequality of less than 13/1000 of an inch. As someone has said, if the earth were reduced to the size of a billiard ball, it would be as smooth as a billiard ball.

It might seem plausible to account for the distribution of continents as merely a matter of chance. Nevertheless, these minuscule surface irregularities are not randomly distributed; and to man, moving about on this planet like an ant on a carpet, the difference between a high mountain and an ocean deep is impressive. He seeks an explanation.

THIS PLASTIC EARTH

What Shakespeare called "this goodly frame, the earth," is in fact quite insubstantial. It is rocked by earthquakes, blown up by volcanoes, inundated

An elevated wave-cut beach in Antarctica, carved out at a time when sea level was higher in relation to the land. (J. R. T. Molholm)

by tidal waves, ground by glaciers, swept by hurricanes and floods. Parts of its surface are rising and parts are sinking, and this is further complicated by changes in sea level over periods of time. Immense amounts of water are tied up in the icecaps; if, through some relatively minor change in climate, these icecaps should increase in area and volume, water would be withdrawn from the oceans, and presently thriving harbors might be left high and dry. On the other hand, if the icecaps should melt, the sea level would rise, seaports would be inundated, fertile valleys go under water and their inhabitants have to flee to the highlands.

Fortunately, changes in sea level generally take place over a long period of time, and man is able to adjust to them without serious inconvenience. But the relation between polar icecaps and sea level must be kept in mind, particularly since man has in recent decades begun to think increasingly of means of modifying weather and climate. It has been proposed, for example, that the climate of regions bordering the Arctic Ocean could be improved and even rendered temperate by building a dam across Bering Strait, then pumping a large amount of cold water from the Arctic Ocean into the North Pacific, whereupon warmer water flowing from the North Atlantic into the Arctic would melt the polar ice. However, it has been calculated that the amount of power required to move the necessary amount of water would exceed the entire power output of the United States.

Quite apart from the feasibility of the project, we must realize that improvement of the climate of northern Canada, Alaska, and Siberia might well cause devastation in other parts of the world. Further, we are not even

13

certain that warming the Arctic Ocean would really improve the climate of the adjacent lands. It would increase the rainfall, which in that latitude would be snowfall, and might precipitate the recurrence of a glacial period.

There is evidence that during the Pleistocene—the geological period of about one million years that immediately preceded our own and gradually merged with it some ten thousand years ago—the sea level fell and rose with glacial and interglacial periods over a range of four hundred feet. The Pleistocene is often erroneously referred to as "the ice age"; it was, in fact, a succession of "ice ages," with periods in between when the ice receded. This did not necessarily involve any marked change in solar radiation or other major factors in our world climate. Where glaciers occur today, we find them sometimes advancing and sometimes receding, depending on whether the ice melts faster in summer than it forms in winter. A change of average temperature of no more than two or three degrees, persisting over a sufficient period of years, could thrust us into another glacial period.

When the glaciers were most extensive, reaching in North America well south of the Great Lakes and covering the northern part of Europe and Asia, sea level was lowered by as much as three hundred feet, and a land bridge a thousand miles wide connected Siberia with Alaska. It was a cold, barren, treeless area, much like the Arctic tundra of today; but people and animals could and undoubtedly did migrate across it. This is the most likely route by which America became inhabited by peoples from Asia, who are today's American Indians and Eskimos.

When the glaciers receded, as occurred from time to time, the sea level rose and the land bridge became narrower or was even covered with water. During that part of the Pleistocene when glacial ice almost disappeared, the sea level was one hundred feet above our present shores. With renewed extension of the glaciers, the water receded and the land bridge again appeared. It was finally broken by the melting of glaciers and increased sea level some ten or eleven thousand years ago, leaving between Siberia and Alaska the shallow Bering and Chuckchi seas and the narrow Bering Strait.

These changes in sea level were of course world-wide, although they have been most carefully studied in Alaska because of the interest in a relatively recent land bridge between Asia and America. It is instructive to consider that a lowering of sea level of three hundred feet would leave San Francisco Bay almost completely dry, whereas a rise of one hundred feet would transform the bay into a large inland sea, covering much of California's populous Central Valley. On a world scale, a lowering of sea level of three hundred feet would increase the land surface of the earth by at least five per cent. It would bring Great Britain and Ireland into contact, and make both into part of the European continent, together with a considerable section of the bottom of the North Sea. On the other hand, a rise of one hundred feet would flood large areas of northern Europe, inundate the valleys of the Mississippi, the Amazon, the Nile, the Euphrates, the Indus, and the Ganges, and submerge the flood-plains of China.

However impressive may be the changes of land and sea effected by alternate freezing and thawing of the ice, these are relatively minor compared with the changes in the earth's surface that have occurred in geologic time through processes collectively known as diastrophism.

A Coast Guard ice-breaker clears ice from the paths of cargo ships in Exeter Bay, Arctic American Coast. (U. S. Coast Guard Photo)

ORIGIN OF THE EARTH AND THE OCEANS

How the earth originated is not known, and there is less agreement on the subject now than there was a hundred or even fifty years ago, when the nebular hypothesis of Laplace was in good standing. This assumed a vast gaseous nebula extending far beyond the limits of the present solar system, which gradually condensed to form our present sun, dropping bands of matter here and there along the way, which in turn condensed to form the planets. The nebular hypothesis gained wide acceptance because there are entities in space, like the great nebula in Andromeda, which look like early stages of this process going on in another part of the universe. But there are mathematical objections to this theory, and such astrophysical objections as that the earth and the sun do not seem to be made of exactly the same stuff.

Early in the twentieth century Professors Thomas C. Chamberlin and Forest Ray Moulton advanced the "planetesimal" hypothesis. They surmised that some passing celestial body exerted sufficient gravitational pull on the sun to cause a solar upheaval, resulting in the throwing off into space of streamers and blobs of solar material, which condensed into a great number of small bodies, called planetesimals, rotating around the sun. Some of these were close enough to each other so that they aggregated, by mutual gravitational attraction, to form planets. Others were left rotating about the sun as asteroids or planetoids, of which nearly a thousand have been discovered by astronomers. This theory is attractive because it explains both planets and planetoids. It is also true to the extent that it assumes that the earth grows by accretion. Through the impact of meteorites it is currently gaining weight at an average rate of perhaps eight or ten tons a day—a very small amount compared with the size of the earth, but fairly substantial over a few millions of years. Moreover, there is evidence of immense meteorites having crashed into the earth from time to time. The famous Meteor Crater in Arizona, believed to have originated from the impact of a giant meteorite, is four thousand feet in diameter and 570 feet deep.

In the late 1920s, James Jeans and Harold Jeffreys modified the planetesimal hypothesis; still assuming that some passing star had pulled streamers off the sun, they believed that these masses of solar material were gaseous and that they condensed to form the planets. Most recently R. A. Lyttleton and Fred Hoyle have advanced the hypothesis that the sun is the surviving member of a pair of twin stars, of which many examples are known throughout the universe. If we assume that the other member of the pair exploded, becoming a "supernova," the debris resulting from its dissolution could have provided the material for the formation of the planets.

The first three of these theories suffer from the disadvantage that the composition of the earth is not identical with that of the sun as known from spectrographic studies. The theory of Lyttleton and Hoyle solves this difficulty by deriving the planets from a different source.

Whatever the origin of the earth, it is now rather commonly assumed to have come into existence some five billion years ago, most likely as a white-hot, molten mass in orbit around the sun. For purely physical reasons it assumed a form approximately but not quite spherical: by reason of the speed of its rotation it bulges a little at the equator and is slightly flattened at the poles, and is thus an oblate spheroid. The earth's diameter at the equator is about twenty-seven miles greater than its diameter from pole to pole.

According to a theory propounded by the late Sir George Darwin, distinguished mathematician and tidal theorist, before the earth became completely congealed the moon was pulled out of it by the gravitational force of the sun. The earth still has solar tides, and when it was molten or only slightly crusted over, these tides could have considerably modified its shape. Some great solar tide, so the theory goes, pulled a big blob of the young earth out into space. Because it shared the earth's rotation, it struck off on a bias and so went into orbit instead of either flying off into space or falling back again to earth.

The moon's diameter is about one-fourth that of the earth, and if it tore away from the earth it must have left a considerable hole. The spinning of the still-malleable earth would quickly restore it to its normal shape, but if it remained just the least bit flattened on the side from which the moon took off, this could account for the origin of the Pacific basin. Proponents

1. Wave erosion of shores, such as this at Victoria, Australia, often leaves towering masses of harder material known as stacks. (Vincent Serventy)

16

2. Left: Icebergs, masses of floating ice detached from glaciers that reach the sea, are a menace to navigation since roughly nine-tenths of their bulk is below sea level. (Sven Gillsäter)

3. Lower left: A churning surf pounds a rocky promontory at Cape Kiwanda on the Oregon coast. (Ray Atkeson)

4. Right: Reid Glacier at Glacier Bay, Alaska, demonstrates the force of moving ice in molding landscapes. (Steve McCutcheon)

of the theory point out that it would explain the known thinness of the earth's crust beneath the Pacific Ocean, and why most of the land is on one side of the earth and most of the water on the other. There is also the fact that the density of the moon is believed to be about the same as that of the rock beneath the earth's crust in the layer known as the mantle. Opponents of this theory argue that the surface of the earth has undergone so many changes in the last three billion years or so that any dent left by the moon would have been completely obliterated. It is also argued that derivation of the moon from a large solar tide on earth is mathematically impossible. The same objection has been offered to every one of the several other theories of the moon's origin. One of the more interesting subjects to be studied by astronauts on the moon is whether it is made of the same stuff as the earth.

The origin of the oceans is almost as problematical as the origin of the earth itself. An earlier view, long held and still not completely discredited, is that the molten earth was once surrounded by a vast cloud of steam. All or most of the water in the world was suspended in air in the form of water vapor. As the earth gradually cooled, this vapor would, it was thought, precipitate as rain. At first, striking a still-warm earth, it would vaporize rapidly and return to the atmosphere. But as the earth continued to cool, it would remain longer in catch basins on the earth's surface, until at last the oceans and the lakes were filled and water vapor would return to the atmosphere only through evaporation by the sun, as it does today.

A more recent suggestion is that water was one of the original chemical compounds of the nascent earth and that it has gradually worked its way to the surface and is continuing to do so. According to this theory the ocean will gradually increase in volume until, in a few thousand million years, it will cover the whole earth. Since the time factor is large, there is nothing to be alarmed about: by the time the earth is completely inundated, man may have become even more versatile than porpoises.

Another problem is how the sea got its salt. The general assumption has been that the ocean was originally a large fresh-water lake, which has become increasingly saline through aeons of time. All rivers carry a small amount of salt, and one of the assumptions has been that the aggregation of all these small contributions has resulted in the saltness of the sea. We know, for example, that the Dead Sea and Great Salt Lake have resulted from everything going in and nothing except water vapor going out. Thus we lean toward the assumption that the saltness of the sea is the result of the gradual accumulation of salts brought in by the rivers. There is even a well-known zoological theory that assumes that the time when various groups of vertebrates emerged from the sea can be deduced from the salt content of their blood.

Some years ago a Dublin scientist, Professor John Joly, attempted to calculate the age of the ocean from the time required for it to reach its present salinity as a consequence of the annual increment of salt from streams flowing in. He came up with a figure of 97,600,000 years—a span so far short of other estimates as to suggest that there is something seriously wrong with the basic premise. Current estimates of the age of the ocean, based on rate of decay of radioactive elements and other data, are about three and one-half to four billion years.

The question is, why did Joly come out with a figure so far short of reality?

5. Mount Pelmo, a 10,000-foot peak in the Italian Dolomites, is limestone made up of marine sediments from the Triassic age. (Werner Friedli)

One answer is that the salinity of the ocean does not increase at a calculable rate; the rate fluctuates, and the total salt content probably decreases from time to time. The end of a glacial period would flood the ocean with melting ice and undoubtedly decrease salinity all over the world. Moreover, at various times, large areas of shallow seas have become landlocked and have finally evaporated, removing from the ocean itself substantial quantities of salt. Important deposits of salt are found on most continents, and most of them are mined for commercial purposes. Some of these deposits, like the one near Moab, Utah, are as much as four thousand feet thick. All of the salt in these deposits has come from the sea, and it is a reasonable assumption that their removal lowered the salt content of the ocean.

In 1942 an engineer, Charles Henry White, advanced the interesting hypothesis that in the cooling of a molten earth the silicates, which have a higher melting point than the chlorides, would solidify first; this would leave the salt on the surface, and as further cooling permitted water to condense, the salt would be dissolved in the water. Thus the sea might have been salty from its beginning. Certainly we must abandon the idea that an originally fresh sea has become steadily more saline, from salts carried into it by rivers. It now appears that salinity, along with sea level, has gone up and down with the accumulation and melting of ice and has also been affected by the removal of immense quantities of salt by the evaporation of ancient seas and by the addition of salts carried by the rivers.

CONTINENTAL DRIFT AND OTHER THEORIES

In 1912 an ingenious German geologist, Alfred Wegener, advanced an idea that has come to be known as the hypothesis of continental displacement or more popularly as "continental drift." This hypothesis can best be understood by looking at a map and noting how well the continents fit each other like the pieces of a jigsaw puzzle. The big bulge on the east coast of South America fits into the deep embayment on the west coast of Africa. If North America were pushed over toward Europe, the wedge of Greenland would pretty well fill any remaining space between. The tip of South America would extend a considerable distance to the south of Africa, leaving a space which Wegener filled in by pushing Antarctica and Australia up against South America and Africa, although here the fit is not quite so good and the picture not quite so convincing.

In other words, Wegener assumed that all of the continents were once part of a single land mass, which broke up into irregular pieces that gradually drifted apart, giving us the distribution we find today. He also assumed that a good deal of this shifting has taken place in the last sixty million years (during and since the Eocene), which is a very short period, geologically speaking, for events of such magnitude.

Wegener's ideas won little acceptance among geologists, but were eagerly espoused by zoogeographers, who were trying to explain why opossums occur in such disparate areas as North and South America and Australia, and why monkeys occur in South America, far removed from their centers of distribution, Africa and Asia. Wegener's theory solved many such problems of animal distribution, but it posed others. If opossums went from

Robeson Channel, separating Greenland (upper right) from Ellesmere Island (foreground), marks the Wegener fault, named for a German geophysicist who, half-a-century ago, predicted its existence in his theory of continental drift. (Dept. of Mines and Technical Surveys, Canada)

Australia to America, why not kangaroos or wombats? Also, if Australia was connected with the rest of the world in the Eocene period, why doesn't it have any mammals besides very primitive edentates, such as the duckbill and the spiny anteater, and the marsupials?

Nevertheless, the Wegener hypothesis is, with some modifications, in considerably better standing among geologists today than it was half a century ago. Significantly, the idea of continental drift is much more widely accepted by scientists in the Southern Hemisphere than in the Northern, mainly because the problems of animal and plant distribution are more troublesome south of the equator than they are in the north.

In the Northern Hemisphere, as we have already seen, a land bridge a thousand miles wide between Asia and North America undoubtedly existed during the Pleistocene period. Over this bridge, geologists, paleontologists, and anthropologists can, in their theories, get people and animals and plants from one continent to the other. In the Southern Hemisphere the water is deeper and the traveling is harder. But there is a possible land bridge across which animals may have moved.

Geologists have for many years postulated a great equatorial continent, now submerged, which they have called Gondwana. This is supposed to have included a good part of South America and most of the continent of Africa during the period from the Devonian to the Eocene, nearly 300 million years. It is presumed to have included Australia and part of India during Cretaceous time. This great equatorial continent is considered to have been separated from the northern continental areas by an ancient sea called Tethys, of which the Mediterranean is a small surviving remnant. To give some idea of the changes assumed to have taken place, a portion of the bottom of Tethys, with its long-accumulated marine sediments, is now presumed to be the summit of the Himalayas, where marine sediments and fossils of the Cretaceous period have been found as high as nineteen thousand feet; there may even be higher deposits buried in perpetual snow.

An old and still widely accepted theory is that the continents and the ocean basins have occupied approximately their present locations since the earth was formed. On all of the continents there are limited areas of very ancient rocks, known as "shields" or "shield lands," which seem to have persisted there since Archean time. Some geologists believe they have always been above water, but it is doubtful that any square foot of the earth's surface has not at some time been beneath the sea. The shield lands, however, were never submerged long enough to have sedimentary rocks laid down on top of them. Among such areas are the Canadian shield in the vicinity of Hudson Bay, the Baltic shield in northern Europe, the Siberian shield in eastern Asia, and similar areas in South America, Africa, and Australia. Many geologists think that these are the original continental areas, and that the margins of the continents have been elevated or submerged around them.

In the present state of knowledge, it is not possible to say which theory is correct. In 1933 a well-known geologist expressed the opinion that not more than two per cent of the geologists of the world accepted the Wegener hypothesis; in 1963 a geologist of equal stature estimated that geologists were about equally divided between those believing in the relative permanence of the continental nuclei and those favoring the idea of continental displacement.

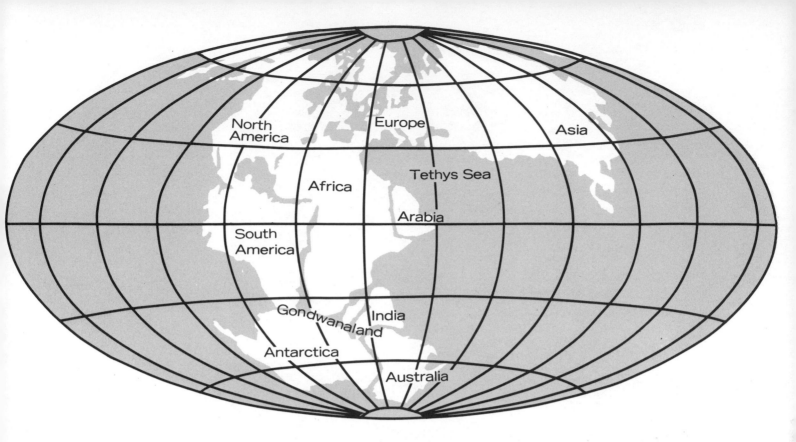

North America
Europe
Asia
Africa
Tethys Sea
Arabia
South America
Gondwanaland
India
Antarctica
Australia

If a single super-continent existed some 150 million years ago, the distribution of land and water might have been much like this. (Adapted from Scientific American)

The debate has been complicated in recent years by new concepts. One of these has grown out of the study of what is termed paleomagnetism. Certain rocks, especially those containing iron, become magnetized by the earth's magnetic field and may retain this property, including positive and negative poles, for long periods, even many millions of years. This directional magnetization of rocks of different geologic age may vary considerably, which has led to the assumption of a shift in the position of the earth's magnetic poles. This is actually an old hypothesis based on the fossil records indicating that areas that are now temperate or even frigid were tropical in earlier geological time; for example, there are extensive coal beds in Antarctica which could have been produced only under much warmer conditions. The shift in position of the earth's poles would provide a convenient explanation. It is only recently, however, that studies of paleomagnetism have produced evidence in favor of polar wandering and thus have given some support to Wegener's assumption of wandering continents.

Another recent idea that has bearing on the Wegener hypothesis is the assumption of an expanding earth. This is vaguely related to the idea of an expanding universe, which is an outgrowth of Einstein's theory of relativity. If the earth was one-half its present diameter three or four billion years ago, it may have been entirely covered by the areas we now call continents. As the earth expanded, its surface would break apart and the areas between the fragments would become the oceans. Mathematical models have been made to show that if the earth were reduced to half its present diameter the continents would form a practically complete skin. An expansion to present size would, if spread over four billion years, amount to less than one millimeter a year, an amount that would be too small to measure. It can at least be said in favor of this hypothesis that it is very difficult to disprove!

Any discussion of these topics among geologists is guaranteed to provide vigorous controversy and extremely divergent points of view—which shows how little we know for certain about the history of our earth.

A stratified rock of marine origin at Starved Rock, Illinois, deep in the Middle West. (Rutherford Platt)

ARE THERE LOST CONTINENTS?

It is easy to tell from marine fossils and from sedimentary rocks of marine origin that vast areas of dry land were once at the bottom of the ocean. It is therefore natural to assume that much of the present sea bottom was once dry land, but this is not easy to prove. Deep borings now being made in the sea bottom may provide important evidence on this question.

If the continent of Gondwana—a vast land mass including South America, Africa and Australia—ever existed, a great portion of it is now evidently under water. A few geologists and oceanographers have assumed a large Pacific continent of which the East Pacific Rise and various Pacific islands represent the last remnants. Madagascar is commonly considered to be part of a former continental area that has been named Lemuria, which connected with and included India south of the Himalayas, these mountains being at that time at the bottom of the sea. If all of the land masses postulated by geologists as having existed in earlier periods—let us say the Devonian, about 300 million years ago—really had existed, it would be hard to find any room for the ocean!

Of all the supposed lost continents the most famous is Atlantis, celebrated in myth as a land that was somewhere to the west of the Strait of Gibraltar and was submerged beneath the sea in relatively recent times. Plato

The sedimentary rocks in this tidal estuary on the coast of Norway have been sculptured by wave action and perhaps by glacial ice. (Toni Schneiders)

26

described it as having been a site of a powerful kingdom some nine thousand years before his own time, but having finally sunk beneath the waves, leaving only a shoal to mark the scene of its former grandeur. Plato attributes the information to Egyptian priests of an earlier generation, and it is hard to tell whether he regarded it as fact or legend. But his mention of it kept the story alive and gave it credit.

It is difficult to believe that any reliable oral record of actual events could have been handed down from generation to generation over a period of several thousand years. But there is scientific reason to believe that portions of the Mid-Atlantic Ridge, now completely submerged, may have been above water during Pleistocene time. One Swedish geologist thinks the final submergence may have occurred since the Pleistocene, which if true would lend substance to the Atlantis legend; this view is, however, not widely accepted. But a very important piece of pertinent evidence was brought to light when the Swedish Deep-Sea Expedition of 1947–1948 took numerous core samples of the Atlantic sea bottom. These were studied by R. W. Kolbe, an expert on diatoms, microscopic plants that have skeletons of silica that will last for millions of years. Some species of diatoms live in fresh water and some in the sea; a fresh-water diatom would immediately die in sea water, and sea diatoms could not live in fresh water. Astonishingly, Dr. Kolbe found many fresh-water diatoms in these deep-sea deposits.

He theorized that they might have been deposited there by rivers flowing into the sea, or been blown out to sea by winds, since they are very small and light. But in one sample, taken 930 miles off the west coast of Africa, he found a layer made up completely of fresh-water diatoms. Being a careful scientist, he records that in this layer he also found "a single fragment of a marine species," and cautiously observes that "this layer gave the impression of belonging to a fresh-water sediment."

A fossil fish *(Acrognathus dodgei)* of the Cretaceous period found on Mount Lebanon, Syria. (Courtesy of the American Museum of Natural History)

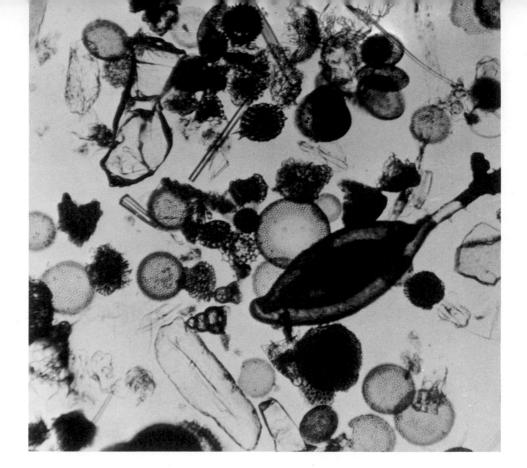

Microscopic fossils of Miocene age (magnified about 105 times), from undersea drilling off Guadalupe Island, Mexico, 340 feet below sea bottom in water more than two miles deep. The largest dark object is a foraminiferan; the circular porous-looking objects are diatoms; the rodlike objects are sponge spicules; there are also several radiolarians. (U.S. Geological Survey)

This thrusts into the middle of one of the scientific adventures of our time. Did Atlantis exist? Was it a continent, or a subcontinent, or a chain of islands? Dr. Kolbe's findings point to an almost inevitable conclusion: there was land in the middle of the South Atlantic ocean that was far enough above sea level to have a fresh-water lake and that lasted long enough to allow diatom deposits to form at the bottom of that lake, to be submerged there by the sea but to leave their message to posterity.

But the idea that any large land mass, center of an important civilization, has gone beneath the waves, may be dismissed as pure mythology. Large areas of the earth's surface once above water may have been submerged; other areas known to have been under the sea are now above water, some of them forming high mountain elevations. But cataclysmic changes of this magnitude all occurred before the coming of man. Lost continents and civilizations that disappeared with them may be relegated to the realm of man's ever-fertile imagination.

2

The Sea and Evolution

There is rather general agreement among biologists that life originated in the ocean and underwent most of its evolution there during a period of the order of three billion years. Life is believed to have originated near the beginning of the Archeozoic era when the earth, if originally hot and molten, had cooled sufficiently to have crusted over and allowed the ocean to be formed by condensation of water vapor already in the atmosphere. By an alternative theory, the water may have been "squeezed out" of the earth itself. This period lasted an estimated two billion years. No proven fossils have been found, although some structures in Archeozoic rocks have been considered fossil algae. The best evidence of the existence of life is the occurrence of sediments containing carbon, which is a basic constituent of all living organisms.

The Archeozoic was followed by the Proterozoic era, an estimated one billion years in duration. Sedimentary rocks of the Proterozoic age reveal unmistakable remains of marine organisms—sponge spicules, worm tubes, brachiopod shells and other organisms, both animal and plant. But in the remains of the end of the Proterozoic era, the fossil record is extremely meager. The beginning of the next era, the Paleozoic, a little less than six hundred million years ago, left fossils representing nearly all of the major groups of animals known today, and in great abundance. This sudden abundance and variety lead to the conclusion that they must have developed during the preceding eras. Why then is the record of those eras so incomplete? It is believed that at least two major catastrophes or "geologic revolutions" wiped out most of the record of earlier eras. When we consider the catastrophic effects of major earthquakes and volcanic activity within historic times, it is easy to understand that still greater catastrophes must have occurred in earlier periods when the earth was even more unstable.

The so-called Appalachian Revolution at the end of the Paleozoic era, when both the Appalachian Mountains and the Ural Mountains rose, almost half the world apart, was a cataclysmic period. The fossil record shows that a substantial portion of the organisms living at that time were destroyed. The elevation of the Alps, Andes, Himalayas, and Rockies at the close of the following Mesozoic era must also have been vastly destructive. The wonder is that any forms survived at all, and that man is here today to contemplate his precarious past.

Rockhopper penguins, found around the Antarctic, are partial to remote islands such as the Falkland, Kerguelen and Tristan da Cunha groups. Awkward on land, the rockhoppers spend at least half their lives at sea. (R. C. Murphy)

About the middle of the Paleozoic era, some 375 million years ago, the first animals, primitive amphibians known as stegocephalians (meaning "roof-headed"), emerged from water onto land. It is not quite clear why they needed armored heads, because there was nothing on the land to attack them. In form they more or less resembled alligators or oversized tadpoles and, as Huxley described them, "they pottered like Falstaff, with much belly and little limb" in the mid-Paleozoic Devonian swamps.

The amphibians never really got away from the water; they made a stab at living on land, but their bodies had to be kept moist, and they had to return to the water to lay their eggs and produce their young as frogs and toads and salamanders still do. Nevertheless, they or their close relatives were in the main line of descent of the land-dwelling animals today.

31

600   405

Near the end of the Paleozoic, the reptiles arose, the first true land animals, completely air-breathing and able to survive for considerable periods
away from water. Present-day desert lizards and snakes are among their
descendants. However, the first lizards were not so independent; they lived
in swamps and were more or less amphibious. But they flourished in a
succeeding era, the Mesozoic, commonly known as the Age of Reptiles.

In the closing millennia of the Paleozoic there was also a small group of
long-limbed reptiles with teeth like modern dogs; nothing is known of them
except their skeletal anatomy, but it is possible that if they were alive today
they would be classified as primitive mammals. Thus the end of the Paleozoic seems to have produced two major groups of reptiles, one leading
toward a greater diversity of reptilian forms, and the subsequent evolution
of birds, the other leading toward the evolution of mammals.

In the Mesozoic era, which began a little more than two hundred million
years ago, the reptiles reached their greatest development. Some of them
became creatures of great size, such as the herbivorous dinosaurs like the
diplodocus, seventy feet or more in length, which had long legs, long tails,

Evolutionary chain
showing (1) microscopic
algae, (2) segmented
worm, (3) coral,
(4) snail, (5) trilobite,
(6) crinoid, (7) giant
nautiloid, (8) hetero-
stracan, (9) primitive
shark, (10) lobe-finned
ganoid, (11) shark,
(12) ichthysosaur,
(13) mosasaur,
(14) whale.

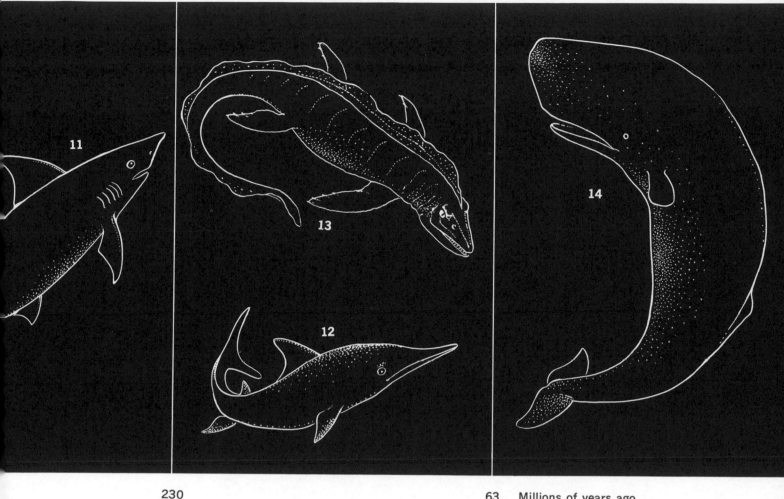

230   63   Millions of years ago

and long necks, and waded about in swamps, living on vegetation. Some became carnivorous dinosaurs, slightly smaller but more terrible, and with tearing teeth such as tyrannosaurus. Some were small, hardly larger than a turkey and apparently made their living running about under the feet of their larger and more cumbersome relatives.

Some of the Mesozoic reptiles either stayed in the sea or returned to it; they were the mososaurs, giant swimming reptiles resembling a modern crocodile, or plesiosaurs with long serpentine necks, resembling a modern idea of a sea serpent. Some, like the pterosaurs, even took to the air and developed wings for at least limited flight or gliding. It is curious and instructive that during the period when reptiles were dominant in the world, they managed to occupy all the available habitats—land, water, and air.

Why did the giant dinosaurs, monarchs of the Mesozoic, become extinct? The principal reasons appear to have been two. One was a change of climate, which altered the living conditions and particularly the food supply: a large dinosaur required a great deal of food. The other was that dinosaurs had much more brawn than brain. Modern man has about one pound of

33

brain to one hundred pounds of body weight; triceratops, a well-known armored dinosaur of the last period of the Mesozoic era, had one pound of brain to ten tons of body weight. In many dinosaurs, in fact, the diameter of the spinal cord was greater than that of the brain. Such creatures, lumbering and unintelligent, could hardly be expected to adapt to changing conditions. Perhaps in the course of their evolution they simply reached the end of the line.

At all events, during the middle and latter parts of the Mesozoic, birds appeared, mammals increased, and the last of the dinosaurs died out, leaving behind such modest relatives as lizards, snakes, crocodilians, and turtles. Only a few of these are marine: a small number of marine snakes, abundant in tropical seas, a single lizard, the marine iguana of the Galapagos Islands, marine turtles, which are quite widespread, and a marine crocodile, which occurs along the shores of southeast Asia and as far as Fiji to the southeast and Palau to the northeast.

BACK TO THE SEA

Reptiles, birds, and mammals as groups have all undergone their major evolution on land, and most of them are still land animals. Those that are today seafaring species are believed to have arisen from land vertebrates that became readapted to the marine environment, most probably as a result of the competition for food. They learned some millions of years ago what man has only recently realized—that the sea is full of things to eat.

How do we come to suspect that a marine animal is a descendant of land ancestors? One important piece of evidence is the habit of coming ashore to lay eggs, as do marine turtles, or to bear young. Little is known of the breeding habits of sea snakes; but of the two major groups, one is believed to lay its eggs on land, while the other bears living young, presumably at sea. One species from the Indian Ocean studied on the *Galathea* expedition was found to produce one or two living young almost half the length of the adult, and able to shift for themselves as soon as they were born. Zoologists tend to believe that the egg-laying species are closer to the ancestral type; those that bear living young have evidently become more completely adapted to the marine environment. Another piece of evidence that sea snakes were derived from land snakes is that they have the same type of venom and venom apparatus as the cobra and its allies.

All marine birds nest on land, even though many of them such as albatrosses, shearwaters, and storm petrels spend the greater part of their lives at sea. Many marine mammals come ashore to bear their young, sea lions and Alaska fur seals, for example, congregating in vast rookeries at that time; but the most specialized mammals, the whales and porpoises, have become so completely adapted to a marine existence that they bear their young at sea.

The most convincing evidence that marine reptiles, birds, and mammals are derived from land-dwelling ancestors is the fact that they are all air-breathing. It was requisite for the evolution of land vertebrates that they be able to breathe air; but the need for air seems a distinct handicap to a marine animal. Thus when air-breathing vertebrates occur in the sea, it is

Brown pelicans off the Florida coast sight a school of fish and start into a steep dive (above). One of the pelicans strikes the water (below), grasps a fish in his beak, and will carry it to the surface before swallowing it. (Kurt Severin)

The wandering albatross *(Diomeda exulans),* found in all southern oceans, is the largest of marine birds, with a wingspread reaching 11 feet. (H. R. H. the Duke of Edinburgh)

generally assumed that they are derived from ancestors that had become more or less completely adapted to life on land.

In some cases the readaptation to the sea has been minor. All or most snakes can swim and they take easily to the water; garter snakes, for instance, will enter a garden pool to capture goldfish. It is therefore easy to understand how snakes could return to the sea, and become increasingly marine in habit in the quest of food. Birds can fly across the water, and all they need for an aquatic environment are such adaptations as webbed feet, waterproof plumage, and the ability to dive for food or pluck or skim it from the surface. In some cases the adaptation has been more extreme, as in the penguins of the Southern Hemisphere and the Antarctic, which have lost the power of flight and use their specialized wings for swimming underwater. This was also true of the now-extinct great auk of the North Atlantic.

Among mammals that have returned to the sea, the ones that have undergone the least change in physical form are the sea otter and the polar bear. The latter spends most of its time on the ice pack, living principally on seals; but in the summer it may come ashore and adopt an omnivorous diet including lemmings, eider ducks and their eggs, and such vegetation as seaweed, lichens, mosses, grass and sedges, cranberries and other berries. Its principal adaptations are its white color, which blends with that of the ice and gives it near invisibility when stalking prey (in late summer the fur becomes yellowish or even golden), and a thick, nearly waterproof fur and a good layer of subcutaneous fat, which enable it to withstand extreme cold. It takes readily to icy water in order to swim across open leads, and swims long distances at speeds up to about six miles an hour without tiring. It can remain under water as much as two minutes at a time. Not inappropriately, the scientific name of the polar bear is *Thalarctos maritimus.*

The sea otter, once abundant along the Pacific coast of North America from Alaska to California, was hunted almost to extinction for its beautiful

6. Steller sea lions on the Oregon coast. They are highly gregarious, and in addition to rookeries they have places such as this where they rest. (Ray Atkeson)

7. Left: Herds of Steller sea lions *(Eumetopias jubata)* are a familiar sight on islands or rocky shores from central California to Alaska.
(Steve McCutcheon)

8. Upper right: Pilot whale spouting. The exhalation is not water but vaporous breath from the whale's nostrils on top of its head.
(John H. Tashjian)

9. Right: Gray-headed albatross *(Thalassarche chrysostoma)* on its nest. This imposing bird ranges the southern seas and nests principally on remote islands in the sub-Antarctic.
(John Warham)

10. The green turtle *(Chelonia mydes),* from 3 to 4 feet long and weighing 300 to 500 pounds, is a species of sea turtle. Although it breathes air like its terrestrial ancestors, it comes to land only to lay its eggs in the sand of tropical or subtropical beaches. (Allan Power)

and valuable fur; now under complete protection, it is increasing in numbers. Its adaptation might almost be called psychological rather than physical, since anatomically it differs but little from related land mammals. It spends a great part of its time floating on its back among the kelp beds, where it is hard to distinguish from the bobbing kelp floats and fronds. When hungry it dives to the bottom in quest of sea urchins or abalones. It is one of a small handful of animals other than man that have learned to use tools. When it dives for a sea urchin it also brings up a stone, lies floating on its back, places the stone on its ventral surface, and pounds the sea urchin against the stone to break open the shell and get at the edible material inside.

Sea lions and seals have undergone considerable modification of their appendages, which have changed from legs into flippers, excellent for swimming but permitting only limited and awkward locomotion on land.

WHALES AND PORPOISES

The most completely adapted of marine mammals are the whales and porpoises, together forming the class known as cetaceans. Cetaceans are divided into two groups, those with teeth and those without teeth. The latter are the whalebone whales, which live on plankton; lacking teeth, they use fimbriated plates of whalebone as strainers to collect the food, simply swimming through vast concentrations of it with open mouth. Since plankton is very nearly the basic food supply in the sea, they are well nourished. Furthermore, the whalebone whales have become the largest animals of all time because creatures of extraordinary size can move about more efficiently in the sea than on land; thus, an elephant must stand on its own four legs while a sea animal is supported by the water. A representative example, the

A section of a porpoise's head showing the separate paths from mouth cavity (1) and nasal passage (2). The esophagus (3) by-passes the larynx (4), which connects the nasal passage directly with the trachea (5).

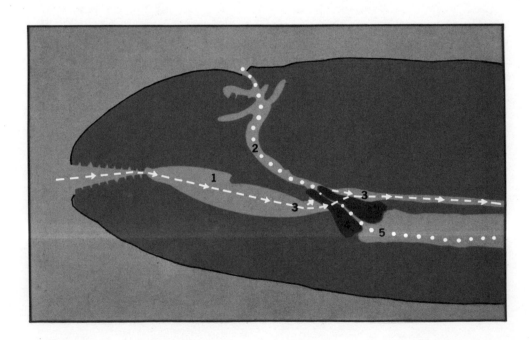

The harbor seal, here seen off the Coronado Islands, Mexico, is a very common seal in both the North Atlantic and the North Pacific oceans. A friendly creature, it often approaches scuba divers to see what they are doing. (Ron Church)

blue whale, known also as the sulphur-bottom, is the largest animal that has ever lived on earth.

The toothed whales are smaller in size, ranging from the porpoises, about four to eight feet long, through blackfish or pilot whales, between eighteen and twenty-eight feet long, to killer whales, up to thirty feet long or more, and sperm whales, occasionally exceeding sixty feet. All of these are carnivorous, but few are dangerous to man. The sperm whale is, of course, a large, powerful animal, dangerous when attacked; it was "the great, white whale" of *Moby Dick,* which was presumably an albino, because sperm whales are usually dark above, with only the underparts white. The killer whale is a vicious predator, living principally on seals and sea lions; it travels in packs and often attacks the much larger whalebone whales, such as the blue whale, the finback whale and the humpback, all of which lack teeth with which to defend themselves and are quickly slashed to pieces. Killer whales have the interesting habit of upsetting blocks of ice on which seals are resting, then devouring the seals. There are no records of their eating men, although this may be from lack of opportunity rather than forbearance.

Porpoises, while equipped with formidable teeth, seem almost man-oriented. They are sportive, easily tamed, and intelligent; there are records of their playing about in the water with bathers, making no move to attack them and apparently just having fun. They are among the most intelligent animals in the world, having a brain weight proportionately larger than that of man. They communicate with each other by audible and supersonic signals; such students of porpoises as Dr. John Lilly have been trying to communicate with them and claim that they can imitate simple words that they hear. Thus far, however, actual meaningful porpoise-to-man communication has not been established.

The gray seal of North Atlantic and adjacent Arctic waters is quite at home among the most forbidding ice floes. (Sven Gillsäter)

42

The adaptation of whales and porpoises to life in the sea is as complete as is possible for any mammal. The nostrils have migrated from their usual position at the front of the head to the top of the head, so that in order to breathe, the animal merely brings its "blowhole" to the surface and exhales and inhales in one quick operation. Porpoises probably breathe about once a minute, but large whales breathe only once in five to ten minutes, and, if necessary, can remain under water forty-five minutes or more. When a whale surfaces after a deep dive it is likely to breathe several times in succession before diving again. The "spouting" of a whale, which looks a bit like a geyser, is its vaporous breath.

Since whales and porpoises bear their young at sea, the nursing of the young presents certain problems. Suckling under water would obviously be difficult. So the female has an arrangement of muscles in the mammary glands for forcing out the milk. When a young whale takes hold of its mother's nipple, it gets an injection of milk not a mouthful of salt water.

The porpoises and the toothed whales have an interesting arrangement of the larynx by which the respiratory system bypasses the esophagus. Practically every human being has at some time choked on either food or water that got into his windpipe—we call it swallowing the wrong way. This never happens to a porpoise. Its larynx, instead of connecting with the esophagus, extends right up into the back of the nasal passage. The esophagus is double at this point, passing to the right and left of the larynx. Oddly enough, this arrangement, which would seem rather useful in swallowing food under water, is confined to the porpoises and toothed whales and is lacking in the whalebone whales, which seem to get along quite well without it.

We cannot conclude the discussion of whales without answering an

A playful bottle-nosed dolphin *(Tursiops)*, a smaller relative of the whale, leaps high out of the waters of the Gulf of California.
(Bruce Markham)

Steller sea lions, all females, on the Alaska coast take to the water. The males reach a length of 10 ½ feet, and a weight of 2,000 pounds.
(Steve McCutcheon)

obvious question: "Why are animals so completely adapted to life in the sea believed to have descended from land-dwelling ancestors?" They are air-breathers, of course; besides that, though whales have no hind limbs, they do have rudimentary pelvic bones, suggesting that their ancestors had hind legs. Another piece of evidence is that the earliest types of whales, known as archaeocetes, which became extinct perhaps twenty-five million years ago, had skeletons more like land mammals than do modern whales.

The famous anatomist, Professor E. J. Slijper of the University of Amsterdam, has written: "From the fact that whales have vestiges of pelvic limbs which arose in the same way as those of normal mammals, we may infer that whales did not originally have their present form but that, in the dim and distant past, they probably had fully developed limbs. In other words, they must have developed from terrestrial mammals . . ."

This, therefore, is the great pageant of evolution—the origin of life in the ocean, the development of all the major groups of animals there, the emergence of land animals, their growth and adaptation until they occupied every available terrestrial habitat, and the completion of the cycle by the return of several groups to the sea, their ancestral home.

45

3
Undersea Geography

Submarine landscapes have many features in common with those above the sea; but there are important differences: they are on a vaster scale, with more extensive and more rugged mountain ranges, and with wider and deeper valleys. If Mt. Everest were to be dropped into the Mariana Trench in the western Pacific, it would be covered by more than a mile of water. Topographical features of underwater landscapes are in general more sharply defined than those on land, because they are not subject to freezing, thawing, and wind erosion. Deep currents are usually considered too slow-moving to be effective agents of erosion, but if they carry particles of sand they can sweep rock faces clean, except for attached marine organisms, and carve considerable channels on the sea bottom. Man uses this principle: in rock cutting for geological or industrial purposes, a rotating steel disk or a rapidly moving steel wire is immersed in water containing sand or carborundum in suspension. The cutting is done by the water-borne abrasive particles.

Submarine topography is of course affected by the same geological forces that affect the land—faulting, volcanic activity, mountain building—and perhaps, because of the greater area of the oceans, in greater amount. Early oceanographic expeditions arrived at the erroneous conclusion that the bottom of the deep ocean consisted largely of flat "abyssal plains" interrupted by occasional rises, volcanic peaks, and coral islands. This misconception was a result of the primitive methods available at the time for investigating the sea bottom.

THE CONTINENTAL SHELF AND SLOPE

In general, the margins of the continents slope gradually into the sea, and continue this gentle gradient for some distance below the water. The gradient then increases rather abruptly, and the sea bottom slopes more or less steeply to a depth of from one to several miles. This change in the steepness of the declivity occurs rather uniformly at a depth of about one hundred fathoms (six hundred feet). The area of gentle gradient within the hundred-fathom line is called the continental shelf, and the steeper region between the hundred-fathom line and a depth of one thousand fathoms is known as the continental slope.

Undersea cliff at a depth of 7,200 feet, east edge of Mexican Basin, Gulf of Mexico. The flower-like form in center foreground appears to be a stalked crinoid, or "sea lily." (D. M. Owen, Woods Hole Oceanographic Institution)

It is convenient to use fathoms in this connection rather than feet or meters, because on sailing charts depths and contour lines are shown in fathoms. The term, meaning in old English "outstretched arms," came into use in early sailing days when depth was determined by dropping a sounding lead, hauling it in and measuring the length of line with outstretched arms. A fathom is six feet or approximately 1.8 meters.

Beyond the thousand-fathom line the sea bottom usually slopes more gently to the ocean depths, commonly known as the oceanic abyss; but in some parts of the world, as off the east coasts of Japan and the Philippines, it may continue abruptly downward to the greatest depths. A continental slope may be thought of as the actual edge of a continent, while the continental shelf is a sort of marginal area, belonging almost as much to the land as to the sea. Considerable portions of the shelf have been alternately exposed and submerged by changes in sea level in fairly recent geologic time.

The continental shelf has caused and will continue to cause problems of international law. For a number of centuries admiralty law has recognized three miles as the distance offshore to which a nation is entitled to extend its sovereignty. This arbitrary distance is said to have been based on the distance one could shoot with an old-time cannon; hence the strip of sea that a nation could defend from its shores. The premise is of course obsolete, but no satisfactory substitute has been arrived at. One suggestion has been that a nation's territory should extend to the edge of its continental shelf, and offhand this sounds logical enough, but it creates more problems than it solves. For example, a good part of the North Sea, including its famous fishing banks, would cease to be international waters; and so would the Irish Sea, the English Channel, the Newfoundland fishing banks, the Bering Sea, and considerable portions of the Gulf of Mexico. Obviously the solution to these problems lies in international agreements.

SUBMARINE CANYONS

At the mouths of various rivers we find, not unexpectedly, canyons cut in the continental shelf. The easiest explanation, and probably in some cases the correct one, is that these are river-cut canyons formed during Pleistocene glaciation, when at various times the level of the sea was considerably below that of today. That the canyons should be wide and deep is compatible with what we observe of river-cut valleys and canyons on land.

But many of these submarine canyons, for example that at the mouth of the Hudson River, are far deeper than can be accounted for by any lowering of sea level in Pleistocene time. Moreover, a number of them occur where no rivers, so far as we know, have ever existed. Such canyons have sometimes been attributed to faulting; that is, under stresses and strains a part of the earth's crust just cracked open and left a deep gash. More recently two other possible explanations have been advanced. One is that of turbidity currents, a transfer of the idea of channels cut by rivers to that of channels cut by currents along the sea bottom. It used to be assumed that the ocean depths are a region of perpetual calm. But it is now known that currents do flow on the ocean bottom and that in certain cases, particularly on the continental shelf, they flow with considerable force, carrying with them silt and sand. These are cutting particles that when river borne have carved out immense canyons on land. Underwater photographs have been taken showing that these turbidity currents are practically moving rivers of sand; their cutting power is obvious.

Another cause of submarine canyons may be sediments, accumulating on the continental shelf to a point beyond what civil engineers call the "angle of repose." When this point is exceeded, stresses are set up, and presently gravity takes over: the accumulated weight of the sediments causes them suddenly to let go and slide down the continental slope. Thus a canyon may be carved out with the force of a glacier, and on occasion perhaps with the speed of an avalanche.

A newborn volcanic island near the west end of Fayal Island in the Azores (above), September, 1957. Another eruption begins (near right) in October, 1957, and soon reaches its height (far right). The new island, joined to Fayal by ash, is now known as the Capelinhos Volcano, after the lighthouse it left standing about a mile from the sea. (Cranbrook Institute of Science)

Each of these forces, along with others yet to be discovered, has probably functioned in one or more of the many submarine canyons over the world.

THE OCEAN DEEPS

Sailors have long practiced sounding with a weighted line in shallow water to avoid running a vessel aground (this is graphically recorded in *Acts of the Apostles* 27:28); but as far as we know Ferdinand Magellan was the first navigator to attempt a sounding in the open sea. Soon after he had worked his way through the tortuous strait that bears his name and onto the broad and, by contrast, pleasant ocean that he called the Pacific, he sought to measure its depth. He lowered a sounding lead with all the line he had— fifty fathoms—without reaching bottom, and thus established that the depth of the world's largest ocean was more than three hundred feet! For some three centuries not much more was known.

During the first half of the nineteenth century many soundings were made for the purpose of preparing sailing charts, but methods were still crude and the results highly unreliable. Rope became waterlogged and difficult to handle; both copper wire and iron wire broke at very moderate depths. The United States Navy for a time adopted waxed flax twine weighing nine pounds per statute mile, but this too had a tendency to break under its own weight plus that of the sounding lead. Moreover, it was difficult to tell when the lead reached bottom in deep water, and some recorded soundings were subsequently found to be in error by many hundreds of feet. The method was to use a line of known length, cut it off when bottom was reached, and measure how much was left.

In 1853–1854, a United States Navy midshipman, J. M. Brooke, invented a sounding device in which the line was carried down by a short tube attached to a heavy weight. The latter would keep the line taut as it was paid out, then automatically detach itself when it hit bottom. This permitted

the line to be hauled in with little danger of breakage. The tube was intended to bring up a sample of the bottom—mud, sand, or shell. If no sample was obtained, the bottom was presumed to be rock.

The famous British physicist, William Thomson (Lord Kelvin), invented a "sounding machine," which came into use about 1872. It consisted essentially of a drum wound with piano wire, which would lower the sounding lead, automatically indicate when bottom had been reached, register the depth, and allow the wire to be rapidly reeled in. Variations on the Brooke and Thomson devices were used for decades to plumb the depths of the sea.

Searching for greater depths became an exciting activity. As depths of three, four, and five thousand fathoms and more were recorded, these "deeps" were usually named after the discovery ship or in honor of some distinguished oceanographer. For example, the Tuscarora Deep off Japan was named for the U.S.S. *Tuscarora,* the Challenger Deep off the Marianas after H.M.S. *Challenger,* and the Murray Deep in the middle of the North Pacific after Sir John Murray, member of the *Challenger* expedition. By the early years of the twentieth century, fifty-seven such deeps had been named, and it was recognized that they were not isolated spots but portions of either great trenches or of abyssal plains. It is customary now to refer to such features by their geographical location, as, the Japan Trench, the Hawaiian Deep, or the Cape Verde Abyssal Plain.

Until the second quarter of the twentieth century, sounding the deep sea was a slow and tedious process in spite of the excitement. Even with the best sounding machine, letting out five or six miles of piano wire and winding it in again would take the best part of a day. Hence our knowledge of

Lightning in the volcanic cloud over the newborn island of Surtsey, Iceland, December, 1963. The lightning is probably caused by a strong positive charge of electricity coming up with gases from the volcano. (S. Jonasson)

the ocean bottom was very spotty and incomplete. But the invention of echo sounding gave oceanographers a new tool for rapid exploration of sea-bottom topography. The method is surprisingly simple: a sound produced under water will travel to the bottom and echo back. The echo can be picked up by a microphone. Since the speed of sound through water is known, the length of time between the original sound and its echo gives a measure of the depth. The apparatus consists of a plate installed in the hull of a ship from which a sound (nowadays an ultrasonic impulse) is given out at regular and frequent intervals, a receiving microphone, and a scale on which the time interval is converted to depth.

One of the first persons to use the sonic depth-finder for plotting contours of the ocean bottom was Captain Claude B. Mayo, U.S.N., who in the early thirties was commander of the tanker *Ramapo*. An ingenious man, he took a piece of plywood and some six-inch nails; every time he made a sounding, he drove a nail into the plywood to a proportionate depth. After a number of crossings of the North Pacific, he had a piece of plywood studded with nails driven in to various depths. Then he plastered some home-made papier-mâché among his nailheads and made the first relief map of the bottom of the North Pacific Ocean. Since then, the world ocean has been pretty well charted by echo sounding, and we know the ridges and trenches and plains and hills and sea mounts. More is yet to be learned, but the basic work has been done.

The greatest depth discovered in the Atlantic Ocean is in the Puerto Rico Trench—27,960 feet; in the Pacific, the greatest depth accurately located is 36,240 feet, in the Mariana Trench about two hundred miles southeast of Guam.

Characteristically we find deep areas of the ocean immediately adjacent to areas of recently elevated land, with a narrow continental shelf and a steep continental slope. Examples are the Philippine Islands with the adjacent Mindanao Deep, Japan bordered by the Japanese Trench, the Aleutian Islands with the Aleutian Trench immediately to the south, and the west coasts of North and South America with deep water close to shore and high mountain ranges on land near the shore. At San Francisco the continental shelf extends out to the Farallon Islands, then the slope drops off rapidly to a depth of two miles. From the summit of the Sierra Nevada to the oceanic abyss off San Francisco, we have a difference of altitude of more than 25,000 feet within a horizontal distance of 180 miles. In South America, where the Andes peaks are higher and come closer to the sea, the drop from mountain peak to ocean depth is even more precipitous, as much as nine miles vertically in a horizontal distance of a hundred miles.

It is to be noted that in all of the areas where there is a sharp difference in height between the land and the nearby ocean bottom, or between adjacent areas of the ocean bottom itself, we have great instability of the earth's crust, as evidenced by frequent earthquakes and volcanic activity.

SEA MOUNTS AND MOUNTAIN RANGES

Sonic depth finding made it possible to explore the ocean bed with unprecedented rapidity. In a single hour soundings could be taken that would have required days or weeks by older methods. It became possible to chart the contours of the deep sea continuously as a ship sailed across them. Vast areas that were supposed to be flat "abyssal plains" were found to be surprisingly rugged. In fact it is doubtful that there is an abyssal plain in any ocean of the world that equals in extent and flatness such land areas as the Siberian steppes or the North American prairies. The bottoms of the oceans are in most areas more irregular and mountainous than any comparable areas on land.

Submarine mountains are sometimes isolated peaks, or groups of peaks, rising from the ocean floors, sometimes to a height of 15,000 feet or more. If they reach the surface, of course, they constitute islands. If they terminate below the surface they are known as sea mounts, except for one particular type, guyots, which have flat tops. If there were only a few guyots, they might be explained as representing some freak of volcanic activity: for example, a submarine volcano might "blow its top" and the crater might subsequently become filled in with sediments. But the guyots are too numerous and too uniform, and they occur in both the Atlantic and the Pacific, though they are considerably more numerous in the latter. One theory is that their tops have been planed down by wave action at a period when either the sea level was lower or these sea mounts were higher.

In connection with guyots we should mention coral atolls, those curious islands of the South Pacific that form a more or less irregular ring with a lagoon in the center. Charles Darwin theorized that these must have been formed around volcanic islands that gradually sank. Coral reefs would form around the island and would continue to build up as the island went down, leaving at last a ring of coral with a lagoon in the center. Guyots must be considered in this connection, since a flat-topped sea mount at or near the surface would seem to form a better base for an atoll than a volcanic island rising to a peak.

In recent years, with better mapping of the sea bottom, attention has shifted to the study of undersea mountain ranges. Early oceanographic expeditions discovered that there was an elevation in the North and South Atlantic oceans, which came to be known as the mid-Atlantic Ridge. More detailed investigations revealed this to be a vast, winding mountain chain with foothills, "abyssal hills," on either side, and branching in a complex way at the southern end, with ridges running toward Guinea, Southwest Africa, and South Africa.

Subsequently a submarine mountain range was found in the Pacific, paralleling the coast of South America and extending northward to about the latitude of central Mexico. This has been named the East Pacific Rise.

Then a complex mountain system was found in the Indian Ocean. Studies made during the International Geophysical Year have revealed that the bottom of this ocean is amazingly rugged. Peaks, ridges and scarps have been found that were previously quite unknown. Recently Bruce C. Heezen and Marie Tharp of the Lamont Geological Observatory of Columbia University have reported a ridge running in a generally north-south direction for a distance of three thousand miles. Because it lies approximately on the ninetieth meridian of east longitude, it has been called the Ninety-east Ridge; its significance is not known.

In studying recent surveys of the sea bottom, geologists of the Lamont

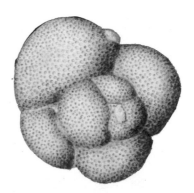

Fossil foraminiferan (*Globigerina ouachita-ensis*) from the Eocene epoch (magnified 112 times). This genus is one of the main groups making up globigerina ooze on the ocean floor. (Drawing by Margaret M. Hanna)

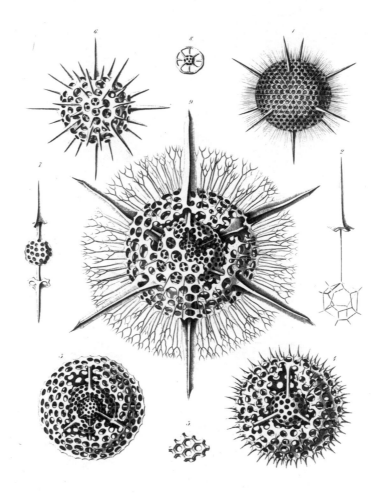

Drawings of some typical radiolarians: three species of *Actinomma* (center and left top and bottom), two species of *Haliomma* (right top and bottom). The smaller drawings are details of the skeletal structure. (From *Die Radiolarien* by Ernst Haeckel, 1862)

Overleaf: San Andreas Fault, Indio Hills, southeast of Palm Springs, California. The extensive movement along the fault through the centuries is clearly shown. (Spence Air Photos)

Geological Observatory, particularly Maurice F. Ewing and Dr. Heezen, saw what they consider to be a continuity of undersea mountain ranges that not only encircle the world but in their winding course, exceed it in circumference. According to their view, this chain of mountains extends from the Indian Ocean, around South Africa, up the Atlantic (the mid-Atlantic Ridge) into the Arctic Ocean between Greenland and Spitzbergen, and across the Arctic Ocean to the coast of Northern Siberia. This would be the largest mountain range in the world, some forty thousand miles in length, and one writer has pointed out that this ridge "has an area equal to that of Europe, Asia and Africa combined and is one of the major features of the earth's crust."

Ewing and Heezen have taken particular note of a rather wide, deep valley running lengthwise at the very crest of the mid-Atlantic Ridge. They have suggested that this is a "rift valley," that is, a valley created by a fracture of the earth's crust, accompanied by seismic and volcanic activity. One theory is that the earth's mantle, although regarded as a solid, behaves like a highly viscous liquid. Over a period of millennia it might flow in such a way as to produce humps in certain areas, which would be mountain ranges, and depressions elsewhere, which would be deep oceanic trenches. If the forces of uplift continued, a mountain range thus elevated might split at its crest, forming a rift valley. Heezen has postulated that this rift may follow the entire course of the 40,000-mile mountain plain, and he and

53

his associates have diagrammed a "rift system" for the entire world.

This is, of course, an assumption based on a limited number of profiles. Obviously no one has taken profiles at reasonably close intervals of a submarine mountain range forty thousand miles long. Not all geologists are in accord with the theory that this great mountain chain has split at the top throughout its entire length, pointing out that there is nothing unusual in finding a valley between two mountains. On the other hand, the "rift" theory has received considerable support from geophysicists. To explain the difference in their explanations of surface features of the continents and sea bed, one might say that a geophysicist thinks of the earth from the inside out, while a geologist thinks of it from the outside in.

ON THE BOTTOM

Over the sea bottom as a whole, exposures of bare rock occur at the tops of sea mounts or on undersea cliffs at the edge of some great fracture of the earth's crust. Much of the bottom is covered with deposited material of various sorts, some of continental origin, some even coming from outer space, but a great deal originating in the sea itself.

Near the shore we find deposits of continental origin—sand, gravel, and various types of mud. A good deal of the sand and most of the mud on the continental shelf is carried into the sea by streams and thence distributed by tidal or other currents. Particles of sand sink more rapidly than particles of mud; hence mud will be carried farther out to sea than sand, to the edge of the continental shelf and even down the continental slope. Mud may be colored black by hydrogen sulphide, blue or bluish black by iron sulphide, more rarely green by the mineral called glauconite, and occasionally red by iron oxide.

The hydrogen sulphide that produces the color of black mud comes from the decay of organic matter, so black muds are generally found only in stagnant regions such as the bottom of the Black Sea or in those Norwegian fiords that drop down to considerable depths behind a shallow sill at the entrance. In such places the surface waters are well oxygenated and teem with life, but the stagnant depths are devoid of oxygen and are habitable only by bacteria, which decompose the organic matter drifting down from above.

Blue muds are the most common and widely distributed muds on the continental shelf. Green muds, which are formed by a complex process not entirely understood (glauconite is a silicate of aluminum, iron and potassium), are found in limited but widely scattered areas, chiefly at the fringe of the continental shelf. Red muds are the least common. They are characteristic of the bottom of the Yellow Sea and the continental shelf of eastern South America.

Sandy beaches are one of the attractive features of seashores in most parts of the world, and a sandy bottom is found in many shallow areas of the sea. As noted, much of the sand is carried to the sea by rivers. This results in the presence of sand bars at the mouths of many rivers and in harbors into which large rivers flow, especially rivers fed by rushing mountain streams which are eroding their rocky channels. One has only to think of the Grand

Canyon of the Colorado to be staggered at the thought of the vast quantity of rock that has been reduced to sand and swept away by that single river.

On the Pacific coast of North America, the famous Oregon beaches and dunes occur south of the Columbia River, in the direction in which river-borne sand is carried by prevailing currents and wave systems. Five miles off San Francisco Bay there is a sand bar—fed from streams originating in the rugged Sierra Nevada and to a lesser degree from streams originating in the nearby Coast Ranges—that has to be dredged at regular intervals to keep a channel open for deep-draft ships to enter the harbor.

Some authorities on beach erosion fear that the very existence of sandy beaches is threatened by the damming of streams for hydroelectric power and for irrigation, thus preventing the rivers from carrying their burden of sand to the sea. This could perhaps be true in certain areas; but the idea that it might be generally true fails to take account of wave action on rocks, itself an important factor in generating sand. There are fine sandy beaches on many tropical islands where stream-borne sand cannot be considered a factor. On the other hand, Arctic beaches have little or no sand because wave action has been prevented by the omnipresent ice. The grinding of ice on shore produces beaches of coarse gravel. It takes either stream action or wave action to produce sand.

The color of sand depends on what it is made of. Granite and sedimentary rocks produce gray sand, and dark lava produces black sand, as on the famous Kalahana beach on the Island of Hawaii, and elsewhere in volcanic regions, such as El Salvador. White sand comes from quartz, also from pulverized seashells and coralline algae, and the whitest sands in the world are the coral sands of tropical beaches.

SAND, OOZE, AND RED CLAY

Deposits that originate in the ocean itself are of two general types: neritic, those originating near shore; and pelagic, those originating in the open sea. Neritic deposits consist of such material as whole or fragmented shells, coralline algae, and remains of true corals. Shell sand and coral sand would be regarded as neritic in origin whether on the bottom or washed up on the beach by wave action. Pelagic deposits are formed from the remains of plant or animal organisms that live in the open sea. The remains of large animals are relatively scarce compared with the extraordinary abundance of small or microscopic forms: diatoms, one-celled plants with siliceous skeletons; radiolarians, one-celled animals with delicate, lacy skeletons also of silica; and Foraminifera, one-celled animals with skeletons of calcium carbonate. There are many other organisms, of course, but these are the dominant types whose remains sink down to form thick deposits on the sea bottom. The upper layers of these deposits have the consistency of thin mud. This type of deposit has been given the not very elegant name "ooze."

Diatoms are found in the surface waters of all oceans, but they are more abundant in cooler waters and become truly dominant in the Antarctic and in the extreme North Pacific. Their shells, or frustules, which are of great variety and beauty, sink to the sea bottom, forming a wide belt of diatom ooze on the floor of the sea completely surrounding the Antarctic Continent, and a narrower belt, just south of Alaska and the Aleutian Islands, that extends from northern Japan to the continental shelf of North America.

The most widely distributed bottom deposits are those made up of the shells of Foraminifera. Of these the most abundant are those of the genus *Globigerina;* hence bottom deposits of foraminiferal origin are referred to as Globigerina ooze. This is the dominant bottom deposit in all of the oceans except the Arctic and Antarctic. In the North Atlantic, where diatom ooze is absent, Globigerina ooze extends north to the vicinity of Iceland and Greenland. It is largely absent from polar seas because Foraminifera become progressively less numerous in colder water. It would probably occur on the sea bottom practically everywhere else except for the interesting fact that its distribution is limited by depth. Calcium carbonate is soluble in sea water under high pressure, and at a depth of around four miles the shells of Foraminifera dissolve before or just after reaching the bottom. Their remains are therefore found only at moderate depths, ranging from four hundred to 3,500 fathoms. The difference in the maximum depth at which it is found in different parts of the oceans may be due to the amount of carbon dioxide in the water, this being a factor in the solubility of calcium carbonate.

Radiolaria are scarcer than diatoms or Foraminifera and are limited to tropical waters. Radiolarian ooze is found as the characteristic bottom deposit in only two areas: a narrow band in the Pacific a short distance north of the equator, extending from the continental shelf off Central America to about mid-Pacific; and a limited area of the Indian Ocean north and west of Australia. The shells of Radiolaria are delicately beautiful and appear fragile, but being siliceous they do not readily dissolve. Radiolarian ooze, in the limited areas in which it occurs, is found in depths of from two thousand to five thousand fathoms.

One other type of pelagic deposit, occasional and rather localized, should be mentioned—pteropod ooze. This is the only pelagic deposit formed by multicellular organisms. The pteropods are a curious group of free-swimming mollusks that occur in the upper waters of all oceans and somewhat irregularly appear in great abundance. They swim by a leisurely flapping of two winglike appendages developed from the sides of the single molluscan foot. They are translucent and delicately colored and are sometimes called sea butterflies. In a very few places their shells accumulate on the bottom in sufficient numbers to be recognized as a bottom deposit. Pteropod ooze is found in small patches in the Mediterranean, in the eastern North Atlantic, near Bermuda, in the eastern and western South Atlantic, and in the central and western Pacific. It is found in relatively shallow water, from four hundred to nineteen hundred fathoms, and nowhere covers a very large area.

In the greater depths of the ocean even the siliceous remains of diatoms and Radiolaria disappear, and we find vast areas of the deep sea—especially in the Pacific but also in the Atlantic and Indian oceans—covered with a substance that when dried has a red-brown or chocolate-brown color and is known as "red clay." This occurs in every ocean but the Antarctic; even the basin of the Arctic Ocean contains a semblance of it. If it occurs in the Antarctic, it has been masked by heavy deposits of diatom ooze found there.

Red clay is the characteristic bottom deposit in very deep water all over the world, extending down to the greatest depths. Chemically, it is a

Ocean bottom life seen from the bathyscaphe *Trieste* at a depth of 4,000 feet in the San Diego Trough. The most abundant organisms are serpent stars *(Ophiomusium lymani)*. Those appearing to have feet and spines are sea cucumbers. (Official Photograph, U. S. Navy)

hydrated aluminum silicate. It contains considerable iron but little or no calcium for reasons explained above. It is believed to be derived mostly from volcanic ash and pumice, along with meteoritic dust and particles. We have pointed out in an earlier section that meteorites add to the earth's substance an estimated eight to ten tons a day. Much of this material falls into the ocean, and microscopic particles of iron or iron oxide found in the red clay are believed to be of meteoritic origin.

Lying on or in the upper layers of the red clay are found irregularly rounded manganese nodules and certain very hard parts of marine vertebrate animals, such as the teeth of sharks and the ear bones of whales. The fact that these occur on or near the surface of the red clay indicates that the rate of deposit of that material is very slow. The teeth of fossil sharks are said to have been found inside manganese nodules, which would be further evidence that these objects have been on the bottom of the deep sea a long time without being completely buried. It is a reasonable guess that the depths of the ocean have existed substantially unchanged through a good many millions of years.

FORMATION OF SEDIMENTARY ROCKS

In contrast to the red clay, the pelagic deposits, especially diatoms and Globigerina ooze, accumulate at a rapid rate. The newer layers press down on the older, forcing the water out and, with time and pressure, forming a solid mass. A core sample thirty feet long, taken by forcing a metal tube into the bottom, may contain sediments ranging from recent time to a million or even several million years ago.

Since there is a limit to the depth that metal tubes can penetrate, extensive studies of the thickness of bottom deposits have been made by seismic sounding, a technique developed by oil geologists for locating structures beneath the continental shelf that may contain petroleum. When a charge of explosive is set off at a depth, an echo will be received from the sea bottom, and a second echo will rise a little later from the solid rock beneath. The time interval between the two echoes gives a measure of the thickness of the sedimentary deposits. Using this technique, the Swedish Deep-Sea Expedition of 1947–1948 reported sediments up to twelve thousand feet thick in the Atlantic basin. In most areas the thickness is much less than this—about one thousand to three thousand feet—and on the tops of undersea mountains there is commonly no sediment at all. It slides or washes down the slopes.

The type of sedimentary deposits that accumulate in deep water is rarely found as sedimentary rock on land, supporting the idea of relative permanence of the ocean basins. The sedimentary rocks that are so prominent a feature of the continents are of materials that accumulate at the margins of the continents or on the bottoms of shallow seas. Where their structure has been exposed either by elevation or tilting, it is not uncommon to find layers of such rock twelve thousand feet in thickness and occasionally up to fifty thousand feet. The reason sedimentary deposits accumulate along the continental margins more rapidly than in the deep sea is probably that they are added to and compacted with materials brought in by streams.

We may feel sure that sedimentary rocks are still being formed beneath the shallower sea as in ages past, and that at some time in the future—as has occurred repeatedly in the past—large areas of them may be uplifted to form new mountain ranges high above sea level. Earth processes are continuing processes, and the more we learn of the present and past of our planet, the better we can predict its future.

BENEATH THE BOTTOM

To achieve an understanding of the changes in the earth's surface that have taken place in the past and are continuing today, it is necessary to know something about the structure of the earth. A hundred years ago the problem seemed very simple. The earth, originally a molten ball, was

Worm tube on sea bottom at 2,095 fathoms. (Lamont Geological Observatory)

60

cooling and contracting. The contraction produced wrinkles in the surface, which became mountain ranges and valleys. The process was often compared to the way a dried apple or prune becomes wrinkled as it shrinks. Volcanoes were places where the still-molten interior of the earth came bursting out.

Geologists rapidly revised this elementary concept. They divided the rocks into two major groups, igneous rocks—that is, those that originated under great heat—and sedimentary rocks—those that were laid down by deposition of sediments at the bottoms of lakes or oceans. Igneous rocks were then divided into granites and basalts. Granites are generally coarse-grained and contain numerous crystals such as quartz and feldspar; basalts are of fairly uniform composition and, although frequently amorphous or irregular in shape, sometimes assume the form of large, upright, parallel columns. Familiar examples are the Giant's Causeway in Northern Ireland and the Devils Postpile in the Sierra Nevada range in central California.

The geologists, of course, went much farther than this in classifying rocks, describing particular formations, and determining their age and probable origin. They reduced to some order everything known about the surface of the earth. Though it is common to discount mining and drilling in the search for gold, coal, or oil as having only commercial value, the fact remains that a great deal of our knowledge of the earth's crust comes from these efforts.

Geologists also discovered that the crust of the earth does not merely fold: it breaks, in immense fractures known as faults. Movement along these faults may be vertical or horizontal, depending on the direction of stress; if it is vertical, one block sinking or its neighbor rising, an abrupt discrepancy occurs, which is known as a fault scarp. Fault scarps one thousand or two thousand feet high are not uncommon. They occur both above and below the sea. Motion along such faults continues at intervals over thousands of years, causing major or minor earthquakes.

How deeply faults extend into the earth's crust is not easy to ascertain, but they may extend horizontally for hundreds or even thousands of miles. An example is the San Andreas fault, which runs from the Gulf of California in Mexico to the coast of northern California, where it turns out to sea. It was movement along this fault that caused the San Francisco earthquake of 1906—in a matter of seconds there was a horizontal displacement of as much as twenty feet. The broken ends of a fence that had been built across the fault were found after the earthquake to be sixteen feet apart. There is geological evidence suggesting a total movement along the San Andreas fault of 220 miles in the last sixty million years. Another example is the famous Rift Valley of eastern Africa, which is a complicated series of faults extending from lakes Nyasa and Tanganyika to the Red Sea, the Dead Sea, and the Jordan Valley, a total distance of nearly three thousand miles.

Volcanoes are commonly associated with major faulting of the earth's crust. We find a string of them along the African Rift Valley, along the west coasts of North and South America, and along the coast of Asia from the East Indies through the Philippines and Japan. There is good reason for this association. Rocks at a depth of about thirty miles are hot enough to be molten but are kept solid by pressure; when faulting occurs, the pressure is reduced, and the superheated rock liquefies and not infrequently finds its way to the surface as lava. The mechanics of volcanoes are much more

Ripple marks on the sea bottom at a depth of 1,800 fathoms on the south side of the Java trench show a strong bottom current. (Official Photograph, U. S. Navy)

complex than this, of course, but this is the basic reason for their relevance to fault lines.

Volcanoes sometimes occur on the sea bottom many miles from land, and may reach the surface and continue far above it, building islands such as the Hawaiian group, where much volcanic activity is still going on. There are many oceanic islands of volcanic origin. In all such cases we assume faulting of the sea bottom as a primary cause.

When the earth's crust breaks, some parts rise and form mountain ranges, while other parts sink and become either shallow seas or ocean basins. The explanation for this is simple—difference in weight. If two ships of similar design are moored side by side, one loaded and one empty, the latter will ride high out of the water while the laden ship will ride low. In much the same way, the fractured blocks of the earth's crust seem to "float" on the superheated rocky layer below.

Gravitation is measured by timing the rate of swing of a pendulum; an increase in gravitational force causes the pendulum to swing faster. This was originally based on the observation that a pendulum clock adjusted to a particular locality gains or loses time if taken to another place on the earth's surface with a different gravitational force. Naturally a delicate measurement of this sort cannot be made on a ship rolling in a rough sea; measurements of gravity at sea have accordingly been made from submarines.

Careful measurements of gravity made at sea level, on the tops of high mountains, and from submarines beneath the sea, indicate that the sea bottom consists of heavier stuff than the continents, and that the high mountains are the lightest of all. Measurements of gravity are an indirect method of weighing. If we could take columns of the earth's surface, cut them all off at a certain level such as twenty miles or thirty miles below sea level, and weigh them, we would find that a column taken through the highest mountain would weigh about the same as a column taken through the deepest sea.

This is known as isostatic equilibrium. The theory of isostasy holds that the earth tends constantly to be in a state of equilibrium about its center, and that any change in the weight of any considerable area will result in a shifting of the load until equilibrium is again attained. An interesting recent example of the way the earth adjusts itself to an increased load is furnished by the area around Lake Mead behind Hoover Dam in Arizona and Nevada. Since the dam was constructed, the entire area has been slightly but measurably lowered by the weight of the water behind the dam, the floor of the lake itself having gone down about six and one-half inches where the weight of the water is greatest. Because the distribution of surface weighting is continually changing through formation or melting of ice, through erosion of the land and through deposition of sediments in the sea, adjustments of the earth's surface are occurring continually.

We need not look for a cessation of earthquakes and volcanic activity in the foreseeable future. Indeed, we should not even wish for such a supposedly comfortable state of affairs, for if the equilibrium postulated by the theory of isostasy were ever attained, we should have—through erosion of the continents by wind and water and ice, and by wave action on the remaining shores—an earth completely leveled and completely covered by an ocean about two miles deep. When we feel an earth tremor or hear of a volcanic eruption, we can reassure ourselves with the old saying, "While there's life, there's hope."

INSIDE THE EARTH

As geological methods developed, it became obvious that the continents are largely composed of granite and that the bottom of the sea is made of basalt, generally overlaid with a thick or thin layer of sedimentary deposits. This might lead one to think that the interior of the earth is composed of molten material that, if it turned up at the surface, would be basalt. This is not necessarily true. The interior of the earth is still a conundrum.

Around the beginning of this century there began to develop a new science: geophysics—the physics of the earth. This science is still in its infancy, but it has made immense strides. Geophysicists quickly developed the idea that the interior was quite different from what had previously been believed. At first they decided that the core of the earth was solid, and about four thousand miles in diameter. This they called the centrosphere. Around this was the lithosphere (rocky sphere), and outside this was the hydrosphere (the oceans). Outside of this was the atmosphere, which could be continued through various concentric layers right up to the ionosphere and the exosphere. But geophysicists began to discover that, however the orderliness of these terms might appeal to the scientific mind, they did not correspond to the actual situation as revealed by new methods and procedures. They thereupon both literally and figuratively got down to earth and, in a reversal almost without precedent in scientific circles, began to describe the structure of our planet in ordinary, everyday language.

What was formerly called the centrosphere is now called the core. It consists of two parts, an inner core that is solid and an outer core that is liquid. Both are extremely hot; the inner core would be liquid except that the tremendous pressure to which it is subjected forces it into the solid state. It has about the consistency of nickel iron. The molten outer core is surrounded by a solid layer, the mantle, about two thousand miles thick. This is undoubtedly composed of rock; what kind of rock nobody knows, although vigorous efforts are being made to find out. The mantle is surrounded by a very thin crust, nowhere more than a few miles deep. This crust makes up both the continents and the ocean basins, and is the only part of the earth that man has been able to study by direct observation.

How then do we know anything about the earth's interior? The greater part of our knowledge has come from the study of earthquake waves. A very rough analogy would be the way a man wanting to hang a picture on a plastered wall locates a wooden stud by tapping with a hammer. He cannot see through the plaster, but from the vibrations that result from his tapping he can tell what is beneath—solid wood or merely lath. By similar means, seismologists and geophysicists study the interior of the earth.

An earthquake produces vibrations that travel in all directions and can be picked up on seismographs all over the world. These earthquake waves are of several types; and all of them travel at different velocities according to the density of the rock through which they are moving. By noting the time of arrival of an earthquake wave at different seismological stations and collating this information with other data that show the type of wave, it is possible to tell a good deal about the material through which it has passed. One type of wave, a lateral wave, will not go through a liquid. On the opposite side of the world from an earthquake, there is an "earthquake shadow" in which these lateral waves do not record on a seismograph; therefore we assume that there is a liquid layer in the interior of the earth. This liquid layer is what we call the outer core; the inner core is assumed to be solid because at the great pressures obtaining there all known substances would be forced into the solid state even at extremely high temperatures. It is not quite clear why the same argument does not apply to the outer core, but the testimony of the seismograph is that there is, deep in the earth's interior, a layer that either is liquid or behaves like a liquid. It should be noted that solid rock, under extremes of temperature and pressure, shares some of the properties of both a solid and a liquid.

Outside the outer core is the mantle of the earth, a solid layer more than two thousand miles thick, which constitutes about 85 per cent of the volume of our globe. Outside of this lies the very thin crust, thicker under the continents, thinner under the ocean basins, but nowhere more than a few miles thick. The distinction between crust and mantle was brilliantly deduced by the Yugoslavian seismologist Andrija Mohorovičić in 1909. He noted that earthquake waves that started at the same time and place became divided into two sets traveling at different velocities. Since the velocity of such waves depends on the medium through which they are traveling, he

11. A tube-dwelling sea anemone *(Cerianthus* sp.*)* with its base surrounded by serpent stars, at a depth of 110 feet off the California coast. (Jim Hodges)

12. Overleaf: Topography of the ocean floors.

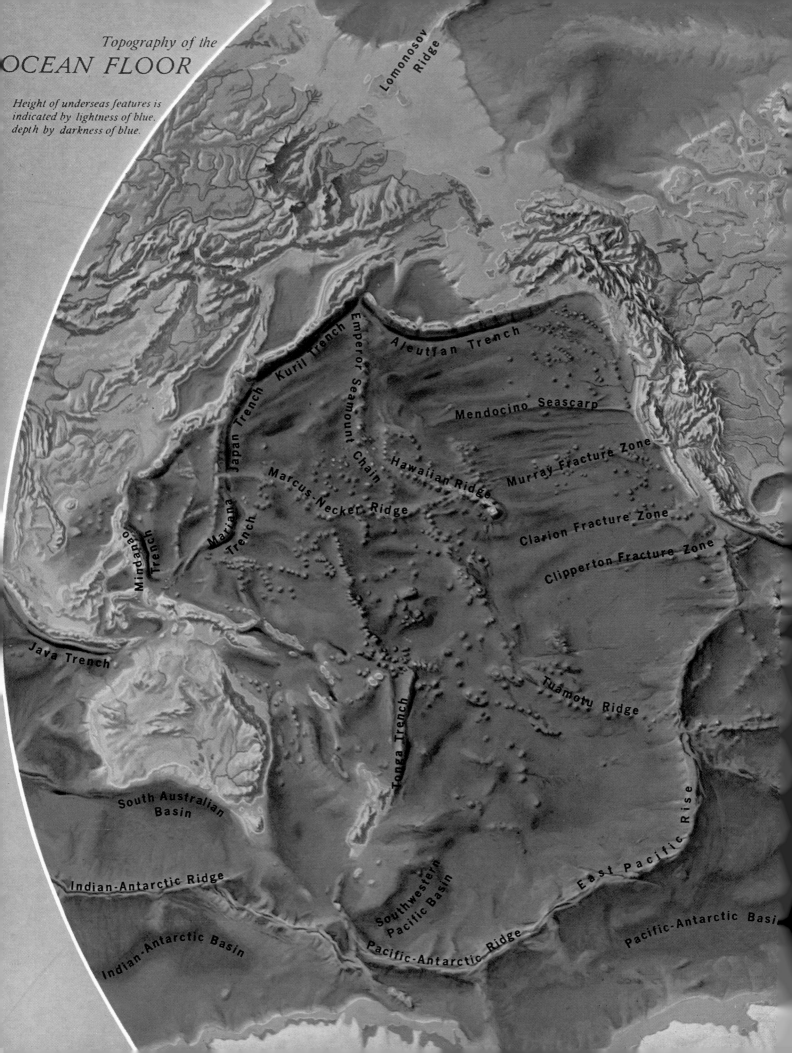

Topography of the
OCEAN FLOOR

*Height of underseas features is
indicated by lightness of blue,
depth by darkness of blue.*

Lomonosov Ridge

Kuril Trench

Emperor Seamount Chain

Aleutian Trench

Japan Trench

Mendocino Seascarp

Hawaiian Ridge

Murray Fracture Zone

Marcus-Necker Ridge

Mariana Trench

Mindanao Trench

Clarion Fracture Zone

Clipperton Fracture Zone

Java Trench

Tuamotu Ridge

Tonga Trench

South Australian Basin

Southwestern Pacific Basin

East Pacific Rise

Indian-Antarctic Ridge

Indian-Antarctic Basin

Pacific-Antarctic Ridge

Pacific-Antarctic Basin

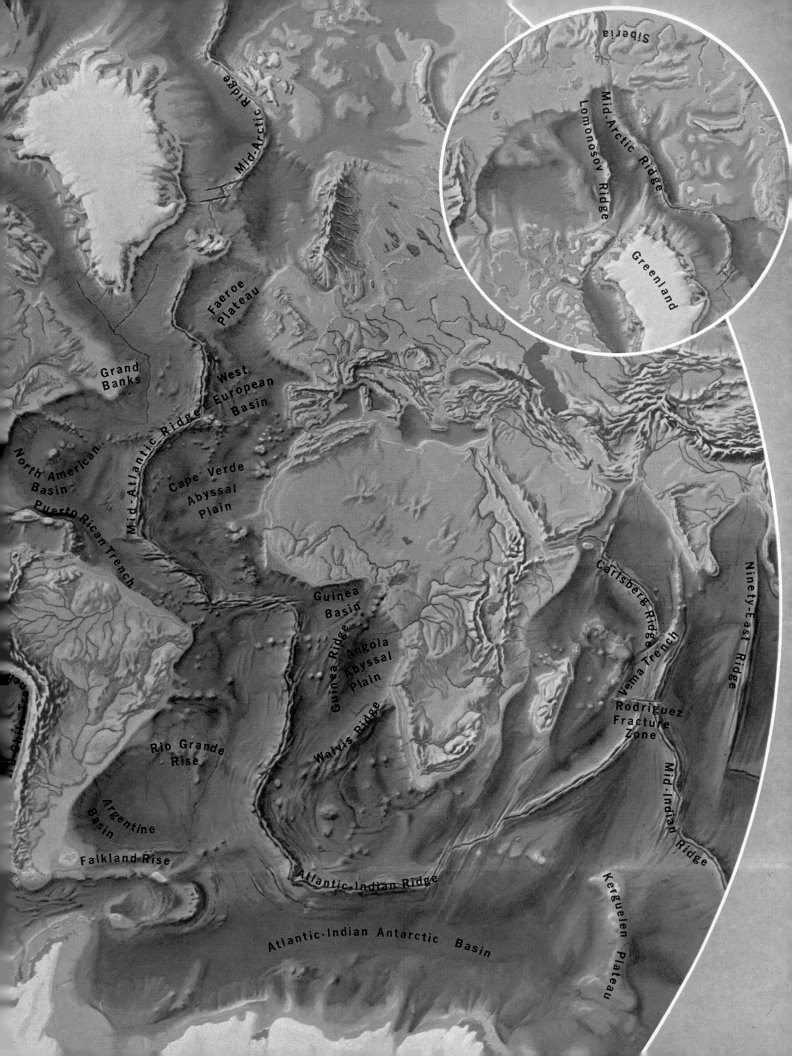

Mid-Arctic Ridge

Siberia

Mid-Arctic Ridge

Lomonosov Ridge

Greenland

Faeroe Plateau

Grand Banks

West European Basin

North American Basin

Mid-Atlantic Ridge

Cape Verde Abyssal Plain

Puerto Rican Trench

Guinea Basin

Guinea Ridge

Angola Abyssal Plain

Carlsberg Ridge

Vema Trench

Ninety-East Ridge

Rodriguez Fracture Zone

Mid-Chile Trench

Rio Grande Rise

Walvis Ridge

Mid-Indian Ridge

Argentine Basin

Falkland Rise

Atlantic-Indian Ridge

Kerguelen Plateau

Atlantic-Indian Antarctic Basin

1. Earth's crust. 2. Moho layer. 3. Mantle (solid). 4. Outer core (liquid). 5. Inner core (solid). Continental area at top, a granite mass, floats on mantle, partially submerged like an iceberg.

concluded that the outer portion of the earth consists of two layers of different composition. The break between these layers, which occurs at depths of roughly five to thirty miles, has been named the Mohorovičić discontinuity—generally known as the Moho.

A great deal of curiosity developed about the precise difference between the crust and the mantle of the earth. There is a peculiar, very basic mineral known as dunite that is believed to originate deep in the earth. Occasionally chunks of it come up in lava flows in the Hawaiian Islands, and since the Moho layer is known to be relatively close to the surface in that area, it is believed that these chunks, quite different from the basaltic lava, may have come from the earth's mantle. St. Paul's Rocks, a small isolated group in the South Atlantic, have yielded samples of peridotite, a mineral related to dunite; these rocks are also suspected of having been extruded from the mantle.

THE MOHOLE PROJECT

There are other areas where it is thought that the earth's mantle may be exposed. But so much uncertainty remained that geophysicists decided to bore a hole through the earth's crust to find out what the mantle is composed of. Since this undertaking meant going down to and hopefully through the Moho layer, it was called Mohole. Offhand, the best place to try such a project would seem to be on land, where drilling rigs could be easily set up and manipulated. But as we have said the crust of the earth is thickest under the continents and thinnest in the deep ocean. Obviously, then, the best place to bore through the earth's mantle is where the mantle is thin.

13. Eruption of the newly formed island of Surtsey, which rose from the sea off the southern coast of Iceland in November, 1963.
(Sigurgeir Jonasson, Almenna Bokafelagid)

Now drilling for oil on the continental shelf, although it utilizes floating platforms, is normally carried on from towers firmly set on the bottom, and the drilling is little different from that on shore. But to drill a hole through the thinnest part of the ocean basin would mean working far out at sea, from a ship subject to winds, waves and currents. Obviously drilling a hole five or six miles deep under a couple of miles of water is not an inexpensive undertaking; so areas characteristically free from storms had to be selected, for a single storm could wreck the entire project. Fortunately, there is a tropical belt of calms, which in sailing-ship days was known as the doldrums because ships were so often becalmed there. The supervisors of the Mohole project have selected several sites where the weather is favorable and where evidence indicates that the ocean bottom down to the Moho is relatively thin.

In 1963, test borings were made, first off the coast of southern California, then in water two miles deep off the coast of Baja California, Mexico. The ship, with three miles of drill pipe attached, was kept in position within a ring of buoys by four outboard motors; if it had drifted outside the ring of buoys the drill pipe would have broken. A hole 601 feet deep was bored in the sea bottom and core samples were brought up that showed they had got through the marine sediments and into the basalt layer beneath; the amount of scientific information gained from these core samples was impressive.

In the meantime, Canadian scientists proposed to establish seismographic stations all over Canada at intervals of about five hundred miles. They plan to drill holes at each of these stations, from one thousand to two thousand feet deep, and to take regular temperature readings to determine the heat flow from the interior of the earth. Heat flow provides a good deal of information. For example, it is still undecided whether the earth is slowly cooling off by radiation into space, or warming up from radioactivity inside.

The Mohole project was abandoned because investigations along the mid-Atlantic Ridge by the Lamont-Doherty Geological Observatory of Columbia University and others have indicated that as continental plates drift apart, material from the interior of the earth is exposed on the sea bottom and can be studied without very deep drilling. It was therefore decided to design a ship for moderately deep drilling (say 4000 feet) in any ocean. This ship, the *Glomar Challenger,* funded by the National Science Foundation and operated by the Scripps Institution of Oceanography and other institutions is investigating the sea bottom to find out more not only about the Moho and the mantle but also about the origin of earthquakes, faulting, radioactivity of the earth's interior, volcanic activity, and plate and continental displacement.

It would be pleasant to think of the cataclysmic activity of the earth's surface as something that happened long ago. But earthquakes of measurable magnitude occur practically every day, usually several times a day, and it is seldom that some volcano is not erupting or threatening to erupt. In 1963 alone, there was a violent eruption of long-dormant Mt. Agung on the island of Bali, and a terrifically destructive earthquake in Yugoslavia that left the city of Skoplje completely in ruins. In 1964 came the great Alaska earthquake and destructive tidal wave. Our planet is far from stable. Yet we live on it in a modest degree of comfort and peace of mind, much as the Italian peasants till the soil around the base of rumbling and smoking Mt. Vesuvius; and well we may, for there is—at the moment—no place else to go!

4
The Ocean Waters

The ocean is important not only because it covers so large a portion of our planet; it is also the most complex chemical substance known to man, and may even hold the secret of life itself. If sea water were found only in some small, remote lake, chemists and biologists would doubtless study it intensively as a most precious liquid.

Sea water is known to contain seventy-five of the ninety-two elements that occur in nature—excluding a small number that have been made in the laboratory, some of which have existed for only a fraction of a second. It is likely that all of the naturally occurring elements will ultimately be found in the sea. It would indeed be difficult to understand why they should not, for all rivers, as they move toward the sea, bear with them all the substances they have garnered from the land.

The Sound of Mull in the Inner Hebrides is one of the many inlets in the rugged northwest coast of Scotland. Fishing is a major industry on the island of Mull. (Toni Schneiders)

THE MOST ABUNDANT ELEMENTS IN SEA WATER
(Values in grams per cubic meter, approximately equivalent to parts per million)

Oxygen	857,000	Potassium	380
Hydrogen	108,000	Bromine	65
Chlorine	19,000	Carbon	28
Sodium	10,500	Strontium	8
Magnesium	1,350	Boron	4.6
Sulphur	885	Silicon	3.0
Calcium	400	Fluorine	1.3

For water is practically a universal solvent. When we say that a substance is insoluble in water, we generally mean that it dissolves so slowly that for practical purposes we can disregard its solubility. Thus we can store water in glass bottles for years on end, knowing that the water will not eat holes in the glass, and that it will remain reasonably pure. But distilled water kept in a glass bottle for a year will not be actually, chemically pure; it will contain traces of substances dissolved out of the glass—silica, borates, phosphates, and so forth, depending on the composition of the glass. Thus it need not surprise us that such unlikely elements as silica, aluminum, tin, lead and nickel occur in measurable quantities in sea water.

Even such rare metals as gold and silver, which we commonly regarded as

Water-bottles are lowered to obtain samples of sea water from various depths on a single haul. (U. S. Fish and Wildlife Service)

completely immune to the solvent action of water, occur in the ocean—in minute quantities per cubic meter, but in an aggregate amount that staggers the imagination. In 1911 a British chemist, L. S. Blackmore, calculated that a cubic mile of sea water contains more than $93,000,000 worth of gold and $8,500,000 worth of silver. Since the oceans of the world contain some three hundred million cubic miles of water, the total value of the gold and silver in the sea is in excess of thirty billion times a million dollars—far more than the total gold and silver reserves of all the nations on earth. The difficulties of obtaining this wealth are made clear, however, by Blackmore's statement that it cost him four to five thousand dollars over a period of several years to extract about five dollars' worth of silver and gold from sea water.

Salt, we know, is in plentiful supply in sea water; more prosaic than gold and silver, still it is not merely seasoning, it is an important and necessary chemical in body fluids. Man has always gone to great lengths to procure it. Naturally occurring deposits have been mined or dug from time immemorial. In early English dialects, "wich" meant a salt pit, and the word survives in such place names as Norwich, Harwich, Greenwich, and so forth—places where salt could be obtained. Julius Caesar describes a crude method of evaporation used by the early Britons: they would build a fire of charcoal, quench it with sea water, and obtain salt from the ashes. The Vikings secured a concentrated brine by allowing sea water to freeze and then removing the successive layers of ice as they formed. (By an interesting reversal of this procedure, one method of obtaining potable water from sea water is to freeze it and use the ice instead of the brine.)

In parts of the world where the climate is favorable, salt has generally been obtained through solar evaporation of sea water, often in large, shallow, man-made ponds. Production of salt by this method is still a thriving industry in Italy, France, Spain, in San Francisco Bay, Baja California, and elsewhere. Not by any means all of the salt produced is refined for human consumption. Great quantities are used in the chemical industries— for example, in the manufacture of chlorine and hydrochloric acid.

Vast subterranean deposits of salt in various parts of the world, as in the United States (particularly New York, Michigan, Ohio, Kansas and Texas), England, Germany, Austria, Poland, Russia and Spain, have been a puzzle to geologists and oceanographers. These deposits are generally agreed to have come from a part of the ocean that occupied these areas in past geological time, some of them as old as the Triassic, Permian or even Lower Carboniferous periods. The layer of salt may be several hundred feet in thickness. It seems unlikely that any large section of the ocean several miles deep should simply have evaporated, leaving its load of salt behind. Much more plausible is the hypothesis that these great salt deposits were formed in broad, shallow seas that alternately evaporated and then were inundated with the not infrequent changes in sea level in geologic time. The incoming water, bearing its own salt, would in time contribute to the deposit.

Less abundant than salt, hydrogen, oxygen, carbon, nitrogen, and phosphorus, all of which are basic to organic life, occur in substantial amounts in the sea. There are smaller but significant quantities of iron and copper, which play important roles in the respiration of animals. Hemoglobin, which gives the red color to the blood of vertebrate animals, is an organic compound of iron that has the property of combining with oxygen quickly but loosely, and just as easily separating again. Thus it can pick up oxygen in gills or lungs, carry it to parts of the body where it is needed, and there release it to the tissues. Hemocyanin is a colorless organic compound of copper found in the blood of mollusks and crustaceans, and probably a large number of other invertebrates having colorless or nearly colorless blood; it functions in the same way as hemoglobin as a means of transporting oxygen throughout the organism. It is likely that many of the minutely occurring or trace elements in sea water will ultimately be found to serve some important purpose as do iron and copper.

THE ALKALINITY OF SEA WATER

Everyone knows that some substances are acid and others are alkaline. Nitric acid, which will dissolve gold, and fluoric acid, which will dissolve glass, are examples of strong acids. An example of a strong alkali is lye. But there are also weak acids, such as carbonated drinks; and there are weak alkalis, like bicarbonate of soda. We mean the weak kinds when we speak of the acidity or alkalinity of natural waters.

Carbonated drinks provide a good illustration of what happens when carbon dioxide and water are brought together. In the preparation of such beverages, carbon dioxide gas is forced into the liquid under pressure. So long as the pressure is maintained, the gas remains in solution; as soon as the pressure is removed by taking the cap off the bottle, the gas emerges in the form of bubbles. Such beverages are commonly referred to as "soda water," not because they contain soda but because carbonated drinks were first prepared by adding a little bicarbonate of soda to a mildly acid liquid such as lemonade, causing it to fizz. One still finds the term "soda springs" applied to various natural waters, although they probably contain no soda whatever and their only resemblance to soda is that they give off bubbles.

Carbon dioxide is almost universally present in both air and water. Whenever the carbon dioxide pressure in the air exceeds that in the water, the gas will go into solution; but if the carbon dioxide pressure in the water exceeds that in the air, the process is reversed—carbon dioxide passes from the water into the air. Oceanographic chemists use the term "carbon dioxide pressure" in stating the relations between carbon dioxide in air and water. Our example of soda water is not farfetched.

When we distill water we get a chemically pure product that is "neutral," that is, neither acid nor alkaline. But as soon as this purest of waters is exposed to the air, it begins to take up carbon dioxide from the atmosphere and becomes a weak solution of carbonic acid. All fresh waters are slightly acid unless they contain alkaline earth minerals dissolved from the earth or rock through which they have passed.

Sea water, on the other hand, is always slightly alkaline because it contains several alkaline earth minerals, principally sodium, calcium, magnesium and potassium. When carbon dioxide is dissolved in sea water, the initial reaction, just as in fresh water, is the formation of carbonic acid. This, however, promptly reacts with the alkaline elements to form carbonates and bicarbonates, rendering the water alkaline. Bicarbonates are less strongly alkaline than carbonates: compare bicarbonate of soda, which is baking soda, with carbonate of soda, which is washing soda.

We have thus a rather complex balance involving carbon dioxide in the air, carbon dioxide in the water, bicarbonates and carbonates, which is known as the carbonate equilibrium. It may be diagrammed thus:

carbon dioxide in air   carbonic acid   carbonates
           ↘ ↖   ↗ ↙   ↘ ↖   ↙ ↗
           carbon dioxide in water   bicarbonates

The double arrows indicate that the reactions may proceed in either direction, depending on whatever portion of the system gets out of balance.

This may seem rather complex and, fortunately for all living organisms, including ourselves, it *is* complex. The complexity of the reactions prevents anything from happening too fast. This is known to chemists as buffer action.

Both plants and animals use up oxygen and give off carbon dioxide in the process of respiration. This would result in a steady decrease in the amount of oxygen in the ocean and an increase in the carbon dioxide until life became impossible, if it weren't that plants have the fortunate capacity of being able to reverse the trend through the process known as photosynthesis—the manufacture of carbohydrates from carbon dioxide and water, using the energy derived from sunlight and giving off oxygen as a by-product. Thus a workable ratio is maintained between carbon dioxide and oxygen.

Since photosynthesis goes on only during the daylight hours, while respiration of both plants and animals goes on day and night, every night there is a building up of carbon dioxide in the water with a resultant shift of the carbonate equilibrium toward decreasing alkalinity. We speak of decreasing alkalinity rather than greater acidity because sea water always remains on the alkaline side.

Many if not most marine organisms are highly sensitive to changes in the alkalinity of water and would be disturbed by any large or sudden change. But because of the buffer action resulting from the step-by-step changes in the carbonate equilibrium, the alkalinity of sea water changes rather slowly, and the ocean thus presents a reasonably comfortable and stable environment for its various inhabitants.

Shifting our attention now from the ocean to the land—and it is the point of view in this book that practically everything that happens in the ocean has a direct and often immediate effect on what happens on land—the relation between oxygen and carbon dioxide is just the same in fresh water or on the land as it is in the sea. Both plants and animals use up oxygen in their respiration, but plants, through photosynthesis, produce more oxygen than they use and thus compensate for the oxygen deficit that animals are continually creating. But in fresh water and on the land there is no buffer action. Changes are immediate and direct. Thus we have had the unfortunate situation of a number of people dying, as in Donora, Pennsylvania, in 1948, and in London in 1963 from respiratory failure due to the sudden development of what is called "smog" in the air they breathed.

Since the industrial revolution in the mid-nineteenth century, there has been a steady increase in the carbon dioxide content of the earth's atmosphere from the output of factory chimneys, blast furnaces, and the growing consumption of coal and petroleum products. The present century has seen more and more use of the internal combustion engine—to the point where in the more highly developed industrialized countries the average citizen drives a smog-producing machine on business or pleasure every day.

At the same time that sources of carbon dioxide have been increasing, the plant life taking up carbon dioxide and producing oxygen has been steadily decreasing, through cutting of forests, use of agricultural lands for building and the paving of millions of acres. Even weeds perform the vital function of removing carbon dioxide and giving off oxygen.

Since carbon dioxide may either be taken up or given off at the interface between air and water, many authorities consider the ocean to be a regulator of the amount of carbon dioxide in the earth's atmosphere. Processes in the ocean have thus far been little affected by man. With growing population and increasing industrialization and urbanization, the ocean may prove to be the key to continued human life on earth.

SALINITY AND TEMPERATURE

It is customary to distinguish between the chemical and the physical properties of sea water, but these are in some ways inseparable. For example, salinity would be considered a chemical property; but salinity can be determined by relative weight (specific gravity), freezing point, or electrical conductivity, all of which are physical properties. In general, the chemical properties of sea water are those that can be determined by chemical analysis, whereas the physical properties are those that can be determined by weighing or measuring. But the differences are mostly procedural; the results of the study of sea water by physical or chemical means generally are in agreement.

Of the various physical properties of sea water, several are of particular interest—temperature, specific gravity, electrical conductivity, pressure, color, and viscosity.

On the Centigrade scale (which is generally preferred to the Fahrenheit scale for ocean temperatures) the total range of temperature in the ocean is from $-1°$ C. to $30°$ C. (about $30.5°$ F. to $86°$ F.). The $-1°$ C. temperatures are found throughout the year in the Arctic and Antarctic Oceans, and the highest temperatures naturally occur in the tropics. Generally speaking, surface temperatures in tropical waters do not exceed $27°$ to $28°$ C. ($80.6°$ F. to $82.4°$ F.), but in partially landlocked areas they may go higher; for example, August temperatures in the Caribbean reach $29°$ C. ($84.2°$ F.) and in the Red Sea, $30°$ C. ($86°$ F.). The Red Sea in summer thus contains the warmest ocean water in the world.

In temperate climates, in both the Northern and Southern Hemispheres, surface temperatures are generally within the range of $15°$ to $25°$ C. ($59°$ F. to $77°$ F.) in summer and $10°$ to $15°$ C. ($50°$ F. to $59°$ F.) in winter. The range is so wide because local conditions vary according to ocean currents, prevailing winds, and upwelling of bottom water.

As a rule the temperature of the sea decreases rapidly from the surface downward. In summer in temperate regions, and almost always in the tropics, there is a layer of warm water at the surface produced by direct heating from the sun. This may be anywhere from one to ten or even more fathoms; but at the lowest level of this layer there is as much as a $3°$ to $4°$ C. (approximately $5°$ F. to $7°$ F.) drop in temperature. Beyond this, the temperature decreases rather slowly and regularly to the bottom.

Persons accustomed to swimming in fresh-water lakes will have noted a similar phenomenon. The surface waters, receiving the sun's radiation, are warm and comfortable; but a deep dive will take one suddenly into colder water. The reason for this abrupt change is that the warm water is lighter because water expands when it is heated; thus it literally floats on top of the colder water. The point at which this sudden temperature change occurs is referred to, whether in fresh or salt water, as the thermocline. This is of practical importance: tuna fishermen drop thermometers into the water because tuna, being warm-water fish, will always be above the thermocline.

Below the thermocline, where the temperature changes abruptly, ocean temperatures decrease gradually with depth till, at a depth of a mile or more, they approximate $0°$ C. ($32°$ F.). This is true even at the equator. Bottom temperatures in the temperate zones are seldom significantly different from those in the tropics. Occasionally small differences may, however, give a clue to whether the bottom water has come from the north or the south.

Surprising as it may seem, the temperature of ocean water in the Arctic and Antarctic may fall below the freezing point of fresh water, and bottom

A mountainous wave in
the open sea.
(Jan Hahn)

water in the depth of the ocean does not freeze although it may be at 0° C.
(32° F.) or below. This will be readily understood by anyone who has ever
melted the ice on a frosty pavement by putting salt on it. Salt lowers the
freezing point of water, thus not only melting the ice but preventing it from
refreezing unless the temperature goes lower.

When salt water does freeze, the salt is not frozen in it but is, so to speak,
"frozen out." For example, the ice that forms at the surface of the Arctic
Ocean is essentially fresh, containing only such particles of salt as may have
been trapped in it during the freezing process; when melted, it provides
good drinking water. A consequence of the "freezing out" of salt is that the
water beneath the Arctic ice pack becomes more saline as the surface freezes.

As we have said, there is a relation between salinity and specific gravity.
Specific gravity is simply the weight of a volume of sea water compared with
the weight of the same volume of distilled water at a standard temperature—
by definition 4° C., but often for convenience 17.5° C. (63.5° F.) or 20° C.
(68° F.). The most accurate way of determining specific gravity is to weigh a
measured sample of sea water at standard temperature on a sensitive analyt-

ical balance. A simpler method, valuable when extreme accuracy is not required, is the use of the hydrometer. This is a glass instrument with a weighted bulb at the bottom that causes it to remain upright in water and a stem at the top marked with a graduated scale. The depth at which the hydrometer floats, as registered by the water level on the stem, gives a measure of the specific gravity of the water. A large hydrometer, with a long enough stem and a sufficiently expanded scale, would be just as accurate as an analytical balance. But glass hydrometers are small because of the danger of breakage; so the readings made on them are not precise. One disadvantage of the analytical balance is that it cannot be used in rough weather.

As has been indicated, both salinity and temperature affect the specific gravity of sea water, and their effects are interrelated. Water with such a high salt content that it would be expected to sink toward the bottom will float at the surface if it is sufficiently warm. Conversely, water with a relatively low salt content, which might therefore be expected to remain at the surface, will sink if it is sufficiently chilled. The latter normally occurs at the edge of the Arctic and Antarctic regions, where the sea water is both diluted and cooled by melting ice.

These factors greatly influence the circulation of water in the ocean. The basic circulation is determined by the differential heating of the water between the tropics and the polar regions, and the swirl created by the earth's rotation. The swirl is emphasized by prevailing winds, which themselves have the same origins—the differential heating between tropical and polar regions, and the rotation of the earth. Local conditions, such as the contours of the floor of the sea and upwelling of bottom water, also affect circulation.

A highly important factor, one without which life could hardly exist in the oceans and might even not exist on earth, is the circumstance that water reaches its maximum density, or highest specific gravity, at 4° C. (39.2° F.), that is, four degrees above the freezing point. As a consequence, freezing water and ice expand and have a lower specific gravity, so that they float on the very slightly warmer water beneath. If water attained its maximum density at its freezing point, the ice would sink, and all of our deep lakes and the ocean itself would be solidly and permanently frozen, with only a shallow layer of water on top, melted by the sun.

SEA WATER AS AN ELECTRICAL CONDUCTOR

The electrical conductivity of sea water is a major problem to engineers who have to deal with various metals exposed to salt water—iron or steel piers, steel hulls of ships, brass propellers, pipes for carrying salt water through the cooling or condensing systems of ships' engines, and so forth.

One of the problems is that (as in an electric battery, where a piece of copper and a piece of zinc immersed in a salt solution create an electric current) whenever two dissimilar metals are immersed in sea water and connected by a pipe line or a propeller shaft, an electric current is likely to be established between them. As in a battery, this results in rapid deterioration, called electrolysis, of one of the metals. Preventing such damage occupies much of the time of experts known as corrosion engineers.

Production of salt by
evaporation of sea
water at Pomorie on
the Bulgarian section of
the Black Sea coast.
(J. Allan Cash)

PRESSURE IN THE DEPTHS

Pressure exerted by the weight of sea water—roughly eight pounds a gallon—becomes an important factor for apparatus that must operate at any considerable depth. Pressure in the sea increases with each mile of depth at the rate of about one ton per square inch. Thus in the greatest depths of the ocean, pressure on the sea bottom or on objects in the water exceeds seven tons per square inch of surface. In utilizing oceanographic equipment it is necessary to provide for equalization of the pressure inside and outside the apparatus as it is lowered to increasing depths, or to build apparatus strong enough to withstand any pressure likely to be encountered.

A spectacular example of the extraordinary effect of pressure is what sometimes happens to metal bottles lowered into the depths for water samples. These bottles have a valve on each end that is set in an open position but is closed when the desired depth is reached by sliding a metal cylinder down the cable. As the open bottle goes down, the water flows freely through it and the pressure on the inside constantly equals that on the outside. Occasionally, the bottle will inadvertently be lowered with the valves closed and therefore with air instead of water inside it. When this occurs, the bottle returns from its journey to the depths as completely collapsed as if it had been pounded with a sledge hammer. Similarly, if a knotty pine board is weighted and lowered by a cable to a depth of a mile, it will be crushed to about half its former thickness, and the knots, much harder than the rest of the wood, will protrude spectacularly above the surface.

Under the tremendous pressure in the sea, the water itself is slightly compressed, the molecules being pushed closer together; thus the density of the water increases with increasing depth. It has been calculated that if water were to become completely incompressible, the sea level all over the world would rise about ninety feet, thus inundating a great part of all seaports. Fortunately the physical properties of the ocean do not suddenly change.

LIGHT AND COLOR

Sunlight falling on the ocean is partly reflected back into the atmosphere and partly absorbed, in the latter case being converted into heat. The depth to which light will penetrate before being absorbed is different for different wave lengths. The red end of the spectrum is quickly absorbed, warming the surface layers; the yellow-green segment penetrates more deeply, while the blue-violet end of the spectrum goes deepest of all, fading gradually into the blackness of the ocean depths.

Offhand it would seem to be a simple matter to lower a light meter into the sea and, with the aid of various filters, quickly determine the rate of absorption of different wave lengths and the depth at which the final blackout occurs. But the problem is more complicated than it appears.

The ocean is a mirror. About one quarter of the light striking it is reflected at the surface and never enters the water. The reflectance varies, moreover, with the roughness of the ocean; surprisingly, more light is reflected when the sea is stormy than when it is calm because an undulating sea presents more reflecting surface and because white caps reflect more light than blue or green water. When the sea is "as smooth as glass," it is absorbing the maximum amount of light and reflecting the least. A ship in a calm harbor may show a nearly perfect reflection in the water, whereas a ship in a rough sea shows no reflection at all; but this has nothing to do with the amount of light reflected. The human eye is not a light meter; in fact, because of its sensitivity, it inclines us to bad guesses about the amount of light present. Reflectance varies also with the angle at which the light strikes the water, and this changes with the latitude and the season. When the sun strikes the water at a low angle, as it regularly does in Arctic and Antarctic regions, the reflectance will obviously be greater and the absorption less than when the sun shines directly down as it does in the tropics.

Everyone who sails in tropical seas is impressed with the deep blue or even ultramarine color of the water. Physicists who have studied this have

Extraordinary concentration of windrows of the minute alga *Trichodesmium* in the Indian Ocean, photographed from a height of 5,000 feet. (Keith Gillett)

come up with several explanations. One is that blue light, being less readily absorbed than red or green, is reflected in greater amount. Another is the phenomenon known as "scattering"; the shortest wave lengths are the ones most likely to be deflected from their normal path by minute particles, perhaps even the molecules of the water itself. A third theory is that the ocean reflects the sky. Several of these factors may be involved. Certainly reflection of the sky is one, because the bluest of tropical seas becomes dull or even gray if the sky is overcast.

For most of us it is sufficient to know that the color of deep, clear water is blue. This is true of fresh water as well as salt. Deep, clear lakes such as Lake Constance in Switzerland and Crater Lake in Oregon are noted for their blueness. The fact that high mountain lakes can be as blue as the Mediterranean is evidence that temperature is not a direct factor. Temperature is, however, indirectly involved. Tropical seas are blue because they are extremely clear, and they are clear because they support only a very small amount of microscopic plant and animal life. One reason for this is that tropical waters as a rule are low in the fertilizing substances (nitrates and phosphates) necessary for a rich growth of organic life. Another reason is that warm water is not able to hold so much oxygen in solution as cold water. The dissolved oxygen content of tropical waters is around four parts per thousand, whereas in temperate and sub-Arctic waters it is likely to be six parts per thousand—50 per cent higher. This oxygen deficiency in the warm-water latitudes puts a brake on various biological processes. The life of tropical seas may be colorful and interesting but, contrary to a popular notion, it is not nearly so abundant as the life of colder waters.

The extraordinarily large anchovy fishery off the coast of Peru, which might seem to contradict this, is due to the influence of the cold Humboldt Current, and to upwelling of bottom water rich in nutrient substances. The tunalike fishes, which are characteristic of warm waters, are exceptionally fast swimmers, and thus able to cover large areas in quest of food.

As one moves away from the tropics the water becomes less blue; presently it becomes green, because of the increasing abundance of microscopic plants.

Where major ocean currents move away from the equator, as do the Gulf Stream and the Japan Current, the blue water of the tropics may be carried to rather high latitudes. When a warm current encounters a cold current the effect can be dramatic. A voyager can tell when he is passing from the Gulf Stream into the Labrador Current, or from the Japan Current into the cold current coming down the Siberian coast, by the change in the color of the water. Often the boundary between the two currents appears to be as sharp as a knife edge.

Inshore waters, even in the tropics, are likely to be green. This is due to the greater quantity of suspended matter in the water, either microscopic plants and animals or just detritus stirred up by wave action. An exception is to be found in coral reefs, where blue water sweeps up on the white reefs. Coral sand is heavy and sinks rapidly, so that the water that pounds upon the reefs is remarkably clear. In contrast we may note the Yellow Sea, in which fine detritus carried by the Yangtze River goes many miles out to sea and colors the water yellow until it sinks.

In sheltered inlets where growth of microscopic plants occurs under the most favored conditions, the water forms a kind of soup and may change from green to brown. In the Red Sea, which presents conditions similar to those just described, the growth of one particular organism, *Trichodesmium*, in immense abundance colors the water red. The occurrence of "red tides" off the coasts of Florida and California, with the killing of immense quantities of fish, is due to the rapid growth of certain dinoflagellates under conditions in the sea favorable to their existence and reproduction. One of the problems of oceanographers is where these organisms live and how they survive between the periods of their maximum abundance.

VISCOSITY

Viscosity is not easy to define. Fortunately most people know something about it because auto service station attendants sometimes ask "What viscosity of oil do you use?" The word comes from a Latin word referring to birdlime made from mistletoe berries and has the connotation of "sticky." Some liquids of high viscosity, such as molasses and tar, are sticky, but stickiness is not a necessary quality. A motor oil with a viscosity of thirty is no stickier than one with a viscosity of ten. The great oceanographer Sir John Murray defined viscosity as "internal friction," and this is probably as good a definition as any. Viscosity is what holds water together.

The viscosity of sea water varies inversely with temperature and is nearly twice as great at 1° C. (33.8° F.) as it is at 32° C. (89.6° F.). This had considerable influence on the speed of sailing ships, although the shipmasters probably did not know it. A ship would move more slowly in cold water because of this greater viscosity and increased friction on the hull. With the advent of steam and of screw propellers, this problem solved itself. The ship's being held back by the viscosity of cold water is partly offset because that viscosity also gives the propeller a greater hold on the water to drive it forward. The main difference would be an increased use of fuel in colder water.

Another practical consequence of the higher viscosity of cold water is the theory—one that most mariners will discount in terms of their own experience—that storm waves (assuming an equal cause) are not so high in sub-Arctic regions as they are in the tropics. This hypothesis is difficult to evaluate, but the conclusion is probably true.

5
Winds and Waves

Everyone knows that high winds produce stormy seas, but it is not too easy to understand how this comes about. The problem can be stated simply enough: as wind blows across the surface of the ocean, the friction sets the water in motion in the same direction as the wind; and through viscosity or internal friction the motion is transmitted in diminishing amount from the surface to successively deeper layers. But one might expect that if the wind were steady it would generate or accelerate surface currents rather than waves.

The most likely explanation is that the wind is not steady, but comes in pulses; moreover, it doesn't flow smoothly over the surface of the water, but bounces up and down. Anybody who has ever had a «bumpy» airplane ride knows that air can move violently in a vertical as well as a horizontal direction. Such up and down movements over water undoubtedly create surface turbulence; as soon as these surface irregularities occur, the horizontal winds, which generally predominate, get a better purchase on the water, build the little waves into larger waves, and if the wind blows long and hard enough, it can produce storm waves of tremendous fury.

Anyone who has watched the surface of the sea, or even of a fresh-water lake or pond, must have seen a version of this process. As soon as a slight breeze comes up, tiny ripples are observed on the surface of the water, usually in patches quite far apart, and looking at first like moving shadows. But if the wind continues, these patches increase in size, and coalesce. The ripples themselves build up into waves. If the wind becomes stronger, the waves begin to break, and whitecaps form. The change from calm to considerable roughness may occur in ten or fifteen minutes.

GREAT WAVES

Nobody who has any knowledge of the sea will ever discount the power of water in motion. One thing that never ceases to amaze is the power of storm waves, for example, to bend iron ladders on the side of a lighthouse. Such a ladder would seem to offer almost no purchase to water. Yet there are numerous cases of iron ladders bent and twisted as if by a giant hand. There are also records of damage done by storm waves to lighthouses

A Dutch rescue boat goes to the aid of a disabled ship in the eastern North Atlantic. (Cees van der Meulen)

Overleaf: Winter storms far to the north send giant waves 100 feet high against lava rocks on the north shore of Oahu. (Werner Stoy, Camera Hawaii)

from one hundred to two hundred feet above sea level. Such records may seem incredible to anyone who has not observed the sea in one of its wilder moods.

On the other hand, the actual heights of storm waves at sea are likely to be exaggerated. Sir John Murray, one of the greatest of oceanographers, mentions waves fifty to sixty feet high, and 560 feet long. This length would be from the trough of one wave to the trough of the next, or from crest to crest. It may help the reader if we point out that sixty feet is higher than a five-story building, and 560 feet is nearly twice the length of a football field.

Waves of this magnitude are of course unusual, but there is little doubt that they actually occur. They cannot, for obvious reasons, be accurately measured, but there are fairly good methods of estimating their height and length: for example, by comparing them with the length of a ship and the height of its masts. The highest wave ever recorded with any real accuracy

was the one sighted from the U. S. Naval tanker *Ramapo* in the mid-Pacific. After the ship had run several days to leeward of a storm, the officer on the bridge saw a mountainous wave astern early on February 7, 1938. Sighting through the crow's-nest to the top of the wave, estimating the angle of the ship and the distance of the wave astern, he then solved a simple problem in geometry by finding the third side of the triangle. The answer was 112 feet. Undoubtedly there was some possibility of error; however, waves of approximately this height are possible under given conditions of wind and sea. Such a wave could last only briefly, for its top would be blown off by any wind sufficient to produce it. In general, however, storm waves probably do not exceed twenty-five to thirty feet, say the height of a two-story house. When such a degree of roughness is reached, the average mariner is willing to settle for what he has, and not look for more. As a matter of fact, wind-driven waves ten feet high constitute a very rough sea.

When a storm is over and the wind has died, the storm waves flatten out into long undulations known collectively as the ocean swell or ground swell, and individually as swells rather than waves. These may travel many hundreds of miles. Persons living along the shore are often surprised to find, in perfectly calm weather, heavy surf rolling up on the beach. This is the aftermath of a storm that may have occurred a thousand miles away.

An aerial view of the "eye" of a hurricane. (Kurt Severin)

In the great southern ocean between Australia, Africa, and South America on the north and Antarctica on the south, where winds sweep endlessly around the world, the ocean swell builds up to heights of thirty or forty feet. These are ordinarily not storm waves, but merely long undulations—the usual condition of the surface of the sea in those latitudes. If a whaleboat must put out from a ship in such a sea, it is immediately lost in a wilderness of swells. The parent ship may be sighted only at intervals of fifteen or twenty minutes, when both it and the small boat happen to be simultaneously on top of swells. To the inexperienced seaman this will seem frightening. But if the whaleboat is in charge of a good boatswain, his situation is hardly more precarious than if he were rowing across a placid lake. The men who work regularly in these great seas put out in small boats on immense swells with no feeling of danger. The only problems are in the launching of the boat and of getting it back aboard.

As for lighthouses damaged high above the open sea, that is not too difficult to explain. A storm wave striking a rocky shore or cliff has no place to go but up, and it may reach a level several times its original height, often carrying with it rocks from the foreshore of sufficient size to do considerable damage. There is a record from the Tillamook light on the Oregon coast of a rock weighing 135 pounds that was carried by a wave to a height of over 100 feet, where it crashed through the roof of the lighthouse keeper's dwelling.

Surprisingly, waves in general do not have a forward component of force; that is, they do not carry objects in the direction in which the waves are moving. It is true that in a high wind the surface water will be carried forward; but once the wind has ceased, objects on the surface, such as a cork, a Japanese fishing-net float, or a small boat, will merely bob up and down as the waves pass under. We should therefore think of waves and swells not as moving a considerable body of water in any direction but merely as undulations.

Measuring the height of a great wave. While the USS *Ramapo* had its stern in the trough between two waves, an officer on the bridge sighted the crest of the following wave on a line with the crow's-nest. Knowing the angle at which the ship was riding, the height of the crow's-nest and the distance from his line of sight to the water line at the stern, he calculated the wave to be 112 feet high.

In the days of sailing ships, wind was a boon to the sailor, for it carried him endless miles across the world. It carried man to lands he would never have known without its aid, and enabled two hardy mariners, Ferdinand Magellan and Sir Francis Drake, to accomplish the first two circumnavigations of the globe.

But wind has also been a hazard. Fair winds have speeded ocean voyages, but opposing winds have hindered them, and high winds have sent many a ship and many a crew to an unrecorded fate. There is a long list of ships that have disappeared without trace. When he signed on for a long voyage on uncharted seas, a seaman knew that he was setting forth on a journey from which he might never return.

In 1805 a British naval officer, Sir Francis Beaufort, devised a system by which mariners might estimate and record the velocity of winds encountered at sea. His system, known as the Beaufort scale, has been almost universally adopted and, with some modifications, is used today for the recording of winds both on sea and land. It originally gave wind velocities a number from zero to twelve.

ORIGINAL BEAUFORT SCALE

Number	Name	Miles per hour
0	Calm	Less than 1
1	Light air	1— 3
2	Light breeze	4— 7
3	Gentle breeze	8—12
4	Moderate breeze	13—18
5	Fresh breeze	19—24
6	Strong breeze	25—31
7	Moderate gale	32—38
8	Fresh gale	39—46
9	Strong gale	47—54
10	Whole gale or full gale	55—63
11	Storm	64—72
12	Hurricane	73 plus

14. A wave explodes in foam on the rugged Oregon coast. (Ray Atkeson)

The Beaufort scale has been expanded by the addition of numbers 13 to 17, the latter figure representing winds from 126 to 136 miles per hour. But even this expansion of the scale does not take into consideration winds of the highest velocity. For a mariner, of course, measuring anything above a hurricane is academic.

The highest wind velocity actually recorded by instruments is 187 miles per hour. Above this velocity the instruments have been wrecked or blown away; but meteorologists believe that winds up to two hundred miles per hour may occur. A full gale produces water as rough as any sea captain cares to encounter. Whether called a hurricane, or a typhoon, as it is off the coast of Asia, or a cyclone or tornado, as it is when it occurs in the Middle

15.   Above: A surf-
boarder rides a 22-foot
wave off Sunset Beach
on the Island of Oahu,
Hawaii. (Carola Gregor)

16. Left: As this wave rushes in on an Oregon beach, the bottom water is retarded by friction, while the crest moves forward and breaks into surf. (Ray Atkeson)

17. Right: Blue water turns green as one looks through an immense wave approaching the shore on Hawaii. (Carola Gregor)

West of the United States, the phenomenon is, usually, basically the same.

Air in motion has a tendency to rotate. The reason for this will be discussed in a subsequent chapter on ocean currents. But the fact is familiar to everyone. In driving across a desert one sees frequent "dust devils," little whirlwinds that pick up the sand or dust and carry it high into the air. At sea these whirling winds frequently produce waterspouts, an awesome though not usually dangerous phenomenon in which a column of water is lifted from the surface of the ocean to meet a funnel-shaped cloud drawn down from above; together they form a wavering, hourglass-shaped structure perhaps a hundred feet high.

The little whirlwinds indicate what may happen on a larger scale. A typhoon, a hurricane, and a tornado all represent swirling columns of air—in some cases several hundred miles in diameter. In the center is a low-pressure area known as the "eye" of the hurricane. When a storm center arrives, there will be calm and even fair weather for a period ranging from minutes to an hour. Then the "other side" of the storm moves into the area, and strong winds again resume. The tag end of a hurricane is usually not so devastating as its advancing front.

Hurricanes are particularly disastrous when they coincide with a high tide and raise water levels to unexpected heights. These disturbances are usually of tropical origin and are commonly thought of in the United States as being peculiar to southern California on the west coast, the Gulf coast and to the West Indies, Florida, Georgia, and the Carolinas in the east. But in 1938 and again in 1944 tropical hurricanes reached New England. In each of these storms several hundred people lost their lives. Property damage in the 1938 storm was estimated at $ 100,000,000 and in the 1944 storm at $ 300,000,000.

Most hurricanes originate in the tropics, but there are extratropical hurricanes of extreme violence. On October 3, 1963, a wind of 92 miles an hour piled up water and ice on the shore of Barrow, Alaska, to a height of twelve feet, destroying homes, wrecking two-thirds of the airport, and creating a channel behind Point Barrow so that what was formerly the northernmost point of the United States became an island.

18. These ripple marks in the sand of Kyushi, Japan, are formed when small waves approach at an angle to the shoreline; large waves erase them. Such marks on the shores of ancient seas are sometimes preserved in geological formations. (Nihon Hasshoku)

WAVES INSIDE THE SEA

It used to be supposed that only the surface of the sea could become agitated and that beyond a few fathoms down the world ocean was a vast region of perpetual calm. Scientists assumed, of course, that water moved along the bottom of Arctic and Antarctic regions to compensate for movement away from the equator due to convection caused by the sun's heat; but this movement was presumed to be too slow to disturb the calm of the depths.

A standard method of studying ocean currents has been to "run sections" across the current, that is, to take a series of water samples at the same depths at stations in a straight line a measured distance apart. From the temperature and salinity of the samples thus obtained, the speed and direction of the current and the areas of upwelling, and so on, were calculated. This method assumed a certain stability in the water layers being studied.

A hurricane hits Miami beach, Florida. (Kurt Severin)

Direct observation, however, cast doubt on this assumption. When a string of water bottles was lowered from a ship the cable would swing in the direction of the surface current, but when the bottles reached a greater depth the cable might swing off at a completely different angle. This indicated that the subsurface waters were subject to complex currents. Occasionally the cable even became tangled, as if the water bottles had been whirled around in a subsurface eddy. Temperature and salinity studies moreover began to show that the thermocline—the interface between the warmer, lighter surface water and the colder, heavier water below—was not a straight line but bounced erratically. Through ingenious methods of recording these bounces, investigators have discovered that the layer of water beneath this boundary behaves as if it were a separate ocean with a surface of its own on which waves are generated. These are known as internal waves. They may travel for great distances, and although their speed is slower than that of surface waves, their amplitude may be very much greater, measuring in exceptional cases from three hundred to five hundred feet from trough to crest.

Among the known causes of internal waves are obstructions blocking

A Dutch vessel trying to beat its way across offshore breakers in the North Sea.
(Cees van der Meulen)

currents on the sea bottom, and different water masses impinging upon each other, as when two currents of different densities meet. Possible causes are variations in atmospheric pressure and strong winds. Internal waves of a certain length have also been found to coincide with tide-producing forces.

This discussion has assumed a surface layer above and the rest of the ocean beneath. But while the major discontinuity does normally occur at the thermocline, the deep ocean consists of a succession of layers of different densities, and the pattern of internal waves may become extremely complex. Further, where opposing currents meet, internal eddies or submarine whirlpools may be formed.

Although water is a liquid and the atmosphere is gaseous, the two media have certain features in common. When a wind is blowing at the earth's surface, it is not at all unusual to observe clouds at a high level being carried in the opposite direction. A plane is occasionally tossed about like a ship in a rough sea. Since the plane is flying *in* the air, not on its surface, the bumps are comparable to internal waves in the ocean. Because air is so much more mobile than water, phenomena common to both occur in the air in a greatly magnified way. An example of this is the planes that have been caught in a

Giant waterspout on
Tampa Bay, as seen
from downtown
St. Petersburg, Florida,
1964. (B. J. Oram)

down draft and have rapidly fallen several thousands of feet before the pilot was able to pull out of the descending column of air.

Leading oceanographers have surmised that something comparable to this, occurring in the ocean, caused the mysterious disappearance of the United States atomic submarine *Thresher* on April 10, 1963. Unusual storm conditions combined with local currents to form a large eddy, perhaps sixty miles across, off Georges Bank at the outer margin of the Gulf of Maine, resulting in a dome-shaped piling up of denser water from the lower layers of the sea. If the *Thresher* was on top of this dome, it could not have moved in any direction without getting into less dense water, which would have caused it to descend. Its descent would have been complicated by violent internal waves, perhaps as large as five hundred feet from trough to crest. Thus the *Thresher* may almost literally have slid off a dome of denser water and, bouncing up and down on internal waves of extraordinary magnitude, been carried toward the bottom more rapidly than it could discharge ballast; when it reached a depth greater than that for which it was designed, it would have been crushed by the pressure of the water.

If this is the correct explanation, we have here a striking example of the potential violence of internal eddies and waves—an undersea ship wrecked in an undersea storm. A naval court of inquiry revealed a number of structural defects in the *Thresher;* but the two explanations are not incompatible, because the ship had successfully test-dived before.

100

Havoc wrought at Hilo, Hawaii, by the tsunami of May, 1960, generated by a severe earthquake in Chile, more than 6,000 miles away. (Werner Stoy, Camera Hawaii)

TSUNAMIS—SEISMIC SEA WAVES

One of the most awesome phenomena in nature is a large seismic sea wave. Such waves have been known through the years as "tidal waves," but this is a complete misnomer, because they have nothing to do with tides. The Japanese term *tsunami* is now being widely adopted. Certainly the Japanese have suffered enough catastrophes from seismic sea waves to be authorities on the subject. Such waves are caused by earthquakes, often under the sea and frequently accompanied by major landslides on the sea bottom. They generally originate along the great oceanic trenches, which are regions of marked instability of the earth's crust.

Waves generated in this manner travel thousands of miles at great velocities—three hundred to five hundred miles an hour. They normally measure a very long distance from trough to crest, and for this reason they generally pass unnoticed by ships at sea, just as a man in an automobile driving across a broad prairie may ascend or descend without any awareness of change of altitude. In the tsunami that devastated the northern end of the island of Honshu, Japan, on June 15, 1896, with a loss of more than twenty-seven thousand lives, fishermen out at sea noticed nothing unusual until they returned home to a scene of desolation and destruction.

Seismic sea waves, just like storm waves or the ordinary ocean swell, build up in height as they move up on a shelving shoreline, and reach their

101

maximum fury when they move into a funnel-shaped harbor. Whenever a severe earthquake occurs along or near the seashore, there is a strong presumption that a seismic sea wave will result, particularly if the movement along the earthquake fault is in a vertical rather than a horizontal direction. This was what happened in the devastating Alaskan earthquake of March 27, 1964. There appears to have been a tilting of a block of the earth's crust, as a result of which Kodiak Island sank about six feet, while the town of Cordova on the mainland was elevated a corresponding amount. The city of Anchorage went down about three feet. A well-constructed government building at Kodiak withstood the earthquake and tsunami, but was permanently lowered to the extent that the first floor became regularly flooded at high tide. One end of Montague Island in Prince William Sound was elevated more than thirty feet.

The tsunami at Kodiak did at least as much damage as the earthquake itself; between the two the town was practically wiped out. The wave then proceeded down the coast toward California, where it arrived at Crescent City on the early morning of the following day and destroyed fifty-six blocks of the main part of the city. A Crescent City official said afterward, "Our greatest problem was the reluctance of people to heed the warning."

The rate of travel and the time of arrival of a tsunami on a distant shore can be calculated with considerable accuracy, but whether the wave will be large or small cannot be predicted. Probably no more than one tsunami out of a thousand does any serious damage; this sometimes gives a feeling of false security when a really big one is on the way.

The tsunami that devastated Hilo, Hawaii, in 1960 originated from a severe earthquake in Chile. Its time of arrival at Hilo was accurately predicted and the people were warned, but many paid little attention. Even observers from the United States Coast and Geodetic Survey, who were watching for the wave, were astonished by its magnitude when they saw it entering the harbor, and had to run for their lives to higher ground. The business district of Hilo was thoroughly wrecked and a number of people were killed.

If more people understood the behavior of such waves many lives might be saved, because tsunamis often provide their own warning service. The first evidence of an approaching seismic sea wave is a great ebb of the water, far beyond the level of the lowest normal low tide. Then the crest of the wave arrives, and the water rushes in with tremendous force. I was in Honolulu at the time of the tsunami of 1957. Noticing dozens of people on the beach gazing seaward, I joined them and saw that all of the coral reefs were uncovered as far out as one could see. Not a single person did the proper thing, which was to head for the hills without a moment's delay. As it happened, little or no damage was done along the Honolulu waterfront by the ensuing wave; but on the other side of the island of Oahu there was some loss of life and considerable damage.

The height of such waves is often astonishing. The wave resulting from the Lisbon earthquake in 1755 is said to have been fifty feet high, and that following the eruption of Krakatoa in 1883 reached a height of 100 feet or more on the coast of Java, and on the island of Sumatra carried a gunboat two miles inland and left it there, high and dry. On October 6, 1737, a tsunami is said to have reached a height of 210 feet at the southern end of the peninsula of Kamchatka. This might be regarded merely as a tall tale, except for the following all-time record, which is fully documented, with photographic proof. On the evening of January 9, 1958, an earthquake at Lituya Bay, Alaska, caused a giant rock slide on the steep northeast wall of Gilbert Inlet, an arm of Lituya Bay. It is estimated that 40 million cubic yards of rock fell from a maximum height of 3,000 feet. The resulting surge of water rushed up the opposite wall of the inlet, which was forested, sweeping the slope completely bare of trees to an altitude of 1,740 feet. Then it moved down and out of the bay as a seismic wave traveling at an estimated speed of 100 miles an hour. Three fishing boats were in the bay at the time, each about 40 feet long. One was sunk and its crew lost. Another was carried across the spit at the entrance to the bay at a height estimated by the owner to be eighty feet above the tops of trees growing on the spit. The owner of the third vessel, seeing a wave that he estimated to be 100 feet high rushing toward him down the bay tried to lift his anchor, but it was wedged among rocks. He then let out all the anchor chain he had, about forty fathoms, started his engine and headed into the wave. It broke his anchor chain—which would probably have pulled him under—and after bouncing the vessel around, left it back in mid-channel, unharmed.

A wave of this sort is not by precise definition a tsunami, because the rock slide occurred above sea level and fell into the water; but the phenomena are closely similar, and the great wave of Lituya Bay gives us an understanding of how earthquakes and landslides at the edges of deep submarine trenches can cause devasting seismic waves by simple displacement of the water.

The owners of the two surviving vessels report experiencing a strong shock wave from the earthquake, transmitted through the water, prior to the immense wave generated by the rock slide. This is not unusual: ships at sea have frequently reported a strong shock as if they had struck a rock. But this is by no means universal, and seems to depend on the distance of the ship from the focus, or epicenter, of the earthquake—perhaps also on certain characteristics of the quake itself.

6

The Tides

Notwithstanding King Canute's vain effort to make the tide stand still at his command, ocean tides have long been known as a recurring and inexorable phenomenon. They were mentioned by the Grecian historian Herodotus in the fifth century B.C.; and the Roman historian Pliny the Elder, in the first century A.D., had learned that they were related to the sun and the moon. But the tides received little study in classical times, perhaps because the Mediterranean tides, having a range of only two or three feet, attracted the interest of only the most curious.

The tides along the coast of England, on the other hand, are very impressive, in some places measuring more than forty feet between high and low water. It was natural that the tides should have been seriously studied there: Britain was a growing maritime power, and the knowledge of the time of high water and of flood and ebb currents was of the utmost importance.

Japanese clam-diggers on a sandy beach at low tide. (Yoichi Midorikawa, Orion)

Even if the ancients had applied themselves to the problem of the tides they could not have solved it, for there was no body of knowledge to which the behavior of the tides could be related. It was not until Isaac Newton expounded the theory of gravitation that a serious beginning could be made. Newton applied his theory in his description of the tide-producing forces, but he left to others the application to the actual tides. For more than two centuries thereafter the latter task occupied some of the best scientists of two continents, including William Whewell, John William Lubbock, George Darwin in England, and R. A. Harris in America.

In the meantime, tide prediction was developed on an empirical basis, that is, from day-to-day observation. It was obvious that the tide had some relation to the moon, for the highest tides came soon after the new and the full moon. It was observed that high tide, like the rising of the moon, came fifty minutes later each day. With such elementary data, during the seventeenth and eighteenth centuries tide tables for the ports of London and Liverpool were published by private individuals. The methods of prediction were a sort of trade secret, and when Whewell and Lubbock, early in the nineteenth century, attempted to put tide prediction on a scientific basis, it was said that they were interfering with private industry!

Scientists, however, encountered problems more serious than this. Since the tides are rhythmical, it is relatively easy to predict their behavior on the basis of careful observations, but there are many complications that early

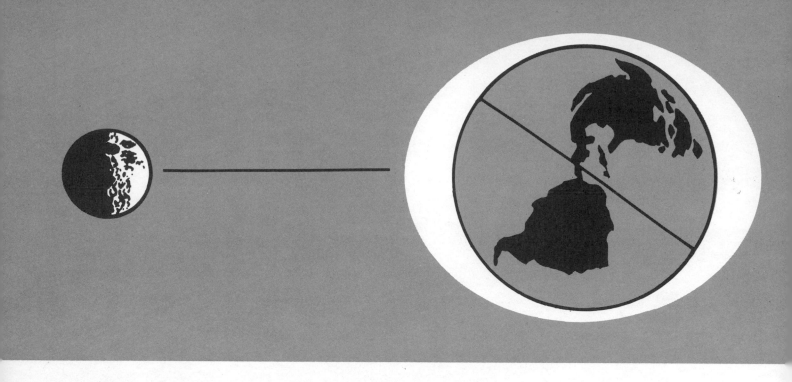

theorists could not explain. Why, for example, does Avenmouth, on the west coast of England, have a tidal range of forty-nine feet, while Heligoland, near the west coast of Germany, has a range of only ten feet? To take an even more striking example, why does the tide at the Atlantic end of the Panama Canal have a range of only about a foot, while at the Pacific end it has a range of sixteen feet? Why do islands in the very middle of the Pacific, such as Tahiti, have a tide of little more than one foot.

The language used in describing the tides needs some explaining. Shakespeare wrote in *Julius Caesar:*

> There is a tide in the affairs of men
> Which, taken at the flood, leads on to fortune . . .

Many people reading this assume that flood tide is the same as high tide. This is not so. A flood tide is an incoming tide that is moving toward high water. The outgoing tide is known as the ebb. Both flood and ebb currents reach their maximum velocity about mid-tide. The velocity of the current then decreases, and at the turn of the tide the water seems for a brief time to stand still. This period is known as slack water and is referred to as high-water slack or low-water slack. Not knowing that the speed with which the tide rises increases from low to mid-tide, many people have been marooned and even drowned by an incoming tide.

Students were for many years puzzled by the fact that some places have only one high and one low water a day, a single tide, and others—these are in a majority—have two tides a day. If there is only one high and one low water a day, this is known as a diurnal tide. If there are two tides a day, with the levels approximately equal, this is known as a semidiurnal tide. If there are two tides a day but the levels are definitely different, this is known as a mixed tide. In describing a mixed tide we have to use such complicated terms as a higher high water, a higher low water, a lower high water, and a lower low. The levels of these also change from day to day.

It is no wonder that early students of the tide were puzzled. But it is now possible to give a fairly simple explanation of such variations.

When the moon is north or south of the plane of the earth's equator, unequal tides result, so that in either hemisphere one of the daily high tides will be higher than the other. Twice a month, when the moon crosses the earth's equator, the two high tides of a day will be approximately equal.

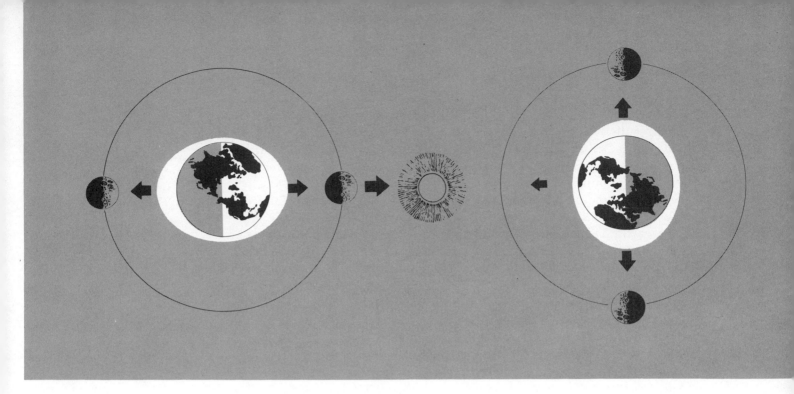

THE TIDE-PRODUCING FORCES

The sun and moon, exercising gravitational force in a straight line (at new moon and full moon), produce large tides known as spring tides. When they pull in opposition to each other (the moon in its first or last quarter), the tides are small and are called neap tides.

To understand the behavior of the tides, it is necessary to know that the tide-producing forces are gravitational and depend on the relative positions of sun, moon, and earth. All of the bodies in the solar system, of course, exercise a gravitational pull on the earth and on each other; but the planets, because of their distance relative to that of the moon and their small size relative to that of the sun, have a negligible effect on the tides.

The moon revolves about the earth in an elliptical orbit, just as the earth revolves about the sun. Notwithstanding the sun's vastly greater mass, it exercises, because of its immensely greater distance from the earth, only two-fifths as much gravitational pull as the moon. Thus the moon is the major tide-producing force, but the effect of the sun is by no means negligible. It is the interaction of the gravitational pull of sun and moon that produces the most significant tidal effects.

As everyone knows, the sun is seen north of the earth's equator during half the year and south of the equator during the other half. Twice a year, at the spring and autumn equinoxes, the sun is on the earth's equator, and twice a year, at the summer and winter solstices, it reaches its maximum distance north or south of the equator. The apparent position of the sun relative to the equator is known as its declination. Thus when the sun is on the equator, its declination is $0°$. Its maximum declination is $23\frac{1}{2}°$, which is the latitude north or south of the equator, respectively, of the Tropic of Cancer and the Tropic of Capricorn.

The moon's relation to the earth is very similar to the earth's relation to the sun, except that its orbit is smaller and is completed in twenty-eight days—a lunar month. Thus the moon crosses the earth's equator twice a month, and twice a month reaches its maximum north or south declination. Because the orbits of earth and moon are elliptical, the tide-producing force of the sun is greatest when the earth is nearest the sun, that is, in its perihelion; and that of the moon is greatest when it is nearest the earth, that is, in its perigee.

It is obvious that the interaction of all these forces must yield very complicated results. We can only consider a few specific cases.

Tidal forces act on the earth as well as the sea, but because the earth is rigid it is only very slightly affected. Water, being fluid and mobile, responds easily to a tidal pull.

Let us for a moment assume that the earth is round, smooth, and uniformly covered with water, and that no friction exists between the water and the earth. The earth would then rotate within an envelope of water. In a polar view of the earth-moon system, there is a tidal bulge on the side that is facing toward the moon. Somewhat unexpectedly, there is an equal bulge on the opposite side; this is due to the gravitational force of the moon which pulls the water away from the earth on one side and pulls the earth away from the water on the other. Now if we assume the earth rotating frictionlessly inside its envelope of water, a given point on the earth's surface will have two high waters and two low waters a day.

Let us now introduce the effect of the sun's gravitational pull. At the time of new or full moon, the sun, moon and earth are nearly in line, and at that time the sun's tide-producing effect is added to that of the moon, producing larger tidal bulges. We have said that sun, moon, and earth are *nearly* in line. At rare intervals they are exactly in line; when this occurs at new moon we have an eclipse of the sun, and when it occurs at full moon, we have an eclipse of the moon. An eclipse has no relation to the tides, except that when sun, moon, and earth are precisely in line the tide should be a very little higher than when they are only approximately in line.

When the moon is in its first or third quarter, its gravitational pull is at a 90° angle to the direction of the pull of the sun. The moon still dominates, but because it is working against the pull of the sun, the tidal bulges are smaller. Thus high tides are not so high, and low tides are not so low, as when sun and moon are working together. Since there is one full moon and one new moon each month, and one first- and one third-quarter moon, we have two periods each month of large tides, known as spring tides, and two periods a month when they are small, known as neap tides. In between these standard phases of the moon, conditions change from day to day. The spring tides gradually become smaller until they are neap tides; then the neap tides gradually increase to the period of spring tides. There is no name for these intermediate phases.

There is one more factor—the declination of the sun and moon. During

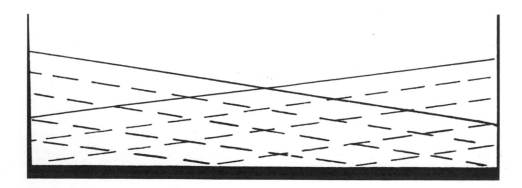

A stationary wave can be demonstrated by taking a tray of water and sloshing it back and forth. When it is high tide at one end of the tray, it is low tide at the other. The nodal point in the middle never changes its level.

A low tide near Bristol, England, leaves a fascinating pattern of ripple marks on a mudflat. (Aerofilms Ltd.)

the maximum northern declination of the moon, the resultant tidal bulges are asymmetrical with reference to the equator, in either hemisphere one high tide (higher high water) being higher than the other (lower high water). This explains why the two tides of a single day are usually not alike. As the moon moves back toward the equator, the two tides of the day become more nearly equal. When the sun and the moon are both on the earth's equator, as occurs about the time of the spring and autumn equinoxes, and in June and December, when briefly the sun and the moon are both at their greatest declination, we have the highest tides of the year.

As complex as the tide-producing factors obviously are, they behave in a predictable way. Spring as well as neap tides occur twice a month, their height influenced by the declination of moon and sun and by the distance between these bodies and the earth as governed by the elliptical orbits of moon and earth. Equinoxial tides occur twice a year. Every 4½ years and every nine years, and at certain longer intervals, the tides have an even greater range than usual. The absolute maximum of tide-producing forces due to the configuration of earth, sun and moon, occurs only about once every 1600 years. This absolute maximum of the tides occurred last in A.D. 1433, and may have been responsible for much of the trouble the Dutch had with their dikes in the Middle Ages; it may even have modified the climate of northern latitudes through increased tidal flow of relatively warm ocean water. The next such maximum will occur in the year 3033.

BEHAVIOR OF THE TIDES

Let us abandon the fiction of a smooth, frictionless earth, and consider the way the tides actually behave. First, friction between earth and water and in

the water itself slows down the movement of the tide, creating a lag between it and the force that produced it. Thus the highest tides of the month do not occur precisely at new and full moon, but a day or two later. It is obvious, moreover, that a tidal bulge cannot run freely around the world in the manner we suggested because the continents are in the way.

The only place where a tidal bulge could run an uninterrupted course around the world is the Antarctic Ocean. Early in the nineteenth century, people believed that the tide originated in the Antarctic and flowed northward into the Atlantic, Pacific, and Indian oceans. This theory, known as the "progressive wave" theory, now seems absurd, because the entire world tide would have to pass through a channel some six hundred miles wide between the Antarctic Continent and the southernmost part of South America. As tidal observations from more ports became available, it grew clear that the tide does not move as a progressive wave from south to north.

It was then reasoned that tides must be generated separately in each ocean basin, and the progressive wave theory gave place to the "stationary wave" theory, which, with some modifications, is still held. This can be easily understood if one takes a rectangular pan partly filled with water and tilts it gently back and forth, causing the water to oscillate. It will rise at one end of the pan as it falls at the other. This is a stationary wave. At the center of the pan, the level will not change, although there will be a flow of the water back and forth. This is the nodal point of the oscillation, known in tidal terminology as the amphidromic point.

Effect of earthquake wave, Lituya Bay, Alaska. Promontory was cleared of trees to an estimated height of 1,740 feet. (U. S. Department of Commerce)

To make our example more accurate, we should have to take the pan by the corners and move it in such a way as to give the wave a circular motion. A ship riding at anchor in a shallow sea—for example, a light-ship anchored near a coast—would swing around in a complete circle every twelve hours and twenty-five minutes if affected only by the tide and not by wind.

An ocean seldom or never constitutes a single unit from the standpoint of tidal oscillation, but is broken up by its irregular bottom configuration into several smaller tidal basins, and thus is likely to have several amphidromic points. It follows, moreover, that where tidal oscillations of different period and magnitude meet and mingle, an extremely confusing situation results. But the stationary wave concept, developed largely by R. A. Harris of the United States Coast and Geodetic Survey, makes it possible to explain in a general way the apparent vagaries of tidal behavior.

An important phase of the stationary wave theory is the concept of resonance, meaning reinforcement of a wave by the surroundings in which it is produced. Resonance is just as significant in a tidal basin as it is in the sound box of a violin or in an auditorium. Every tidal basin has a period of oscillation natural to it, depending on its size and shape. The liquid in a cup of coffee and that in a plate of soup have a different period of motion; it may be noticed that when a person carrying both of these on a tray stumbles, one may splash over while the other does not.

If we revert to our pan of water, and tilt it back and forth at a rate cor-

Rear view of a tidal bore passing up the Severn River, near Gloucester, England. It travels 21 miles from Awre to Gloucester at an average speed of 5 miles per hour. (British Information Service)

responding to the natural oscillation of water in a pan of that length, the stationary wave will increase in range till it slops over the edge. If, however, we change the rate at which we tilt the pan, this will interfere with the wave and cause it to decrease. Similarly, if a body of water constituting a tidal unit in an ocean has a natural period of oscillation corresponding to the period of the tide-producing forces, large tides will result; but if such correspondence is lacking, recurrence of the tide-producing forces will interfere with the oscillation of the water and the tides will be small.

This concept also helps us to understand why some ports have a diurnal tide, others a semidiurnal tide and still others a mixed tide. If a body of water has a natural period of oscillation of about twenty-four hours and fifty minutes, it will have a diurnal tide—one high and one low water a day. If its natural period of oscillation is twelve hours and twenty-five minutes, it will have a semidiurnal tide. If its natural period is in between these two, it will have a mixed tide, which is the most common type of tide.

If the reader finds this confusingly complex, it may comfort him to know that Aristotle is said to have fallen into despair after attempting to find an explanation for the particularly puzzling tides in the Strait of Euripos off the Aegean Sea. There the tides, after behaving more or less normally for several days, ebb and flow twelve to fourteen times a day. There was no theory known to Aristotle which could explain this. But with the stationary wave theory we can at least begin to explain it as the result of normal tides in the Aegean Sea complicated by local oscillations in the Strait of Euripos.

TIDE PREDICTION

All this would seem to suggest that it is nearly impossible to predict tides; but in fact tide prediction is fairly easy for the simple reason that the tides in any locality repeat themselves from year to year, and variations resulting from astronomical factors are also predictable for years or even centuries in advance.

Sir George Darwin, a son of the famous biologist, worked out an ingenious method of predicting the tides, but his system required a discouraging number of mathematical calculations. The difficulty was solved by the invention of a tide machine, which is amazingly simple in principle. If a string is threaded through a series of pulleys operated by plungers, each plunger representing a different tide-producing factor (e. g., sun, moon, declination of sun and moon, apogee, perigee, aphelion, perihelion, etc.), the string will integrate all of these factors and, if attached to a pen moving on a revolving drum, will record the result. In other words, the string pulled this way and that by a series of pulleys performs a great number of operations in integral calculus.

To predict the tides for any locality in the world, it is necessary to have reliable observations for a period of only one year. If these records are fed into the machine, it can furnish predictions for any year in the future. Such tide tables, issued by the United States Coast and Geodetic Survey, and by the British Admiralty, are accurate almost to the minute, except as the tides are occasionally affected by weather. An offshore wind can delay a tide, while an onshore wind can accelerate it and build it up. Devastating floods

19. Right: Ripple-marked mudflats have a beauty all their own, and at low tide they uncover a host of interesting organisms. Wrightsville Beach, North Carolina. (Jack Dermid)

20. Upper left: Low tide in a narrow inlet, North Cornwall, England. The dark line along the shore indicates the average high tide. Lower left: High tide in the same inlet. (D. P. Wilson)

21. Where lava rock is eroded by the sea, black sands are formed, as on St. Vincent Island, West Indies. (Nancy Palmer)

22. Surf beating on stratified rock wears away the softer portions, leaving the harder, and providing this terraced effect. Aoshima Island, Japan. (Orion Press)

have been caused in low-lying areas near the sea when a high tide, driven onshore by a strong gale, has exceeded the predicted level.

THE GREATEST TIDES

As we have said, at various points along the coast of England there is a range of forty feet or more between high and low water. Along the coast of southeastern Alaska a range of thirty-six feet is not uncommon. But the greatest tides in the world occur in the Bay of Fundy, which lies between New Brunswick and Nova Scotia. Here the tide has a range of fifty feet, that is, about the height of a four- or five-story building. Fishing boats resting on the mud at low tide will, six hours later, be floating in water fifty feet deep. To avoid being stranded at low water, cargo boats must come in at high tide, unload rapidly, and depart.

One reason for the large range of the tide there is that the bay is eighty-seven miles wide at its mouth and narrows toward its head, thus crowding the incoming water into a narrower and narrower channel. But the principal factor appears to be that the size and shape of the bay are such that the normal period of oscillation of its waters would be about twelve hours. One tidal expert, H. A. Marmer, calculated it to be 11 hours and 15 minutes, but such calculations, based on length, width and depth of an irregularly shaped body of water, are necessarily only approximations. In the Bay of Fundy the normal period of oscillation of the water corresponds almost exactly to the rhythm of the tide-producing forces, resulting in the largest tide in the world, and lending convincing support to the stationary wave theory.

It has been mentioned that the rate of flow of the water is greatest at mid-tide. In very large tides, or those confined to a narrowing channel, the rising tide may come in as a great surge of water, known as a bore. This phenomenon occurs in the Bay of Fundy, in the Severn and Solway rivers in England, in the Amazon River, and in Cook Inlet near Anchorage, Alaska, and in Hangchow Bay in North China. The tidal bore in the Bay of Fundy moves at a speed of 8 ½ miles an hour, with a sound like that of a distant train. At times it reaches a maximum height of about five feet. In Hangchow Bay the moving wall of water is said to reach the extraordinary height of ten feet.

It is obvious to anyone watching a phenomenon of this sort, or even the more ordinary ebb and flow of the tide, that a tremendous amount of energy is involved; and many men over many years have dreamed of harnessing the tides as a source of power. H. A. Marmer calculated that a flood tide brings into the Bay of Fundy more than 3.5 billion cubic feet of water. But to harness this energy would require building a dam eighty-seven miles long with an average height of 280 feet!

President Franklin D. Roosevelt was deeply interested in a more modest project to harness the tides of Passamaquoddy Bay, an arm of the Bay of Fundy. This was to have been a cooperative project undertaken between Canada and the United States but since the United States has declined to appropriate sufficient funds for the Passamquoddy project, Canada is studying the idea of proceeding independently to develop the tidal resources of the Bay of Fundy.

23. A river entering the sea at Cape Siar, New Ireland, New Guinea, creates an eddy or countercurrent contrary to the main current. (Eric Read)

A great wave called a tidal bore is created by water rushing from the Bay of Fundy into the Petitcodiac River, New Brunswick. It sometimes reaches a height of 5 feet and the amazing speed of 8½ miles per hour, depending, like the tides, on lunar influence.
(New Brunswick Travel Bureau)

Gill-nets set at low tide in the Bay of Fundy catch shad on the flood tide; at the next low tide the catch is removed. The work can be hazardous since the tide comes in very fast and the fishermen must travel several miles in their rounds.
(Richard Harrington)

In the meantime, France completed, in 1966, an experimental 226-megawatt tidal power plant in the Rance Estuary near Saint-Malo. The experiment was considered a success; but the larger project—of which this was to be the forerunner—that of using the 220 square miles of the Bay of Mont-Saint-Michel for a tidal plant that would produce an amount of electricity equal to about half the total now produced in all of France, was temporarily abandoned because of the expense. Now, with the shortage and sharply increased cost of petroleum, the original plans have been reconsidered and improved, and what once seemed to many to be a visionary scheme may become a reality.

Britain and Russia are also experimenting with means of harnessing tidal power. There seems little question that this can be done in suitable localities; but there are rather few good localities, and it has to be demonstrated that the amount of power derived from a tidal plant will justify the cost of construction and maintenance, and be competitive with other sources of power.

Whether or not man becomes able to control their energy for his own advantage, the tides accomplish a remarkable amount of work. A tidal current of one-half mile an hour will begin to move sand along the bottom; a current of one mile an hour will move fine gravel; and a current of 2.5 miles an hour will move coarse gravel up to perhaps an inch in diameter. In areas where tides are strong, currents up to twelve miles an hour have been measured. It is plain, therefore, that tidal currents are important agents in transporting sand and gravel. They are, in fact, responsible for building the bars that obstruct the entrance to many harbors throughout the world.

7

The Ocean Currents

If the earth did not rotate on its axis, and if it were not for the compelling influence of the wind, we should have a very simple system of circulation in the oceans: a north-south movement deriving its energy from the differences in temperature between the tropics and higher latitudes. At the equator the water is warmed by direct and reasonably constant radiation from the sun. Heated water expands, causing a rise in sea level in the tropics. Wherever gravity exists, it is an inviolable rule that water seeks its own level; hence this equatorial mound of warmed, expanded water flows to the north and to the south, to be replaced by cooler water from below, which immediately is subjected to the same process. In other words, under the heating of the tropical sun convection currents are established.

The heating by the sun has the further effect of increasing the rate of evaporation in the tropics, so that water flowing away from the equator has a greater salt content, which has important consequences. As this warm, salubrious surface water moves into higher latitudes, it is gradually cooled, thus becoming more dense. There comes a point at which it is little or not at all warmer than the waters of the latitude into which it has moved. Originally lighter because it was warmer, the water from the tropics is now heavier because of its greater salinity; and it sinks slowly to the bottom, and creeps back toward the equator, whence surface water is constantly being removed by the process we have described.

There is a smaller replica of this system in reverse, in both the Arctic and the Antarctic, which for the moment may be described as a counter-current. But more of that later.

We have now established a basic principle of oceanic circulation—a slow but constant drift of warm tropical water along the surface to higher latitudes both north and south, and a compensatory drift of cold bottom water toward the equator, where it rises again to greet the warming sun. This is oversimplified, and is subject to endless variations, some of them not yet understood. For example, there is evidence that bottom water from the Antarctic creeps far north of the equator before it rises to become surface water in the Pacific.

Now let us consider the complications introduced by the rotation of the earth, which has the effect of deflecting all freely moving bodies over the earth's surface from a straight to a curved path, the curve being to the right in the Northern Hemisphere and to the left in the Southern. Baseball players need not be concerned—the effect over a short distance is small, and besides, the effect on every pitched ball is uniform. But if one were able to throw a baseball a hundred miles, the effect of the earth's rotation would be startling. This deflection is called Coriolis force, after a nineteenth-century French mathematician and engineer whose name has now been rescued from obscurity by the development of ballistic missiles. It is impossible to aim a long-range missile without taking account of the rotation of the earth. This rotation, which, as the rising sun tells us, is to the eastward, imparts an easterly momentum to all objects on the earth's surface, be they liquid, gas, or solid. Because the diameter of the earth is greatest at the equator, objects there will travel faster than in higher latitudes. A man standing on the equator, though he feels no sense of motion, is traveling eastward at a speed in excess of thousand miles an hour—or 25,000 miles in twenty-four hours.

At latitudes to the north or south of the equator, the circumference of the earth becomes progressively smaller. At latitude 45° N.—the latitude of Minneapolis, and approximately that of Bordeaux—the distance around the earth is 17,640 miles. Here our traveler would be going only 735 miles per hour, staying in the same place. A man standing eight miles from either the North or the South Pole would complete his circuit of the pole, a distance of about twenty-five miles, at a speed of hardly more than one mile per hour, that is, one-thousandth of his speed at the equator.

Now let us substitute for our standing man a moving object. The farther and faster an object moves, the more dramatically it will illustrate Coriolis force. An intercontinental ballistic missile launched from a spot on the equator and aimed at Minneapolis would miss its target by many hundreds of miles. The reason for this is that the missile, propelled northward at supersonic speed, is also being carried eastward with the speed of the point at which it was launched, something like 1,040 miles an hour. When it arrives at Minneapolis, that city traveling eastward at only 735 miles an hour, will not have arrived at the rendezvous. In other words, the path of the projectile, although aimed due north, will be a curve to the eastward that grows greater as the missile moves into latitudes where the circumference of the earth is smaller. In the Southern Hemisphere, of course, the situation would be completely reversed.

Understanding Coriolis force, we can see why ocean currents, moving to the north or south, will be deflected to the right, or in a clockwise direction, in the Northern Hemisphere, and to the left, or in a counterclockwise direction, in the Southern Hemisphere. This explains the great, slow-moving vortices in the North and South Pacific, in the North and South Atlantic, and in the Indian Ocean.

But there are countercurrents, too—currents moving opposite to the general course of oceanic circulation. A countercurrent is best explained as an eddy, and may be observed in any swiftly moving mountain stream. Wherever a widening of the banks permits, an eddy will form; if a stick is

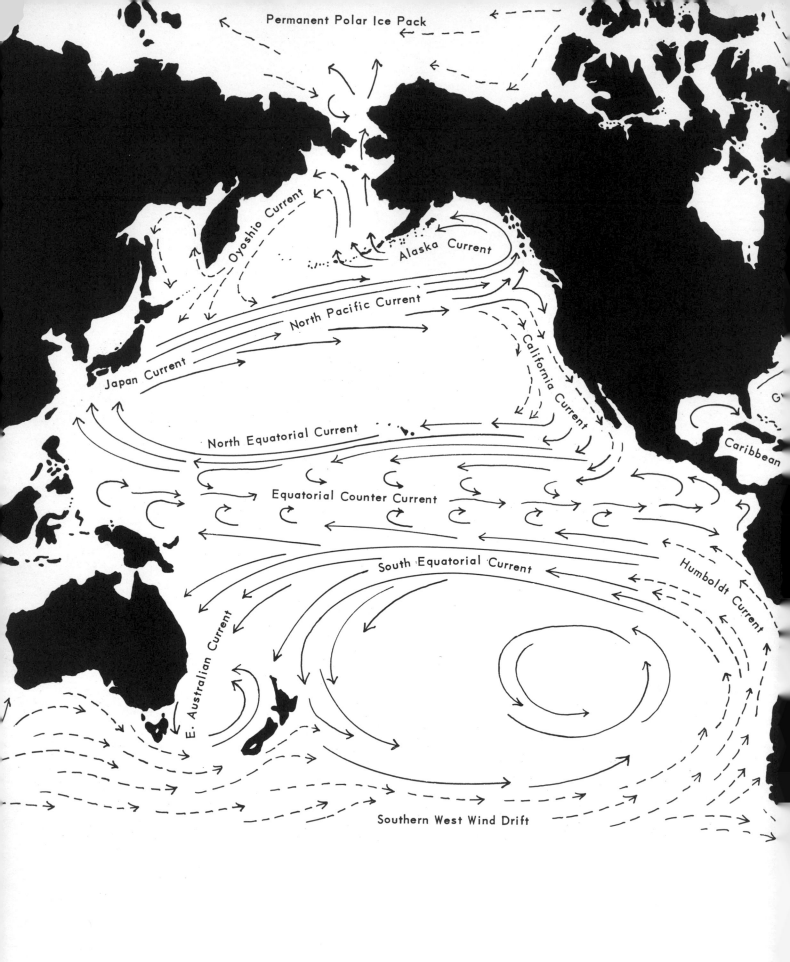

Permanent Polar Ice Pack

E. Greenland Current

North Atlantic Current

Canary Current

Sea

Equatorial Current

Guinea Current

South Equatorial Current

Brazil Current

Benguela Current

Mozambique Current

Agulhas Current

SW and NE

Monsoon Drift

Equatorial Counter Current

South Equatorial Current

W. Australian Current

Southern West Wind Drift

Major Ocean Currents of the World. Warm currents are
shown by solid lines, cold currents by broken lines.
Currents are considered warm or cold in relation to
latitude and effect on climate, a "warm" current in the
Aleutians, for example, having a lower temperature than a
"cold" current along the northwest coast of Africa.

123

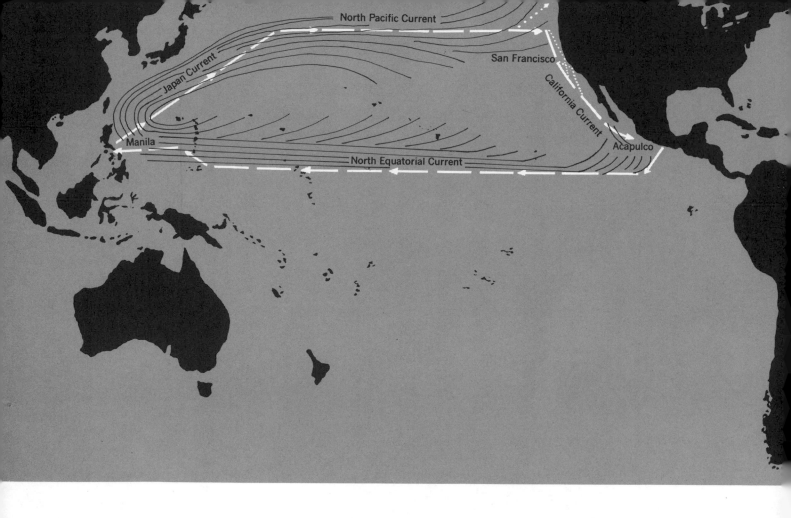

thrown into the stream, it may be swept along in the main flow or it may be carried to the edge of the main current and then move upstream close to shore.

The mechanics may be understood by thinking of two intermeshed cogwheels; if one moves, the other moves automatically in the reverse direction. Now if we substitute friction—which, because of the viscosity of water, is always present when water is in motion—we can understand how the great ocean currents tend to produce countercurrents at their edges. The best example of this is the equatorial countercurrent in the Pacific.

In the great circulation system of the oceans, we have two giant whorls of water in the Pacific, one moving in a clockwise direction in the North Pacific, one moving counterclockwise in the South Pacific. These two mighty streams do not impinge. Each contributes along its equatorial edge to a slow, eastwardly moving countercurrent that extends all the way across the equatorial Pacific to the Central American region, where it breaks up into a complex system of eddies that is still under study.

Winds have such a strong effect on ocean currents that surface currents are often referred to as "wind currents," and many oceanographers consider winds the primary cause of ocean currents. But most of these authorities will acknowledge that winds are only the proximate cause of ocean currents, and that if there were no wind, we still would have a circulation of the ocean waters not too dissimilar to what exists today, although it would undoubtedly be much slower.

Perhaps the most accurate statement is that ocean currents and prevailing winds have the same causes—differential heating between the tropics and

Route of the Manila Galleons. The course, shown in broken lines, followed the great clockwise gyral formed by the North Equatorial, Japan, North Pacific, and California Currents.

124

higher latitudes, convection currents, and the rotation of the earth. Because the air is so much more mobile than the water, and takes up and gives off heat so much more rapidly, it can either accelerate the surface currents of the ocean, slow down, or even turn them back, as at the northern edge of the Indian Ocean, where the current reverses itself twice a year under the influence of prevailing winds.

THE PACIFIC OCEAN

The system of currents in the Pacific may be regarded as typical, since this is the largest of the oceans and the currents are least affected by land masses. The North Equatorial Current streams westward toward the coast of Asia where, in the vicinity of the Philippine Islands, it turns north, becoming the Japan Current or, as it is known to the Japanese, the Kuroshio (meaning dark, i.e., blue water). Off the coast of Japan it is met by a cold current, the Oyashio, coming down from the north along the Kamchatka coast. This is recognizable over great distances by its greenish color. The reason for the difference in color is that the cold water from the north is rich in microscopic plant and animal life, while the warm water of the Japan Current is relatively devoid of such life, and hence transparent and blue. These two currents meet and flow eastward across the North Pacific, forming the North Pacific Current, which is warm along its southern border and cold along its northern edge. When this current reaches the coast of North America, at about the latitude of Vancouver Island, it divides into two parts, one flowing northward into the Gulf of Alaska as the Aleutian Current, the other flowing southward as the California Current.

Here we run into a momentarily confusing phenomenon: the Aleutian Current behaves as a warm current, but the California Current behaves as a cool current. The reason is that temperature is a relative matter. The Aleutian Current has all the effects of a warm current because it is moving northward into a colder latitude, producing fog, mist, and rain along the Alaskan coast and in the Aleutian Islands.

The California Current, on the other hand, behaves as a warm current at its northern end, off the coasts of Washington, Oregon, and northern California, because it is in a rather cool latitude. So along the northwest coast, the California Current may be considered a warm current, ameliorating the winter temperatures in those latitudes, and at the same time producing a considerable rainfall. Somewhere along the northern California coast the temperatures on land become equal to the temperature of the current, and from there on south it is a cooling current until it merges again with the North Equatorial Current, is warmed by the benevolent tropical sun, and continues its endless journey around the North Pacific. It has been estimated that a drop of water in the periphery of the North Pacific gyral would require about two years to complete one circuit of that ocean.

In its journey southward the California Current receives an assist in its role as a cool current from the rotation of the earth. It has already been explained how Coriolis force deflects a southerly-moving current in the Northern Hemisphere continually to the westward. Off the coast of central and southern California this effect becomes of considerable importance. The

California Current is deflected away from shore, and since sea level must remain the same, this westerly moving water must be replaced. The only source is deeper water from the basin of the Pacific; so as the California Current swings away from the coast, a mass of colder bottom water comes up from the depths between it and the shore. The shoreside water may be several degrees colder than the California Current itself.

This phenomenon is known as upwelling. It occurs in various places in the world, and is quite important in bringing up bottom water, rich in nutrients that contribute to an abundant growth of plant and animal life in surface waters. Since upwelling involves the flowing of surface currents away from the place of upwelling, regions in which this occurs are known as areas of divergence. The opposite process, in which surface currents flow together and the surface water drops to a lower level, is known as convergence. Since sea level must remain approximately constant, areas of divergence and convergence must be about equal. But areas of divergence are a good deal better known, since they produce, among other things, water that is uncomfortably cold for swimming, and considerable fog.

Along the California coast upwelling is particularly a phenomenon of the spring and summer months, because during that period the prevailing winds are from the northwest. Coriolis force explains the seemingly contradictory fact that a northwest wind can produce a southwest current. The force of the wind accelerates the California Current, while the earth's rotation makes the accelerated current swing increasingly to the right or away from shore, causing cold water to well up on the shoreward side.

In the winter, when upwelling is at a minimum, we find a countercurrent moving northward along the Pacific coast at the inner edge of the California Current. This is known as the Davidson Current. Coming from the south, it is to some extent a warming current. Its effect can sometimes be noted as far north as the Strait of Juan de Fuca. In summer the Davidson Current is obscured or obliterated by upwelling.

In the South Pacific Ocean the major currents move, for reasons already explained, in a counterclockwise direction, and in general the current system is the reverse of that found in the North Pacific. However, there are

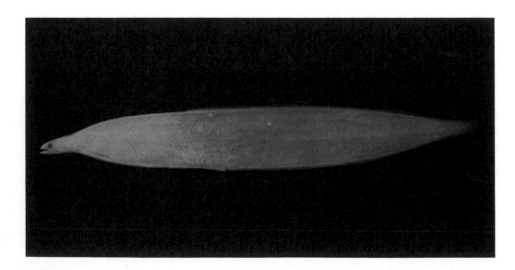

The sea-going larva of the common fresh-water eel, at first considered a new kind of fish, was named leptocephalus. It becomes an elver and finally an adult European eel. (J. H. Fraser)

The European eel,
which develops from
the intermediate stage
known as an elver.
The adult eels live in
fresh water, but return
to the ocean to spawn.
(M. Pasotti)

special features due to the arrangement of land and water masses in the Southern Hemisphere. A glance at the map will show that the South Pacific Ocean is actually southeast of the North Pacific; much of the west coast of South America is farther east than New York City.

A second point is that in the western half of the South Pacific the movement of the water is influenced by numerous island systems and by such larger land masses as Australia, New Zealand, and New Guinea. There is no real counterpart of the Japan Current in the South Pacific, its nearest equivalent being the East Australian Current.

A third and major point of difference is that in contrast to the North Pacific, which receives only as much Arctic water as can make its way through Bering Strait, the South Pacific is wide open to the Antarctic. The southern edge of the South Pacific gyral is in fact a part of the southern west-wind drift, that rough and stormy belt of frigid water that encircles the Antarctic Continent, throwing immense cold currents into every southern ocean. It flows constantly to the eastward, moved by prevailing westerly winds. This current, sometimes also called the Antarctic Current, is first encountered at about latitude 45° S., and because of strong winds and heavy seas that area has been known to many decades of seamen as "the roaring forties."

127

The Peru or Humboldt Current (so called after the famous German geographer Alexander von Humboldt) is a southern counterpart of the California Current, but colder because of its burden of Antarctic water. This current flows northward as far as the Galapagos Islands before turning westward to merge with the South Equatorial Current, which forms the northern edge of the South Pacific gyral.

The Indian Ocean presents peculiarities of its own because, although a vast body of water, it is in a sense only half an ocean. Instead of having another ocean to the north of it, it is bounded on that side by the continent of Asia and the subcontinent of India. This gives a curious interplay of oceanic and continental climates. During about half the year, when the continent is warmed by the northern sun, the wind blows steadily from the sea to the land and, being deflected by the earth's rotation, produces the northeast monsoon. When the sun is in the Southern Hemisphere the situation is reversed and we have the wind blowing steadily from the land to the sea, producing the southwest monsoon. These prevailing winds naturally affect the movement of the water.

In the limited area of ocean between the equator and the south coast of Asia the clockwise movement of currents characteristic of the Northern Hemisphere occurs only during the summer months, when the wind is from the southwest. In winter, when the wind blows steadily from the northeast, the current system is reversed, moving counterclockwise. Arab traders have been aware of this for centuries, and have timed their voyages to Zanzibar and the coast of Africa to have the wind and sea in their favor both coming and going.

South of the equator the Indian Ocean behaves in a conventional manner, with a South Equatorial Current moving westward and swinging south, where it flows on both sides of the large island of Madagascar. Between Madagascar and the mainland of Africa the current is constricted and flows more rapidly; this flow is given the special name of Agulhas Current. All of the southern-flowing water moves at last into the southern west-wind drift where it flows eastward toward Australia, then swings north as the cold West Australian Current, which compares in a smaller way with the Humboldt Current in the South Pacific. The Indian Ocean south of the equator presents a well-developed counterclockwise gyral, which is the correct way, theoretically, for a southern ocean to behave.

THE ATLANTIC

Now we come at last to the Atlantic Ocean. We have left it for last because it is an atypical ocean, with many features that are best understood after we have become acquainted with currents in the Pacific and Indian oceans.

Considering the Atlantic Ocean as a whole, it is a long, narrow ocean of extremely irregular shape. It did not seem narrow to Columbus because he crossed it at the widest part. At its narrowest part, where South America extends to the eastward just south of the equator and Africa bulges toward the west just north of the equator, the width is only eighteen hundred miles. Comparing this with the Pacific, which has its greatest width at the equator—approximately ten thousand miles—we can anticipate the fact

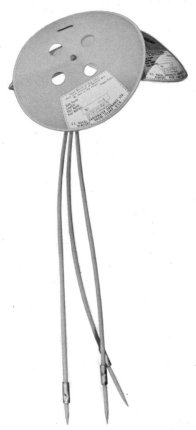

Plastic "drifters" sink to the bottom and are then carried along by underwater currents. They are most often recovered from the nets of trawlers. (Official photograph, U. S. Navy)

that the system of equatorial currents and countercurrents in the Atlantic will be markedly different. In addition to the equatorial bulges, there are other irregularities and obstructions to the free flow of currents—large embayments, submarine ridges, and various islands, including the West Indies, Newfoundland, the British Isles, Iceland, and the subcontinent of Greenland.

In describing the surface currents of the Atlantic it is best to start at the south, where the southern west-wind drift feeds cold Antarctic water into the South Atlantic. This impinges on the west coast of Africa, along which it flows northward as the Benguela Current. Residents of Capetown have a dramatic experience of the effects of ocean currents: when the water in Table Bay is too cold for swimming, they need only drive a few miles to the east of the Cape of Good Hope to bask in the warm waters of the Agulhas Current, which comes southward from the equatorial regions of the Indian Ocean.

The Benguela Current, under the influence of Coriolis force, swings westward as it approaches the equator and becomes the South Equatorial Current. Off the east coast of South America a portion of this current turns southward as the Brazil Current. Thus we have a moderately well-developed counterclockwise gyral in the South Atlantic. Approximately off the Rio de la Plata the Brazil Current meets the cold, northerly moving Falkland Current, which has no counterpart in any other ocean, and is generally explained as being due to prevailing winds. It might also be considered an eddy current created by the tip of South America's projecting as far as it does into the southern west-wind drift.

The most remarkable feature of the South Equatorial Current is that much of it crosses the equator and gets into the North Atlantic! Where it strikes the easterly-extending shoulder of South America, it is split into two parts; one turns southward, becoming the Brazil Current, as we have seen; the other part is diverted northeasterly into the Caribbean Sea and the Gulf of Mexico. It is joined by a part of the North Equatorial Current, the portion of which flows east of the Antilles directly into the North Atlantic gyral.

We thus have a sizable portion of the South Equatorial Current, plus the southern part of the North Equatorial Current, streaming together into the Caribbean and the Gulf of Mexico with no place to escape except the narrow channel between Florida and Cuba and between Florida and the Bahamas. This causes a piling up of water at the western end of the Florida Strait and a rapid flow through the narrow channel. This is the origin of the Gulf Stream, which may justly be termed the most famous ocean current in the world.

THE GULF STREAM

At its narrowest portion the current is about fifty miles wide, and has a maximum velocity of about four miles an hour. As it moves to the north and east, it widens and the velocity rapidly decreases; but it retains its character as a distinct and important current all the way into the eastern Atlantic. Oceanographers have divided it into three main sections: the

Florida Current, the Gulf Stream proper, and the North Atlantic Current.

The current was discovered by Ponce de Leon in 1513. Among other frustrations encountered by this hardy adventurer, he noted one day while working along the coast of Florida that, although under full sail with a good wind, he was unable to make any progress against the opposing current. Whether or not he was looking for a fountain of youth, his discovery of the Gulf Stream may be rated as a pretty good consolation prize.

It is recorded that one of Ponce de Leon's pilots subsequently used his knowledge of the Gulf Stream to speed up a return voyage to Europe. But for more than 250 years any knowledge that mariners had of this current and its possible use in transatlantic navigation remained a trade secret. It was not until Benjamin Franklin interested himself in the matter that knowledge of the Gulf Stream became common. In 1770 it came to Franklin's attention that ships of New England registry consistently made better time crossing the Atlantic than English ships, the difference sometimes amounting to as much as two weeks. With his perpetually inquiring mind, Franklin wanted to know why. He put the question to a Nantucket sea captain of his acquaintance, Timothy Folger, who told him about the Gulf Stream, with which the New England captains were familiar and which the English captains ignored. Captain Folger explained that in a light wind it was easy for a westbound ship to be set backward by the current farther in a day than it could sail forward. At Franklin's request, the captain sketched for him a map of the Gulf Stream, which Franklin had redrawn and engraved on a chart of the Atlantic Ocean. He passed out some copies of this, but the map received little attention till 1786, when he published a paper on the Gulf Stream in the *Transactions of the American Philosophical Society*.

Drift bottle. The finder is offered a small reward for returning the enclosed card with information on the time and place of recovery. These bottles can be used for study of surface currents or, by ballasting, to register underwater currents. (Canadian Dept. of National Defence)

Facsimile of a card
found in a drift bottle.

This was by no means Franklin's only contribution to oceanography; he studied and commented on the design of ships, and was, as far as we know, the first person to take ocean temperatures and to suggest that they could be used to determine whether currents were coming from the south or from the north.

The Gulf Stream, after turning east from the approximate latitude of Cape Hatteras, widens and slows down, but it still continues as a major current. As it approaches the coast of Europe it divides into two or more branches, only one of which we shall for the moment consider. A tongue turns south, washes the coasts of Spain and North Africa, and returns westward as the North Atlantic Current.

THE SARGASSO SEA

This North Atlantic circulation is the strongest of all the gyrals, and it has at its center—like the calm that traditionally exists in the center of a storm—the Sargasso Sea.

The Sargasso Sea is truly a fabulous area. It has been regarded by seamen for centuries as a place where ships become becalmed or enmeshed in weed, and where objects from the North or South Atlantic drift in and go circling forever in a forgotten wasteland of the sea. Actually the Sargasso Sea is not a place to fear. It is simply the nodal area in the great gyral of the North Atlantic Ocean. It is distinguished by the absence of current, and by the presence of large aggregations of the Sargassum weed, or gulfweed.

Sargassum is a tropical seaweed that grows, breaks away from its moorings, drifts out to sea, and is capable of vegetative reproduction without any attachment to the sea bottom. There are several kinds and it occurs in several oceans; but only in the Sargasso Sea does it form large aggregations, with a specialized group of fishes and other marine animals that live in and

131

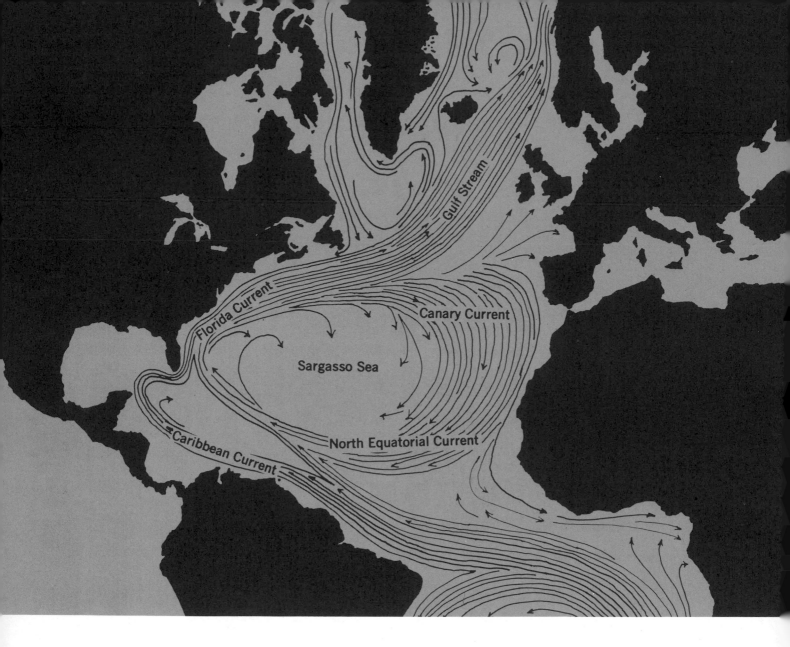

Florida Current

Gulf Stream

Canary Current

Sargasso Sea

Caribbean Current

North Equatorial Current

among it. The Sargasso Sea is in this respect a particular feature of the Atlantic gyral. It is best explained in relation to the fast-flowing Gulf Stream, and may be regarded not improperly as the "eye" of a kind of vast Atlantic whirlpool.

There is a similar node or central area in which there is little or no current in each of the great oceanic gyrals of the world. These others differ from the Sargasso Sea in being less conspicuous, chiefly by reason of the absence of large aggregations of Sargassum.

Two seas adjacent to the Atlantic must be mentioned in connection with it, the Mediterranean and the Arctic. The Mediterranean is one of the few seas in which evaporation plays a conspicuous role (the Red Sea is another). There is a sill at the entrance to the Mediterranean, averaging just over two thousand feet in depth. At the surface, because of the high rate of evaporation in this tropical sea, water is constantly drawn in through the Strait of Gibraltar; but at a depth, cooler water is constantly moving out across the Mediterranean sill and mingling with the deeper waters of the Atlantic. One reason the Atlantic remained so long unexplored was that it was difficult for seafaring men of the Mediterranean to get their ships west-

The Sargasso Sea lies at the center of the gyral formed by the currents of the North Atlantic Ocean.

ward through the Strait of Gibraltar on account of the strong eastward current at the surface.

The Arctic Ocean, which differs from the Mediterranean in every other way, resembles it in being a kind of appendage of the Atlantic. Northward currents from the Gulf Stream flow into the Arctic along the Scandinavian coast, move slowly around the North Pole, and emerge again into the North Atlantic along the east coast of Greenland and the east coast of North America. This last is the Labrador Current; flowing southward, it is pressed by Coriolis force to the westward and clings to the North American coast all the way to where it meets the Gulf Stream. Here part of the Labrador Current swings eastward along the northern edge of the Gulf Stream, part of it moves southward along the Atlantic coast, mingling with eddies from the Gulf Stream, and a part dives under the warm Gulf Stream to contribute cold water to the depths of the Atlantic.

A glance at the map will show that the surface currents of the Atlantic are continually contributing more water to the north than flows out along the surface. But deep currents from the Arctic compensate for the inequality of the surface flow.

8

The Ocean and World Climate

Although we apply different names to the major areas of ocean—the North and South Atlantic, the North and South Pacific, the Indian, the Arctic and the Antarctic, their number corresponding to the pleasantly alliterative phrase "the seven seas"—the ocean is a unit, with all its areas interconnected. But all the continents are not interconnected; and some of them are widely separated. Their area is relatively so small that they may be thought of as a group of irregularly shaped islands of varying size completely surrounded by the sea. Thus by one of those curious accidents of history we have returned to a version of the basic view of the ancients, who believed that the land was surrounded by Oceanus, a then unknown and terrifying body of water that extended to the rim of the world.

Although the ocean is actually a unit, its different sections perform different functions—warm currents carrying heat from tropical to higher latitudes, cold currents having a reverse effect, and the ocean as a whole serving as a major regulator of the climate of the land.

Water has what the physicists call a high specific heat. This means that water can, under appropriate conditions, take up and store a considerable amount of heat, from the sun or any other source, hold it for a substantial time, and give it off slowly. The old tradition of the use of a hot-water bottle to keep one warm in bed on a winter night is an example of the importance of water's high specific heat and of its value as a thermoregulator. In contrast, air has a very low specific heat. A hot-water bottle filled with heated air would be cold and useless in a few minutes. Because the atmosphere and the oceans are in constant contact, it should be obvious that the oceans in large degree regulate the temperature of the air. They also regulate its humidity.

Land is intermediate between ocean water and air in the rate at which it stores and gives up heat. Like an aluminum kettle, it warms up quickly, cools off quickly, and is also a middling good reflector of heat. We often speak of "the hot desert sands," and the desert may indeed be almost unbearably hot during the day, but it cools off rapidly after sundown and may be uncomfortably cold at night.

Sun shining through air warms it hardly at all. The temperature of the earth's atmosphere is determined chiefly by the amount of heat absorbed from earth radiation, plus heat that is released when water vapor condenses.

Stratocumulus, a principal cloud type, usually composed of small water droplets. (J. Allan Cash)

Overleaf: Four stages in a cloud-seeding experiment over the Caribbean Sea in August, 1964. Upper left: normal tropical cumulus clouds at beginning of seeding with silver iodide from airplane. Upper right: 9 minutes later, showing rapid vertical growth. Lower left: 19 minutes after seeding, showing rapid horizontal growth. Lower right: giant cloud as it appeared 38 minutes after seeding. (U. S. Weather Bureau)

134

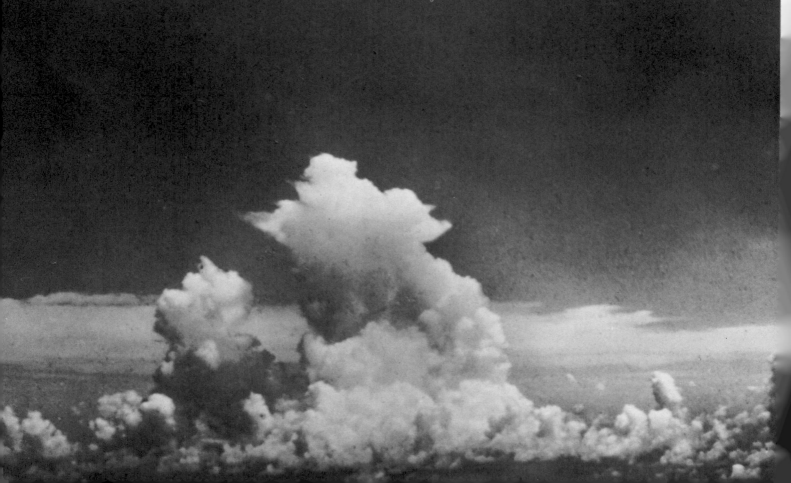

Because of the ocean's capacity to gain heat and return it slowly to the air, the islands of the sea and the margins of the continents have an oceanic, that is, a rather equable type of climate. The interiors of the continents, being more subject to the vagaries of rapid heating and cooling, have a continental type of climate, exhibiting far greater extremes of temperature.

Because the oceans cover seven-tenths of the earth's surface, this amount of water, along with the heat it absorbs from the sun and carries from place to place with the movement of ocean currents, plays a major role in influencing weather and climate all over the world. The late oceanographer Harald U. Sverdrup referred to the ocean as the world's hot-water heating system. Even the interiors of the continents do not completely escape the influence of the ocean. Storms originating at sea often pass inland, and the greater part of the rain that falls anywhere originates in evaporation from the sea's surface.

Weather and climate involve the same factors; the difference between them is summed up in a British scientist's comment that Britain has an excellent climate but abominable weather. What he meant was that in spite of a certain amount of rain, fog, chilling winds, and other inclement weather, Britain seldom has excessive heat, freezing weather, or droughts. In general, the average conditions there are favorable to man and his enterprises.

Weather consists of small pieces of climate and, conversely, climate is the aggregate result of the weather. If it rains on a holiday and spoils everybody's outing, that is weather; but if it ordinarily rains 7.2 inches a year, that is climate; in fact, this is the dry climate of Phoenix, Arizona. If it rains sixty inches a year, that is the wet climate of Neah Bay, Washington. Every type of climate has its advantages and drawbacks.

Weather, of course, involves not only rain or snowfall, but such additional factors as sunshine, cloudiness, fog, temperature, humidity, direction and velocity of wind. Climate consists of the average of such factors over a period of years, usually several decades. In the western portions of both the Atlantic and Pacific, several hurricanes occur every year, and thus constitute a recognized aspect of the climate of those areas. Similarly, summer thunderstorms are a standard feature in any part of the United States east of the Rocky Mountains and are thus part of the climate there. Because they rarely occur on the Pacific coast, they would there be regarded as weather.

Lens-shaped cloud, a type often formed in rising air in the lee of a mountain. It may remain stationary, dissipating at one edge as rapidly as it is formed at the other.
(Toni Schneiders)

AN OCEAN OF AIR

It is instructive to compare the air with the ocean, for their behavior has many features in common. First we should consider the differences, which are impressive. Because of its greater mobility, the air moves vertically and horizontally with a velocity unknown in the ocean. The largest ocean waves (excluding seismic waves) seldom exceed sixty feet in height and have a wave length of upwards of six hundred feet from crest to crest. Air waves may be several thousand feet high, and have a wave length of five hundred to one thousand miles. The most rapid ocean current probably does not exceed four miles per hour. Air currents of twenty to forty miles per hour are standard. At this point, the contrast ceases to be meaningful: there is

Altocumulus, another
principal cloud type,
composed of water
droplets.
(Toni Schneiders)

nothing in the ocean to compare with hurricanes of a velocity of one
hundred to possibly two hundred miles per hour.

Nevertheless, the ocean and the atmosphere have many things in common.
First of all we must remember that air is an actual substance. It has weight
and therefore exerts pressure; at sea level it can support a column of
mercury about thirty inches high. In motion, it can blow automobiles off a
highway, demolish houses, and support jet planes thirty thousand feet above
the earth. It is just as real as water, but its behavior, while in many respects
similar, is considerably less predictable.

Under the heating of the sun, re-radiated into the atmosphere, air rises
in the tropics and moves toward the poles—it has nowhere else to go.
Gradually chilled, it sinks at some higher latitude and moves back toward
the tropics, not directly but in giant swirls created by the earth's rotation.
This is also the basic feature of the circulation of water in the ocean; but in
the atmosphere it happens more rapidly. In the ocean only the surface
waters are warmed; but the atmosphere is warmed literally from the
ground—or the water—up. Thus things happen faster in the atmosphere
than they do in the ocean.

In general the prevailing winds at the earth's surface correspond to the

24. Rain forest, west
side of the Olympic
Peninsula of the Pacific
coast. Although thought
of as characteristic of
the tropics, rain forests
occur well northward
under the influence of
the warm North Pacific
Current.
(Joseph Muench)

140

25. Left: From mid-California south, as here at Sobranes Point, near Carmel, a relatively cold ocean current contributes to a semiarid climate. Summer coastal fogs are quickly dissipated as they move toward the heated interior. (Cole Weston, Rapho-Guillumette)

26. Upper right: Fog forest, Bosque de Fray Jorge, near Coquimbo, north central Chile. A belt of coastal fog permits considerable vegetation in what would otherwise be barren desert. (E. S. Ross)

27. Lower right: Peruvian desert coast, north of Lima, with an irrigated valley in the background. (E. S. Ross)

Hole bored in a layer of supercooled clouds near Goose Bay, Labrador, by seeding with dry ice, permitted airplane flights that would otherwise have been canceled. (Air Force Cambridge Research Laboratories)

28. In the short Arctic summer, the barren Greenland tundra briefly becomes a garden, contrasting with the glacier in the background. The plant in the field is Arctic cotton, *Eriophorum*. (J. Molholm)

ocean currents, except that the latter are limited by the margins of the continents, while the winds are not. The wind systems of both the Atlantic and Pacific may be described as follows: the Northeast and Southeast Trade Winds parallel respectively the North and South Equatorial currents, being separated by a tropical belt of calms known to sailors as "the doldrums." The northern and southern portion of each ocean is swept by the prevailing westerlies, corresponding in the Pacific to the North and South Pacific currents, in the South Atlantic to the southern west-wind drift, and in the North Atlantic to that portion of the Gulf Stream known as the North Atlantic Current. The Indian Ocean, having no northern counterpart, has the southern half of this type of wind system, modified by the monsoon winds presently to be described.

In each ocean, between the trade winds and the westerlies, there is a belt in which the winds are light and variable; this belt is known to sailors as the "horse latitudes," a term whose origin is uncertain. According to the early American oceanographer Matthew F. Maury, sailing ships bound from New England to the West Indies carrying horses as a deck load were sometimes becalmed in this area and had to throw the animals overboard for lack of water. Another explanation is that this zone between the westerlies and the

145

trade winds was first described by a German geographer named Ross, and hence was known for a time as the Ross Latitudes, which soon became corrupted into horse latitudes.

The importance of these areas to world climate is that in contrast to the lower atmospheric pressures of the trade winds and westerlies, the horse latitudes are areas of high pressure and descending air, and are thus cloudless. The ocean takes up much heat here.

There is a separate system of polar winds blowing more or less continuously in an east-west direction; and at high altitudes (six to eight miles) a jet stream blows constantly from the west at speeds of one hundred to three hundred miles per hour, its latitude changing somewhat with the seasons. This situation in the Northern Hemisphere presumably has its counterpart in the southern. The jet stream is of interest to aviators, but need not concern oceanographers except for its possible effects on the lower atmosphere. The polar winds are another matter.

The polar air system expands and contracts with the seasons, being minimal in summer and maximal in winter. Polar air is, as it were, in a constant struggle with warmer air from the south. They push each other back and forth, now advancing and now retreating. The edge of the advance of cold air from the polar regions is known as a cold front, while that of the warm air from the lower latitudes is a warm front. Where these two meet, much of our weather is generated—storm, rain, hail, snow, sleet. Occasionally the polar air goes on a rampage and, as in America in the winter of 1963–1964, pushes clear down to the Gulf of Mexico, bringing frost to Miami and snow to New Orleans, and even bringing chilling winds to the Isthmus of Tehuantepec.

The North American continent is peculiarly susceptible to this; all its major mountain ranges run north and south, so there are no mountain barriers to interfere with the progress of cold air from northern Canada down the Mississippi Valley to the Gulf of Mexico. In Asia the Himalayas form a barrier to polar air, protecting the Indian subcontinent from extremes of cold. In Europe, the Alps likewise protect the western Mediterranean area, especially the Riviera, but with interesting side effects; the deflected cold air sometimes flows down the Rhone Valley to the west or the Dalmatian coast to the east, producing a strong, chilling wind known in France and western Italy as the "mistral," and along the Adriatic as the "bora." These winds often blow several days at a time, detracting from a generally salubrious climate.

The polar front, of course, extends around the world. One place where storms are generated is the northwestern Pacific when a polar front encounters the warm air over the Japan Current. In winter in the Northern Hemisphere it is customary for a series of storms to originate in the vicinity of the western Aleutian Islands, proceed southeasterly across the Pacific, deluge the Pacific Northwest and northern California with rain—which turns to snow in the mountains—and then proceed eastward as a series of blizzards, heavy snowfalls, and bitter weather clear across the United States to the Atlantic seaboard and even out into the Atlantic Ocean. All along their course they follow the edge of the polar front. But the Atlantic has its own storms, many originating off Cape Hatteras; it does not need to rely on storms originating in the Aleutian Islands, although these, after crossing

One of San Francisco's summer fogs moves in over the city in late afternoon. The warm, humid air from the open sea is chilled by upwelling of cold water near the coast, precipitating fog. (Pirkle Jones)

North America, may be rejuvenated by energy released to the air from the Gulf Stream.

The climate of northwestern Europe is similar to that of northwestern America, the coastal regions of Oregon, Washington, and British Columbia, with mild winters, cool summers, and a good deal of cloud cover. The winter storms originate from a low pressure area in the vicinity of Iceland, which extends toward the northeast in winter, bringing severe weather to central and east Europe. The mild winter climate of the British Isles and of the adjacent portion of continental Europe is due to the warm surface waters of the North Atlantic, carrying the heat of the Gulf Stream and the North Atlantic Current.

MONSOON CLIMATES

A monsoon climate is one in which the wind blows rather regularly from the sea to the land for approximately half the year, then reverses itself and during the remainder of the year blows from the land to the sea. Such a climate is particularly characteristic of south and southeast Asia. The word itself is derived from an Arabic word meaning time or season, and refers to the regularity with which the summer and winter monsoon winds recur.

147

It has already been noted that the Indian Ocean lacks a northern counterpart and is, so to speak, only half an ocean; in addition, if we exclude the ice-bound Arctic, which borders all the northern continents, the continent of Asia is unique in being bounded by ocean only on its southern and eastern shores. This provides the setting for a typical, indeed *the* typical monsoon climate.

In summer the interior of the continent is heated by the sun, causing the air to rise and to be replaced by warm, moist air drawn in from the tropical ocean. This results in hot, humid summers. In winter the reverse happens: the interior of the continent becomes cold while the ocean remains warm. Thus air rises over the ocean, drawing cold air from the interior of the continent, producing the winter monsoon. There are interludes in spring and fall when temperatures are balanced and the wind is still. But there is no mistaking the onset of either the summer or the winter monsoon; the temperature may change twenty or thirty degrees in a matter of hours. There comes a day in autumn when the man wearing a sun helmet, a thin shirt and shorts suddenly decides to go home and put on a woolen suit. In spring the change is equally dramatic; when the summer monsoon begins, the man in a woolen suit knows that the weather will be hot and humid for several months. He also knows that he will need an umbrella, for the summers are wet and the winters are dry.

The summer monsoon is strong enough to reverse the currents that would otherwise be expected in the northern sector of the Indian Ocean. The winter monsoon corresponds in direction to the Northeast Trade Winds in other oceans, but the summer monsoon blows from the southwest. Arab traders have for many centuries taken advantage of the winter monsoon to make their voyages to the coast of Africa, and the summer monsoon to return.

Monsoon climates exist in lesser degree in various other parts of the

Shore winds form striking patterns in sand mingled with small stones. (Carola Gregor)

Shifting dunes and wind-rippled sand in the Sahara in eastern Algeria, an area in the rain shadow of the Atlas Mountains. (Pierre Pittet)

world—northern Australia, west Africa, portions of North, Central and South America. Any area that has warm, humid, rainy summers and cool dry winters partakes in some degree of the characters of a monsoon climate.

DESERTS BY THE SEA

An ocean current flowing along a coast has different effects in different latitudes. We have seen that water has a marked tendency to take up or give off heat very slowly; land, on the other hand, takes up and gives off heat very rapidly, and tends to have a temperature appropriate to the latitude in which it lies. This produces interesting consequences wherever the ocean comes in contact with the land.

Take, for example, the current system in the eastern North Pacific Ocean. The North Pacific Current, a continuation of the warm Japan Current, impinges on the coast of North America approximately at Vancouver Island, where it divides into two streams, the northerly flowing Aleutian Current and the southerly flowing California Current. The Aleutian Current is, compared with the latitudes into which it is moving, a warm current juxtaposed with cool or cold land. Therefore it brings heavy rainfall to British Columbia and southeastern Alaska, and both rain and dense fog to the Aleutian Islands. Juneau, the capital of Alaska, has an average annual rainfall of 54.7 inches.

Coming down the coast with the California Current, we find Portland, with an average rainfall of 42.4 inches, San Francisco, with an average of 20.1 inches, Los Angeles, with 14.8, San Diego, with 11.3 inches. When we get to Baja California, we find a desert peninsula where significant rainfall occurs only at intervals of several years.

A closely similar condition is found in comparable latitudes on the Atlantic. Northern Europe, like the northwest coast of America, has a great deal of rain and fog. The climates of Portugal and Spain are similar to that of California. Baja California may be compared to Morocco.

What is the relation between the ocean temperature and the rainfall? When moisture-laden sea air blows across land that is cooler than the sea wind, moisture will be precipitated either as fog or rain. The greater the difference in temperature the greater will be the precipitation. The wettest place in North America is believed to be at the headwaters of the Hoh River in the State of Washington, where Pacific air strikes the snow-covered Olympic Mountains. During the International Geophysical Year, a manned station on the nearby Blue Glacier recorded 160 inches in one year. The forest covering the lower slopes of the western side of the Olympic Peninsula is a dense, almost impenetrable rain forest, with moss hanging from the trees.

As we move into lower latitudes, the difference in temperature between the sea air and the land becomes progressively less, and the rainfall decreases accordingly until it reaches a point where rainfall is occasional and unusual. It should be mentioned that on the rare occasions when rain does come to the desert region of Baja California, it seems to make up for lost time, for it is torrential, and sometimes results in devastating floods. The same is true of the Sahara, the Atacama, and other deserts.

It would be an oversimplification to attribute the gradual reduction in rainfall in areas from the Pacific Northwest to Baja California entirely to a diminution of the temperature of the California Current relative to that of the adjacent coast. An important element is the upwelling of cold bottom water to replace the surface water which, owing to the rotation of the earth, swings west as it moves south. Upwelling of bottom water is a regular occurrence from approximately mid-California south, and it is responsible for the famous summer fogs in San Francisco. The faster the California Current flows, the more rapidly it swings to the west. Since the rate of its flow is largely determined by the strength of the northwesterly winds, the stronger these winds are in summer, the more fog there will be.

The explanation is very simple. Warm, moisture-laden air from the Pacific, drawn toward the coast in summer owing to the rising air resulting from heating of the continent, strikes a cold belt of inshore water and the result is fog, which then moves in over the land. Thus, by what seems a curious anomaly, the hotter the summer weather in the Sacramento Valley, the more fog there will be in the San Francisco Bay area.

Giant tree ferns grow 40 to 50 feet high in the rain forest on the windward side of the volcanoes of Hawaii. In the rain shadow of the mountains semi-desert conditions prevail. (Werner Stoy, Camera Hawaii)

In the Southern Hemisphere, we have the cold Humboldt Current, derived from the southern west-wind drift, moving northward along the coast of Chile, and producing one of the famous and more extreme desert areas of the world. Similarly the west coast of Africa, swept by the Benguela Current, is a desert area until we approach the tropics, where the warm Guinea Current takes over and produces the lush, warm, moist climate of the Congo and adjacent lands.

The Sahara, most famous desert in the world, is not so easily explained. The Canary Current sweeps southward along its Atlantic coast; but there are strong areas of upwelling close to shore, so that the shoreward water is really cold compared with the temperature of the land. Also the Atlas Mountains of the northwest African coast interpose a barrier to sea winds. There is historical evidence, and even evidence from prehistory in the form of ancient rock paintings, that this was once a well-watered land, inhabited both by man and by a variety of native animals. There has obviously been a shift in the atmospheric pattern, perhaps coinciding with the disappearance of glacial ice from northern Europe. The dominant wind in the Sahara now is a hot, dry wind that gets hotter and drier as it blows across the desert sands; when it reaches the Mediterranean area it is known as the "sirocco."

It appears that once a desert has formed for whatever reason, it tends to perpetuate itself. In the Sahara the infrequent but sometimes torrential rains average less than two inches a year, and in the central portion less than one inch; they provide sufficient ground water to maintain the occasional oases.

Inland deserts, such as the Mongolian Desert and the Great Basin in North America, are regions in which mountain ranges intercept the rainfall before it reaches the desert area. As an example of the effect of mountains on rainfall, the town of Sequim, Washington, which lies in what is called the "rain shadow" of the Olympic Mountains, has an average annual rainfall of only fifteen inches, although it is no more than forty miles to the east of what we have described on a preceding page as the wettest place in North America. Ben Nevis, the highest mountain in Scotland, receives 171 inches of rain; the town of Nairn, in the rain shadow of the Scottish Highlands, receives only twenty-six inches. Bergen, on the Atlantic coast of Norway, has an annual rainfall of eighty-one inches, while that of Oslo, in the shadow of a range of mountains, is only twenty-three inches. Perhaps the most striking case of all is found on the Hawaiian island of Kauai, where Mt. Waialule receives 471 inches of rain a year, while fifteen miles to the southwest the rainfall is only twenty inches.

CAN MAN CONTROL THE WEATHER?

Through the centuries mankind has generally taken the weather as something he had to make the best of—certainly something produced by forces beyond his control. A saying of Charles Dudley Warner, often attributed to Mark Twain, has it that "Everybody talks about the weather, but nobody does anything about it." Nevertheless, the idea has persistently recurred that man may directly or indirectly influence the weather.

The Roman historian, Plutarch, about the end of the first century A.D., declared, "Extraordinary rains pretty generally fall after great battles." The same idea was advanced during the Franco-Prussian War, the American Civil War, and the First and Second World Wars, the theory being in these cases that precipitation was induced either by the explosive force or the smoke of gunpowder. However, since the type of warfare carried on in Plutarch's day could hardly influence the weather any more than a Hopi Indian rain dance, any rain following a battle may be attributed to coincidence.

The theory that rain might be produced by explosions in the atmosphere was tried out, following an appropriation for the purpose by the United States Congress in 1890. The results were unsatisfactory. The first attempt appeared successful: following bombardment of the atmosphere, there came a rain. But subsequent attempts proved generally futile, and after two or three years the project was abandoned.

The old belief in modern guise is the fairly widespread popular notion that atomic explosions have influenced or may influence our weather. But meteorological records show that all of the vagaries of the weather in recent years have also occurred in times past, long before the atom bomb was invented. It is the consensus of meteorologists that atomic blasts have thus far had no observable effect on weather.

The idea that smoke might provide nuclei around which, under appropriate conditions, raindrops could form, led to experiments, with interesting but somewhat inconclusive results. One of the early attempts at rainmaking occurred in 1916 when the city of San Diego, after a prolonged drought, engaged a man who claimed to have a method of producing rainfall. The rainmaker thereupon went about his work, which seems to have consisted mostly in setting up smoke pots. A terrific downpour followed, which not only filled the reservoirs but broke a dam, causing a serious flood. Neither the city nor the rainmaker wanted to assume responsibility for what had happened, each preferring to consider it "an act of God." The city refused to pay, and the rainmaker did not press his claim.

This points up one of the difficulties of rainmaking experiments; it is extremely difficult to establish scientific controls. If rainmaking efforts are followed by rain, it cannot be proved that the rain might not have come anyway. Comparisons with average rainfall are of little significance, because there are often years—sometimes a number in succession—when the rainfall is either above or below normal.

Two methods of rainmaking have been developed in recent years, both of which show some evidence of being able to produce results under appropriate conditions. Both are forms of "cloud seeding," that is, introducing into a cloud composed of water droplets some substance that will induce precipitation. The substances that have been used successfully are dry ice (frozen carbon dioxide) and crystals of silver iodide. In a number of experiments "cloud seeding" by either of these methods has been followed promptly by rain, but neither has been proved uniformly successful. It will almost inevitably rain somewhere every day, and sometimes rain that had fallen two thousand miles away has been attributed to cloud seeding.

Considerable success has been achieved in one area of weather modification without attendant complications, namely, in seeding with dry ice to dissipate super-cooled fogs—that is, fogs that are below the freezing point of water. Such fogs are common in high latitudes. During an experimental period of two winters (1963–1965) the United States Air Force was able to "punch holes" in super-cooled fogs blanketing northerly airports, permitting two hundred scheduled airplane flights that would otherwise have been canceled. The rate of success was better than eighty percent.

During the Second World War a proposal was advanced to put a dam across the Gulf Stream between Florida and Cuba, and thus change the climate of western Europe to something approximating that of Labrador. Quite apart from the question of feasibility of the plan, it appears obvious that such an undertaking would have done as much damage to the allies of the United States as to the enemy. Moreover, nobody knows what such a change in circulation of the waters of the North Atlantic would do to the rest of the world. It might conceivably create deserts in what are presently well-watered lands.

Weather control by man is still a long way in the future. There are complex problems from both scientific and legal standpoints: if any substantial degree of weather control is ever achieved, it will have to be by interstate and international agreement. A much more promising field for the immediate future is long-range weather forecasting. As our knowledge of oceanic conditions all over the world continues to increase, and to the extent that weather on land is dependent on what goes on at sea, seasonal forecasts of temperature and rainfall many months in advance become increasingly feasible.

9

In the Tidal Area

Although a long stretch of wide sandy beach may be just right for sun-bathing, biologically speaking it is a rather sterile environment. Except for small leaping crustaceans known as beach-hoppers or sand fleas (which fortunately do not bite), the principal residents of a sandy beach are a few harmless sand crabs and a number of clams adapted to a surf-swept shore.

Among these are the wedge clams and the razor clams, with species occurring in most parts of the world. As indicated by their names, they are narrow in shape and adapted to rapid burrowing in sand frequently shifted by the action of waves. One razor clam, removed from its burrow and laid upon the wet sand, took only seven seconds to bury itself again. Attempting to dig razor clams can be a frustrating experience, because the clam often goes down faster than the digger can follow it with a spade.

Another beach inhabitant is worthy of mention even though it has a rather restricted distribution: the pismo clam. It occurs only from the central California coast to Mexico, but closely related species occur in Florida and the West Indies, and the family (Veneridae) to which it belongs is widely distributed through the world. Unlike the wedge clams and razor clams, the pismo has a large and heavy shell; individual specimens may weigh four pounds or more. It is not a particularly rapid burrower. Yet it is so completely adapted to a surf-beaten sand environment that it can live no-where else and will die if removed to quieter waters. Doubtless its heavy shell gives it substantial protection; in addition, its incurrent siphon is protected by a network of fine papillae that admit water and microscopic organisms on which the animal feeds, but exclude grains of sand, which might clog its gills and smother it. Its relatives elsewhere in the world also have filtering mechanisms on the incurrent siphon, but these are not so well developed as in the pismo clam.

Many times a sandy beach reveals windrows of organisms swept in from the open sea. If they are nearly transparent but slightly bluish, they are probably made up of *Velella*, the "by-the-wind sailor," a rather small colonial jellyfish that has an upright transparent sail. If they are pinkish, they are likely to be pteropods, commonly known as sea butterflies, a group of mollusks only occasionally seen onshore, but whose tiny shells are the source of large deposits on the sea bottom known as pteropod ooze (see Chapter 3).

The common bay scallop *(Pectens irradians)* of the Atlantic coast of North America; the dark spots on the edge of the mantle are eyes. (William Amos)

However remarkable the adaptations of animals dwelling in surf-beaten sand, even more extraordinary are those of animals on rocky shores, exposed to surf that, as we have already noted, can bend iron ladders on lighthouses. An extensive array of both animals and plants are able to survive in this environment. At first glance, such a location appears at low tide to be a mélange of barnacles, snails, shore crabs, starfish, sea urchins, sea anemones, sea cucumbers, crabs, mussels, and numerous other animals together with miscellaneous seaweeds ranging from tiny species encrusting the rocks to large ones with stalks and fronds many feet in length. But a little observation reveals that nearly every species of plant and animal occupies a defined zone between high and low water, and when the tide is out in an area of large tides, one can often see distinct transverse bands of organisms—sometimes as many as eight or nine of them.

The reason for these horizontal bands along the shore is that the dominant organism composing each band, whether a seaweed, a barnacle, or a mussel, is adapted to living at a particular height above low water, and in that particular zone it becomes the most successful and the most numerous. Most obvious of these adaptations are the ability to withstand heavy surf without being broken up or swept away, and the capacity to survive either drying when the sun shines or a fresh-water bath when it rains.

157

Let us explore some of these horizontal bands; the four major zones. As we saw in the preceding chapter, the range of the tide varies greatly in different places and during the various phases of the moon. In a region where the range of the tide is thirty feet, the zones will obviously be wider than in an area where the range is six feet. In places where the tidal range is small, say three feet or less, zonation is inconspicuous, but wherever tides are medium to large, one can determine these zones either by direct observation or from readily available sources.

Let us take mid-tide—the average of all the mid-tides of the year—as our starting point. From mid-tide to the average high tide, we have the *upper intertidal zone*. From mid-tide to the average low tide, we have the *lower intertidal zone*. Plants and animals living above mid-tide are exposed to sun, rain, and wind more than half the time. As one progresses from low tide to high tide, the physical conditions become more and more rigorous. Mid-tide is a convenient point of reference, one that anybody can establish by direct observation, by consulting tide tables, or in seaside communities by using the times of high and low water as given in the local newspaper. Given the highest and lowest tides, mid-tide can easily be approximated by dividing the distance between them.

Above the upper intertidal area we have what may be called the *splash zone,* which supports an interesting and extremely rugged population. Animals living here have to be tough. They are out of the water most of the time, but are intermittently wetted by splash and spray. When the tide is out, they are subject to drying by sun and wind or to being drenched by rain. In winter they may experience freezing cold. When the tide is in they are pounded by the surf. During the high tides of the month, they may be completely under water for an hour or two at a time. Yet a considerable number of animals manage to survive under these conditions—barnacles, limpets, periwinkles, and two crustaceans: the common shore crab and a somewhat distant relative of it, which is flattened in shape and is called the rock louse or sea slater.

Both the shore crab and the sea slater can run rapidly, and if conditions become too rough they merely move higher up on the shore or wedge themselves into a convenient crevice. But the limpets and periwinkles move very slowly, and the barnacles are anchored fast; they have to take things as they come. The higher one goes in the splash zone, the smaller are the anchored or slow-moving organisms. They lead a marginal existence, like itinerant workers with an unreliable income. That they can exist at all in this inhospitable environment is a testimonial to the fact that life seeks to perpetuate itself under whatever difficulties.

At the lower edge of the splash zone, there is generally a dark band resembling a stain on the rock. On inspection this will be found to be very small, encrusting, dark brown algae of the genus *Ralfsia*. This line can be seen on almost any rocky beach in the world, and it marks the average height of high water and the lower edge of the splash zone, almost as if someone had gone around the world and marked the border between these zones with a giant pencil.

In the upper intertidal zone we find great masses of large brown algae known as kelp. Among them are smaller species of red and green algae. It is impossible to do justice in one or two paragraphs to the vast number of the

A ghost-crab, running sideways, leaves its tracks in the sand. (Jack Dermid)

159

A young explorer with
a stalk of kelp in Acadia
National Park, Maine.
(Jack Dermid)

world's algae (as many as eighty species have been recorded from one limited surf-swept rocky shoreline), but certain kinds are easily recognizable. One is the palm alga, found on many rocky promontories. It has an erect, flexible stem from one to two feet high, and is topped with a mass of fronds so that it looks like a miniature palm tree. Algae do not have roots like those of land plants, but many of them have suckerlike disks at the bottom of the stem, known as holdfasts. The palm alga has massive holdfasts to anchor it to the rock and, with its flexible stem, it is able to withstand the sweep of the heaviest surf.

Other algae resident in the upper intertidal zone are the coralline algae. They belong to the group known as red algae, of which about three hundred species are known. They often form considerable deposits, and when this occurs they are listed on sailing charts as "corals," although they are plants, whereas true corals are animals. Some of the coralline algae are branched, but many of them have solved the problem of coping with the waves by simply flattening out and covering themselves with a heavy calcareous skeleton, often pink or white, and clinging so tightly to the rock that they seem to be a part of the rock itself.

Although called red algae, they can be either pink or white because the classification of algae is determined not by color but by structural relationship to other species of algae. Marine algae, other than those that are microscopic, were divided by early botanists into three general groups—brown, green, and red—and these terms are still in rather general use, although the classification of algae has become considerably more refined. Color, which once seemed an important matter, is actually minor.

Adding to the confusion of colors, another common and easily recognized alga of the upper intertidal zone is a "red" alga that is actually olive green! Because it has no common name, we shall call it by its generic name, *Halosaccion*. It looks like a small toy balloon, is filled with sea water, and if one squeezes it, water comes squirting out of several tiny pores. Another alga that anyone can recognize is *Ulva,* a bright green alga commonly known as sea lettuce. There are several species, ranging from the upper intertidal zone into the lower, but all are distinctively green. They cannot withstand too heavy surf, and on rock shores are most frequently found in tide pools where the water is calm when the tide is out.

In the lower intertidal zone we find various large brown algae; beyond identifying them as kelps it is impracticable to try to describe these in a general work on the sea. A very common one is *Laminaria,* which can be recognized by its broad, leaflike but ribless fronds.

Between the level of the average low tide and that of the lowest tides of the month or year is a zone that has been called the demersal zone, because the organisms living there are not really intertidal in the ordinary sense, but belong to deeper water and are only occasionally and briefly uncovered by the tide. One of the most common kelps of the demersal zone is *Macrocystis,* which is almost worldwide in distribution. In addition to having holdfasts to anchor it to the bottom, it has developed floats to keep its fronds at the surface, for one of the major requirements of plants is

Intertidal barnacles are out of water much of the time; at high tide they open the valves of the shell and feed on small organisms brought in by the waves.
(Gordon S. Smith)

sunlight. More spectacular, though less widely distributed, is *Nereocystis*—giant kelp—of the Pacific coast. This kelp grows in water sixty feet deep or more and, together with its fronds at the surface, may have a total length of ninety feet. The fronds are supported at the surface by a single bulbous float, which may contain two quarts of gas—mostly air, but, curiously, mingled with twelve per cent or more of carbon monoxide. These kelps are not intertidal, but they do have an important relation to the intertidal belt; they grow far enough out and in sufficient density to break the force of the waves and provide considerable protection to both animals and plants on rocky shores.

Two very interesting groups of animals characteristic of the upper intertidal zone are the mussels and the goose barnacles, both of which often form large colonies on surf-swept rocks. They are completely adapted to this environment and, notwithstanding what we have said about the power of storm waves, it is practically impossible for the surf to dislodge them from their seemingly precarious habitat. The mussels are firmly attached to the rock by a group of powerful threads forming what is called the byssus. If the collector finds a large mussel, five or six inches long, wedged into a crevice and anchored there by its byssus, he can pull with all his strength without breaking it loose. The goose barnacles resist dislodgment in a different way. They are attached to the rock by a long flexible neck, which bends with the surf but which, like the byssus of the mussel, is exceedingly tough. It is difficult to get one loose from the rock without cutting the neck.

The goose barnacle gets its name from the fact that its form resembles the head and neck of a goose. This gave rise to a myth that wild geese originated from barnacles, much as a caterpillar becomes transformed into a butterfly. An English writer of the sixteenth century claimed to have actually seen the metamorphosis of a barnacle into a goose. And there is a wild goose of northern latitudes in the Atlantic Ocean, whose range extends from eastern America through Iceland and the British Isles to northern Europe, which is commonly known as the barnacle goose.

Of the little barnacles that encrust every shore and cling tightly to the rocks, there are numerous species. A very few are limited to the splash zone, but most extend into two or more zones. Those that start in the splash zone are likely to extend into the upper intertidal, and those that start in the upper intertidal usually are found also in the lower intertidal and in the demersal zones. Some extend their range down to a depth of many fathoms. Quite a few species grow on the hulls of ships and thus are distributed practically everywhere. A few even attach themselves to whales or to the shells of marine turtles.

In the lower intertidal zone we find the most common species of starfish, and various species of crabs, clams, and marine snails. Among the last is *Thais,* a representative of a group from which the ancients derived their famous dye, Tyrian purple; *Murex,* a related genus used for the same purpose, is usually demersal. We also begin to find occasional sea urchins, sea anemones, and chitons—those curious flattened mollusks, most of which have a visible row of overlapping dorsal plates, making them look as if they were buttoned down the back.

In the demersal zone we find all these in greater abundance and represented by a greater number of species. There are kelp crabs, spider crabs,

A bed of giant kelp in the Kerguelen Islands. Kelp forms an important food and industrial resource in many parts of the world.
(E. Aubert de la Rue)

and the crabs of the genus *Cancer,* so well known to the ancients that a crab of this type became one of the signs of the zodiac. There is the remarkable decorator crab, which is camouflaged and often completely concealed by seaweed, sponges, and other organisms; this crab (of which there are a number of species and several genera widely distributed along the shores of most continents) is known to select organisms to conceal it, pluck them with its claws and carefully transplant them to its back!

We should also examine tide pools, small, clear basins of water among the rocks that, when the tide is out, form natural marine aquariums. The pools are likely to be lined with corallines and other small algae and to be occupied by an extraordinary number of animals. Among these will be small fishes such as gobies, blennies, and sculpins. There will also be sea anemones, colorful, flowerlike animals that may be mistaken for plants, but that when disturbed pull in their tentacles and become simply motionless mounds of flesh clinging tightly to the rock.

An omnipresent inhabitant of tide pools is the hermit crab, which is represented by numerous species distributed widely about the world. For some strange reason, evolution left them with the head, legs, and forward

Hermit crabs in textile-patterned *Conus* shells in the Indo-Pacific. (Bernard Villaret)

164

body of a crab, but with a posterior half that is naked and completely unprotected, so that any predator could quickly bite it off. They deal with the problem by finding the empty shell of a dead marine snail and backing into it. This protects them from the rear, while their sturdy claws defend them in front. Since they grow, while the shell does not, they must move to larger shells from time to time. One of the most amusing sights in nature is to see a hermit crab selecting a new shell. It will try one after another, like a human being trying on new suits. At length it finds one that fits and settles happily into it.

MUD FLATS AT LOW TIDE

A muddy tide flat is to the casual observer the least inviting of all seashore habitats. He is even likely to think such an area noisome and unsanitary. For these reasons, mud flats in the vicinity of any metropolitan area are likely to be filled in and converted to industrial sites or residential subdivisions. But to a marine biologist, a mud flat is an interesting and exciting place. It is filled with thousands of organisms belonging to hundreds of species. Even the odor attracts him, for when he detects it he knows the tide is out. Unless contaminated by wastes produced by man, the odor is to him a clean one deriving from a variety of organic compounds.

A large number of the inhabitants of a mud flat will be worms. It is hard to develop enthusiasm for worms, but it took nature more than a billion years to develop a good worm—meaning one that has specialized organs for digestion, respiration, circulation of the blood, and excretion of wastes. All organisms perform these functions—amoebas, flagellates, bacteria or even filterable viruses; but the worms—at least the higher worms—do all these things better. They also developed segmentation or reduplication of parts, permitting increase in size with completely coordinated function. Contemporary architects call this modular construction. It is found in man in the spinal column, in the segmental arrangement of spinal nerves, and in some other features that are especially prominent during embryonic development.

Segmented marine worms are related to common earthworms, but differ from them rather generally in having a head, eyes, tentacles, in many instances jaws, and a row of sometimes complicated flaps down each side of the body, which in free-living forms serve the double purpose of being swimming organs and of oxygenating the blood; in other words, they are both fins and gills. These are adaptations to the complexities of a marine environment. There are many species and they are extremely adaptable, living in mud, sand, under rocks, or among the barnacles and hydroids on wharf piles. They range in length from one or two inches to as much as three feet. The most common forms are known to fishermen as clamworms, if they have to be dug, or as baitworms or pileworms if found on wharf piles. There is one rather curious mud-dwelling form, dark brown in color and with the gills borne only on the anterior half, known to fishermen as the lugworm.

Some of the segmented marine worms have a curious and rather remarkable method of reproduction. During most of the year the sexes are not

One of the larger sting-
ing jellyfish of the
North Atlantic, beached
by wind and wave,
Terschelling, Holland.
(E. van Moerkerken)

distinguishable, at least by ordinary observation. But as the reproductive
season approaches, the posterior half of the animal undergoes a remarkable
change. The swimming organs referred to above (serving both the function
of swimming and respiration) become enlarged and the color of the body is
likely to change, particularly in the females (for example, from green to
pink). The two halves of the animal become distinctly different in appearance and also in function. The posterior end develops reproductive cells,
either eggs or sperm. Then, in late summer or autumn, the worm breaks in
two. The front end remains in its accustomed place; the posterior end swims
gaily off. Male and female elements swarm to the surface and release their
eggs and sperm, thus providing for the continuance of the species. Then
these sexual portions of the worm, having no mouth with which to feed,
either die off or are eaten by predators. The most famous swarming of
marine worms is that of the palolo worm of the mid-Pacific. Regularly, in
the last quarter of the moon in October and November, the palolos come to
the surface, in such numbers that the Samoans and Fiji Islanders fish for
them for food. But the same phenomenon occurs in greater or lesser degree
wherever the segmented marine worms are found.

Not all segmented worms are free-living. Some have become tube dwellers,
building tubes for themselves with secretions from their own bodies—either
calcareous or parchmentlike tubes. In the parchmentlike tubes grains of
sand or other particles are sometimes mingled with the body secretions.
Since tubeworms must perform all the functions of life from the open end

A horseshoe crab bull-
dozes its way across
the sand. Found on the
Atlantic coast of North
America and the Pacific
coast of Asia, it is the
only living represent-
ative of a class dating
back to the early Paleo-
zoic. (Gordon S. Smith)

166

of the tube, they develop various faculties in that area. Their tentacles multiply till they resemble a floral growth, and literally hundreds of eyes are developed along each tentacle. Nobody knows what tubeworms see, but it is certain that they are sensitive to light, because the moment a shadow falls on them, every tentacle is drawn in.

Some tubeworms live on wharf piles; some form little curled tubes on the shells of clams, on rocks, or on other solid substrate; some form colonies of calcareous tubes; some form parchment-like tubes in the mud, anchored so deeply that it is almost impossible to get them out intact.

A number of groups of worms living in mud are not segmented. Their ancestors, in the long history of life on earth, either never learned of modular construction or learned it and then gave it up. Evolution may proceed either up or down or sidewise. It is a continuing experiment on a cosmic scale; if a line of organisms survives, whether in a mud flat or on a mountain top, the experiment is a success. A worm that is alive is obviously more successful than a dinosaur that is extinct.

There is a group of worms, found commonly in the mud and in adjacent flats of sandy mud, known as ribbon worms. They bear this name because they are somewhat flattened and are often rather colorful. They vary in size from a few inches to an alleged twenty-five feet and they seldom can be pulled out whole. However, any piece of reasonable size will regenerate into an entire worm, and it has been suggested that fragmentation may be a normal method of reproduction. They are equipped with an eversible proboscis, which can be rapidly thrust out and drawn back, rolling itself in by muscular action much as one inverts the finger of a rubber glove by pulling it from the inside. They also have a stinging apparatus with which they may attack animals larger than themselves, although they seem to be harmless to human beings.

Somewhat less prepossessing are the sipunculid (from a Latin word meaning a little tube) worms, which, when found in mud, look like wet peanuts. But after a few minutes in sea water they elongate and begin to look like worms. These, too, have an eversible proboscis. Another of these unsegmented mud-dwelling worms, and one that has been intensively studied, has been referred to as "the innkeeper" because of the number of other animals that move in to share its dwelling. It is a fairly large worm, reaching a length of 1 ½ feet or more, although eight to ten inches is a more common size. It lives in the mud within a broadly U-shaped tube open at both ends. Its doors are literally never closed, and strangers naturally take advantage of this. Its tube is likely to contain, in addition to the owner, a species of segmented worm whose somewhat flattened shape adapts it to living in crowded quarters, one or two small pea crabs and anywhere from one to five small fishes called gobies. There is no evidence that the host welcomes these guests or that they do anything for their host. They appear rather to be roomers whom the owner is unable to evict.

Worms are by no means the only denizens of mud flats. A majority of the kinds of clams, including most of the favored edible species, occur in mud or in sandy mud. The deeply burrowing clams have long siphons, known to the clam-digger as a "neck." This is frequently a long, tough structure containing two channels, one of which takes in water while the other passes it out; these are known respectively as the incurrent and the

29. A bright green alga, called "sea lettuce," frequently forms a narrow band on rocky shores just above midtide. It also occurs in tidepools. (Donovan Roberts)

30.   Upper left: The reticulate sea-star *(Oreaster reticulatus)* is the largest and one of the most abundant starfish in subtropical American waters. (Douglas Faulkner)

31.   Lower left: A green sea anemone *(Anthopleura elegantissima)* common on the Pacific coast of North America. (Al Giddings)

32.   Right: An orange starfish *(Ophidiaster* sp.) and two "biscuit stars" *(Pentagonaster dubeni)* against a background of yellow sponge and purple coralline algae at a depth of 90 feet along the west Australian coast. (Allan Power)

33. Far left: The sand crab, Cape Hatteras National Seashore. Ordinarily this crab merges so completely into its sandy habitat that it is scarcely visible and hence is commonly known as a "ghost crab." (Jack Dermid)

34. Near left: A sand dollar from the Red Sea, showing the characteristic pentagonal pattern of this flattened relative of the sea urchin. (Douglas Faulkner)

35. Lower left: Fiddler crab, so called because of the enormously enlarged claw of the male. It makes good use of the claw in fighting and in blocking the entrance to its hole. (Jane Burton, Photo Researchers)

36. Right: A young hermit crab *(Eupagurus)* has made itself at home in the empty shell of a dog whelk. When it outgrows this shell, it will move on to a larger one. (D. P. Wilson)

37. Left: Two of the wonderfully delicate shell-less mollusks known as nudibranchs, *Glossidoris westraliensis* (above) and *Hexabranchus imperialis,* are shown on the Great Barrier Reef, Australia. The latter is known as the "Dancing Lady" from the way it flexes its body. (Keith Gillett)

38. Upper right: *Actinia tenebrosa,* about one inch in diameter, is the most common Australian sea anemone. The young develop inside the parent and are emitted through the mouth. (Keith Gillett)

39. Lower right: Green sea anemones *(Anthopleura xanthogrammica)* at Cape Johnson, Washington. Those in the foreground, with tentacles expanded, are under water; those with tentacles drawn in are out of water. (Victor B. Scheffer)

excurrent siphons. They are retractile, and when a person walking across a tide flat observes little spurts of water coming out of the mud at his approach, this means that clams, disturbed by his footsteps, have "pulled their necks in," squirting out the water that the siphons contained.

The siphons enable the clams to burrow deeply and still maintain contact with the surface, taking in water from which they obtain both oxygen and food. For clams in general do not eat mud, but subsist on minute organisms that they strain out of the water; thus they feed only when the tide is in.

INHABITANTS OF A SAND FLAT

A true sand flat, as distinguished from an open surf-swept beach, will support a highly interesting group of animals, although both the number and variety of individuals will be considerably less than found in a mud flat. Among the best known are sand dollars, cockles, and scallops.

More people are more familiar with the bleached white skeletons of sand dollars than with the animals themselves. A live sand dollar is round and flat—only by a stretch of the imagination resembling the coin after which it is named—and is covered with short, dark-colored, movable spines, which give it a small amount of locomotion and enable it to burrow into the sand. When covered with water, live sand dollars are found lying edgewise obliquely in the sand with about two-thirds of the body buried. When the tide is out, they may lie flat or be entirely buried in the sand. An occasional solitary individual is found, but most commonly they occur almost crowded together. They prefer extremely sheltered flats where there is minimal wave action, or better yet, flats in which shallow pools remain even when the tide is out. So special is the habitat they prefer that many persons who have spent a great deal of time along the shore have never seen a single living specimen.

As everyone knows from Mother Goose rhymes, it was "Mary, Mary, quite contrary" whose garden was decorated with "silver bells and cockle shells." However pleasing cockle shells may be as decorations, the living animals are far more interesting. (Viewed endwise, cockle shells are heart-shaped, which may explain the origin of the old expression, "warm the cockles of one's heart.") Because their siphons are extremely short, the clams live very close to the surface of the sand to obtain the life-giving water necessary for food and respiration. This renders them likely to be uncovered by wave or current action, so they have to be able to dig in again rapidly. This is accomplished by a large muscular foot. If a cockle is taken from the sand, it will close its shell tightly for protection; but if left alone for a few minutes, it will open up, extend the foot and become amazingly active, even hopping short distances by violent movements of the foot. This is hardly a satisfactory means of locomotion, but perhaps it assists the clam to get into position for a new dig.

One of the most familiar and beautiful of shell shapes is that of the scallop. This bivalve is also known to gourmets as a marine delicacy. Scallops are found in most parts of the world. There are numerous species, many of them favorites among shell collectors. Mostly they occur in moderately deep water, and for commercial purposes they have to be obtained

40. A red sea anemone *(Tealia)* and, in the foreground, small orange anemones *(Corynactis)* at a depth of 50 feet in Monterey Bay, California. Both genera occur along the coasts of Europe. (H. Stellrecht)

by dredging or trawling; but individual specimens may be found on the beach at low tide. Some species seem partial to sand flats or beds of eel grass.

Scallops are the most active of all the bivalve mollusks. They can swim vigorously and rather rapidly by clapping the two halves of their shell together, forcing the water out and thus engaging in a kind of primitive jet propulsion. Moreover they have a row of eyes along the edge of the mantle (a part of the body that secretes the growing margin of the shell). These eyes are colorful—for example, a deep blue-green—and useful. It is doubtful that they can see an object as such, but if a shadow passes over them, instead of closing their shells as most clams do (a response that has given rise to the colloquialism, "clamming up"), they flap the two valves of the shell with great energy and swim quickly off. Their swimming is poorly directed and aimless, but undoubtedly their fast getaway saves them in many dangerous situations.

A gnarled buttonwood tree on the southern coast of Puerto Rico, source of much of the driftwood on the southeastern coast of the United States. (Charles E. Lane)

178

Clams that hop and clams that swim, worms that run a caravanserai—these are only a few of the surprises that await any person who becomes a diligent student of the life of the seashore.

ANIMALS THAT BORE IN ROCK AND WOOD

In the lowest level of the lower intertidal zone and in the demersal zone we find animals that actually bore in rock, finding thus a refuge from the pounding of the waves. Conspicuous among these are the boring sea urchins. Most sea urchins cling to a rock—as do the starfish—by a large number of suction cups known as tube feet, and defend themselves with a formidable array of spines. But a few species embed themselves in the rock so solidly that a human being can dislodge them only with great difficulty. They obviously do this by sheer persistence, working themselves slowly round and round by their tube feet until they have worn a hole. As they grow, they enlarge the hole, and presently they are working beneath the surface of the rock. After awhile they are found occupying a hole with an opening smaller than the diameter of the sea urchin itself, and they are secure from being dislodged by the surf.

A number of mollusks, chiefly the pholad borers and the date-shell borers, have a similar boring habit, working themselves into the rock and making their own home or, as some may regard it, their own prison. They are there for life, and they have both security and food, for they feed on the multitude of minute organisms in the water in which they are constantly or intermittently bathed.

There has been much discussion on the question of how clams can bore in rock. One theory is that they do it by chemical action; another is that they do it by moving the valves of the shell. The latter view seems reasonable for the pholad borers, because they have regular rows of corrugations on the shell, which could serve as a file. But the date-shell borers—so named because they are brown and elongated—have shells that are smooth or only slightly rugose; it is believed that they have some chemical means of dissolving the rock. Whatever means the pholad borers use, they become completely embedded in quite hard rocks, with their siphons protruding in order to bring them water, oxygen and food. In the course of providing shelter for themselves, the rock-boring mollusks act as geological agents, honeycombing the rocks and assisting the sea in its erosion of the land.

It is worth noting that the mollusk *Zirphaea* bores in a clay so solid that a man would need a pick to break it up. *Zirphaea* has wavy ridges on the forward part of the shell, and it doubtless uses these for boring into the clay. *Zirphaea* seems to be an intermediate stage between ordinary mollusks and those that bore into solid rock.

Rock-boring mollusks have been known to damage concrete structures in harbors. Generally the damage has been minor, but was considerable in the concrete in caissons during construction of the Panama Canal. The harder concrete used today in reinforced concrete piling and in concrete seawalls is not likely to be seriously damaged.

Closely related to the pholad borers is a rather large group of mollusks, known as shipworms (though they are not worms), that bore in wood. They did great damage to wooden ships in earlier days, and to wharf piles. In recent decades the damage has been reduced to a minimum by the use of steel hulls and concrete piling.

How mollusks developed the habit of boring in wood is an interesting subject. Most probably they began with waterlogged wood in which the surface layers had become softened. The most primitive group of molluscan wood borers, the Xylophaginae, bores only in wood that has been at the bottom of the sea so long that a fingernail can scratch its surface. Most wood borers have a more specialized organization than the primitive Xylophaginae: the body has become elongated, and the shell has been reduced in size and serves only as a tool for boring, the forward surface bearing rows of very sharp teeth and resembling a file. Shipworms bore in wooden hulls, wharf pilings, mangrove roots, and in wood floating in the sea. One species, known only from the Pacific Ocean, is found almost exclusively in drifting logs. Shipworm burrows range from less than an inch to several feet in length and are as smoothly polished as if sandpapered.

In their long evolution the shipworms have also found a way to digest wood. Since the animals had no other convenient way of getting rid of the wood in which they were boring, they took the wood particles into the mouth and passed them through the digestive tract. Since wood is a carbo-

The giant red sea urchin of the Pacific coast is found from Alaska to northern Baja California, Mexico, in deep tide pools or rocky shores at low tide. It sometimes reaches a diameter of 7 inches. (Fred M. Roberts)

Gooseneck barnacles attached to a floating bottle that drifted in from the sea; some species are found on rocks along the shore, others only on floating objects. (J. H. Fraser)

hydrate and contains considerable potential nourishment, in due course, the shipworm developed enzymes for digesting the wood. It derives a great deal of food from the wood in which it bores, though it still depends, for proteins and essential vitamins, on the minute organisms drawn in through its siphons. The shipworm may be disagreeable to man, but it is one of the most highly specialized and well adapted animals in the world.

The mollusks are not the only animals that destroy wood in salt water; certain crustaceans also do this. A small crustacean, *Limnoria,* related to the sow bugs we find under an old board in the garden, occurs almost all over the world. It burrows in wood, and what it lacks in size it makes up in numbers. There may be millions of individuals in a single wharf pile. *Limnoria* is the organism that whittles wharf piles down to an hourglass shape. It can largely be controlled by using heavily creosoted piles and, of course, it can make no headway whatever in concrete, which is now increasingly used for marine structures.

One might be inclined to think that wood-destroying organisms in the sea are simply pests. But in the order of nature they are quite useful. Wood is a durable substance that does not readily break down in water. Roman galleys predating the Christian era have been dug up out of mud and found to be in pretty good condition. If wood that finds its way into the ocean were left alone, we might after a few hundred thousand years have either gigantic oceanic log jams or great deposits of sunken wood in various areas of the sea. The work of shipworms and woodboring crustaceans prevents this accumulation. It is only when boring organisms interfere with the works of man that we consider them pests.

10

Coral Reefs and Tropical Beaches

Coral reefs and coral islands are characteristic of tropical seas all around the world, in general where the temperature of the surface water does not fall below 70° F. They are made up principally of the calcareous skeletons of coral animals. As a rule, living corals are found only at the upper and outer edge of a reef, approximately from low tide to a depth of twenty or twenty-five fathoms. The great bulk of the reef is made up of the skeletons of dead corals, compacted with the shells of mollusks and of coralline algae, which are plants that use calcium from sea water in building their tissues. It was mentioned in the preceding chapter that coralline algae were for a long time confused with true corals.

Corals are closely related to sea anemones, which are extremely common in the intertidal zone in temperate and even cold waters. Sea anemones are among the most common animals photographed on the sea bottom at depths of a mile or more. Corals are plankton feeders, subsisting on the smaller forms of animal plankton, which they paralyze by means of stinging cells on their tentacles. They then use the tentacles to carry the food to the mouth. There has been a good deal of debate about whether they take in vegetable plankton; recent evidence indicates that some types of coral are omnivorous.

An individual coral animal, known as a coral polyp, resembles a small sea anemone but builds itself a supporting or protective skeleton. Because the skeleton is on the outside of the body, it is called an exoskeleton; it is commonly composed of calcium carbonate, the stuff of which limestone is made. A few kinds of corals are solitary, each occupying its own little calcareous home, attached to a rock. The majority are colonial, forming aggregations of from hundreds to countless millions of organisms dwelling side by side, each contributing to the growth and substance of the community.

The great majority of corals reproduce by budding and growth, much like a tree or shrub, but they also produce small ciliated larvae, which drift in the ocean currents and can thus become established in new localities. Vast numbers of these larvae are eaten by plankton-feeding organisms, or die without finding a suitable place to undergo further development. But if one of them settles on a hard surface, it transforms into a polyp with mouth and tentacles, forms a hard skeleton around itself, and then begins to branch out to form other polyps—and thus a new colony of corals begins.

Coral formations in the Red Sea provide refuge for an abundance of brightly colored tropical fish. (O. Sacher-Woenckhaus)

The form of the colony is often determined by the conditions around it. Some species form branching colonies in relatively quiet water but build low, encrusting colonies in areas pounded by heavy surf. Such different growth forms long caused considerable confusion in the classification of corals. It is a common misconception that corals are restricted to warm waters. Reef-building corals are, but other species are found as far north as Alaska, the New England coast, and the fiords of Norway, and at least as far south as the Cape of Good Hope. Some of these are solitary and some are colonial in a small way, forming limited aggregations. There are also related forms—sometimes called false corals—the flattened sea fans found in temperate and warm waters, the curious organ-pipe coral of tropical waters and the precious red coral of commerce, found in the Mediterranean Sea and nearby Atlantic, with a related species occurring off Japan.

The reef-building corals, whose heavy calcareous skeletons entitle them to be regarded as an important geologic agent, are largely limited to the tropics, and only stray out of bounds where warm-water currents produce tropical conditions, as, for example, in Bermuda. The reef builders are often referred to as stony corals, or sometimes as "true" corals, which is a misnomer because there are true corals that do not build reefs, and there are organisms that are not in any sense true corals but that do participate in reef-building.

Why then are coral reefs restricted to the warm-water areas of the world? The most plausible answer is that calcium carbonate is much more soluble in cold water than in warm; if we heat a beaker of sea water over a Bunsen burner, one of the first substances to precipitate is calcium carbonate. It is even thought that some limestones have been formed by direct precipitation of calcium carbonate in warm sea water, without the action of animal or plant intermediaries.

Coral heads exposed at low tide on the Great Barrier Reef, Australia. (M. J. Yonge)

184

The difference in the solubility of calcium in warm and cold water means that warm-water organisms need do less work to get calcium out of sea water than must cold-water organisms. This theory is borne out by the fact that the largest mollusks in the world, with the heaviest shells, the tridacnids, are tropical, and are found on coral reefs.

KINDS OF CORAL REEFS

Coral formations in tropical areas may take the form of fringing reefs, barrier reefs, or coral atolls. Atolls are curious, ring-shaped islands with an inside lagoon connected by one or more passages to the open sea. A fringing reef is simply a reef growing out from shore, whether of a tropical island or of a land mass such as Florida or northern Australia. Coral grows most rapidly at the outer edge of a reef, and tends to die on the inner edge because of silting, warmer temperatures, and other reasons. The reef itself will grow seaward, while the breaking of surf or the flow of water in surge channels may excavate a shallow channel inside the reef, sometimes deep enough to be navigable by native canoes.

In a sense, the difference between a barrier reef and a fringing reef with a small channel behind it is one of degree. A barrier reef is some distance offshore, forming a kind of breakwater, with a channel between it and the land that is navigable by fairly large ships. The most famous reef of this kind is the Great Barrier Reef off the northeast coast of Australia; it extends well over a thousand miles in a northwest-southeast direction and the distance between reef and shore ranges from twelve to considerably more than one hundred miles. Ships regularly use the channel inside the reef, although this requires an expert pilot, because minor reefs and coral heads are distributed apparently at random along the course. Actually their occur-

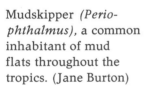

Mudskipper *(Perio-phthalmus),* a common inhabitant of mud flats throughout the tropics. (Jane Burton)

The peacock worm *(Sabella)* of the Atlantic coast of Europe is a tube-dwelling annelid. The colorful gills at the anterior end are quickly drawn in if the animal is disturbed. (Jacques Hérissé)

rence is not random, but depends on geological and biological factors, which are only partially understood.

Coral atolls have been a fascinating subject ever since Charles Darwin began their study in 1836, near the end of his famous voyage as naturalist on HMS *Beagle*. An atoll may be anywhere from one to eighty miles in diameter. Although we describe it as ring-shaped, an atoll is seldom if ever actually circular, and may be very irregular in shape. This is at least partly due to the fact that coral grows more rapidly on the windward side of a reef, where the water is clean and clear, than on the leeward side, where sand and detritus tend to accumulate in the backwash of a wind-driven current.

Reef-building corals do not grow at depths much greater than twenty fathoms. It is obvious, therefore, that coral islands in mid-Pacific could not have started at the bottom and gradually built up to the surface. Darwin concluded that atolls were formed by the growth of fringing reefs around islands that were subsiding, the upward growth of coral keeping pace with the subsidence of the island; when at last the island disappeared beneath the waves, it would leave only the coral, which would continue to maintain itself by growing up to the surface of the sea as fast as the former island went down. This process could over a long period of time result in coral formations hundreds or even thousands of feet in thickness, of which only the surface layer would consist of living and growing coral.

Various other theories were advanced, one of which was the precise opposite of Darwin's: namely that atolls were formed on land recently elevated. If a submarine mountain, a volcano for example, came almost but not quite to the surface, coral growing around this seamount would form an atoll. A lagoon would remain in the center because conditions for the growth of coral are better at the outer than the inner side of a reef.

A theory deserving more than passing mention is that suggested by Professor R. A. Daly of Harvard University; it depends on the effect of glacial periods on sea level, referred to elsewhere in this volume in connection with a Pleistocene land bridge across Bering Strait. Professor Daly pointed out that when glaciers covered great areas of the earth, sea level was lowered by the amount of water frozen into ice; in interglacial periods, sea level rose. Changes in sea level due to these phenomena have been variously estimated at from 150 to 400 feet. As the sea went down, there would be wave-cut benches at successively lower levels around continents and islands; seamounts might, as they emerged at the surface, have their tops entirely planed off by wave action. As sea level rose with the melting of the glaciers, the benches would form platforms for the growth of fringing or barrier reefs, and the flat-topped seamounts would become crowned with atolls. This theory, while possibly true in certain cases, could explain coral formations only a very few hundred feet in thickness.

Deep borings on coral islands have given strong support to Darwin's view. Several drillings have shown coral extending to a considerable depth. Drilling on Eniwetok Island brought up coral from one thousand, two thousand, three thousand feet; but slightly beyond four thousand feet a basalt founda-

A common small translucent sea anemone *(Diadumene)* of wide distribution in temperate waters.
(William H. Amos)

Sting rays *(Dasyatis)* commonly lie half-buried in sand, and if stepped on may inflict a painful wound with a poison spine on the tail. More than thirty species occur around the world. (Alfred Schuhmacher)

tion was reached. There is no way to explain a coral formation four thousand feet thick in mid-Pacific except on the assumption of a gradual subsidence of a former island or seamount. On the other hand, on the island of Timor in the Malay Archipelago, massive coral formations are found at an elevation of nearly four thousand feet *above* sea level. They have been described as "atolls on a mountain."

It seems fairly obvious that no single explanation can be made to fit all of the known cases. The subsidence of one island area and the elevation of another is, of course, in accord with the idea of isostasy discussed in Chapter 3. Darwin himself almost hit on the theory of isostasy when he stated that if some portions of the earth were elevated, other parts must necessarily have subsided.

CORAL ORGANISMS AND THEIR GUESTS

The bodies of reef-building corals almost without exception contain an immense number of tiny brown algae known as zooxanthellae. These are no more than a one-hundredth of a millimeter in diameter, and they occur in many thousands in each coral polyp of the reef-building type. As many as 7,400 have been counted in a coral larva one millimeter long.

The function of zooxanthellae has been widely debated. The coral can apparently get along without them; yet it never lives in depths of more than twenty or twenty-five fathoms—it seems this is because the zooxanthellae, being tiny pigmented plants, require sunlight for their existence. The general theory is that the zooxanthellae help the coral by using up its waste products, such as ammonia, nitrogen, phosphates, and carbon dioxide. They also

188

contribute oxygen. There is no sound evidence that the coral needs the oxygen, although tropical waters are less rich in oxygen than those of temperate or sub-Arctic regions. But corals are not active animals and require much less oxygen than, say, a fish. The presence of zooxanthellae may, however, enable the corals to survive at times and in places where oxygen in the water is insufficient. At all events, the corals do not live off their house guests. When short of food, they do not digest the zooxanthellae, but evict them.

The precise relationship between the corals and their zooxanthellae is still unclear, but the relative permanence of their association suggests that there are advantages to both partners. Such a relationship, known as mutualism, is not infrequent in nature, and involves two organisms of different kinds living together in mutual helpfulness. In several species related to the reef-building corals experiments have shown that the animals obtain nourishment and perhaps certain enzymes from their zooxanthellae.

Curiously, a group of mollusks living on coral reefs have also taken on the habit of including zooxanthellae in their tissues. These are the tridacnids, one of which, *Tridacna gigas,* the "giant clam," is the largest mollusk in the world; one specimen has been measured at four and one-half feet. The shell is heavy as well as large, and may weigh three hundred to

A school of young porgies or sea bream off the Canary Islands at a depth of about 40 feet. They are common in the Mediterranean, eastern Atlantic and African waters. (Alfred Schuhmacher)

four hundred pounds. There are several smaller species, but all of them grow zooxanthellae in their tissues.

Immense numbers of these organisms, which require sunlight but not too much sunlight, live in the highly colored mantle of the mollusk evidently because the pigmented tissues of the mollusks filter the light and thus provide an ideal environment. But even less is known about the relation of zooxanthellae to mollusks than to corals. Periodically the mollusks evict their tiny guests in large numbers and eat them along with any other plankton that is available. But the zooxanthellae are not digested, and emerge from their passage through the mollusk still alive and able to reproduce in large numbers. The entire relationship of zooxanthellae to mollusks remains one of the most puzzling phenomena in the organic world.

REEF-DWELLING FISHES

The waters surrounding coral reefs are inhabited by some of the most bizarre and brilliantly colored fishes to be found anywhere in the world—schools of bright blue damselfish and orange-and-white anemone fish; the multicolored angel fishes; the amazing pink-tailed triggerfish and its colorful relatives; the oddly shaped Moorish idol marked with black, white, and orange; the striped zebra fish—also known as the turkey fish because of the resemblance of its trailing fins to feathers—parrot fish and wrasses of a multitude of hues, to mention only a few.

Several theories have been offered to explain the bright colors of reef fishes. One is that, because the corals themselves are of various colors, the fish blend into the reef; an objection to this is that the fish are often brighter than the corals and certainly more conspicuous by reason of their movements. Another theory is that the bizarre shapes and markings break up the outline of the fish, thus reducing its visibility—the principle of camouflage. A third idea is that, because they can quickly dart into cavities in the reef to escape predators, it really doesn't matter what color they are.

That none of these theories is satisfactory to the fish themselves is

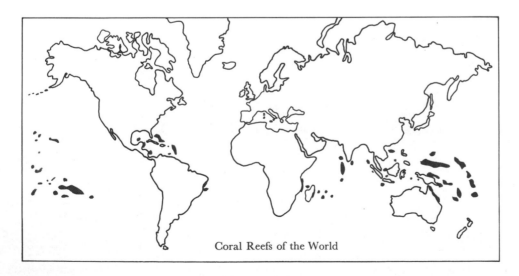

Coral reefs of the world.

Coral Reefs of the World

190

Unicorn fish being cleaned of parasites by the Hawaiian rainbow wrasse, seen just in front of the unicorn's fin. (Stephen Skolnick)

indicated by the fact that many species have definite means of defense. A triggerfish can elevate a sharp spine on its back, with which it can inflict a nasty wound. A porcupine fish is covered with spines and can inflate itself into a round ball very difficult for a predator to seize. A turkeyfish is armed with a whole battery of poison spines, which can produce really dangerous wounds. The stonefish is so venomous that it can cause death to a wader unfortunate enough to step upon it. The colorful anemone fish gets protection at second hand by taking refuge among the tentacles of a sea anemone, whose stinging cells do not affect it but are effective against other organisms. There are small, slender reef fish known as shrimpfish that take shelter among the long, sharp spines of tropical sea urchins.

A coral reef is a fascinating place, but not exactly a safe one for its animal inhabitants or even for human observers.

LIFE AMONG THE MANGROVES

It would be pleasant to think of tropical beaches as consisting only of white coral sand washed by shimmering blue water, with sea shells of varied form and hue awaiting the eager beachcomber. But mud is fairly universal, and it occurs in the tropics in reasonable abundance even on most coral islands.

Mud flats in the tropics are likely to look more interesting than those in higher latitudes, though, because they are nearly always rimmed by a dense growth of mangroves. As one approaches closer, mangroves come into view. The mangrove is a shrub or small tree that grows on a muddy shore in the intertidal zone. It stands up out of the mud on branching roots, suggesting a small version of a banyan tree. Oysters frequently grow on the roots, which are out of the water at high tide, giving rise to the tales of early sailors of "oysters that grow on trees." They grow in thick organic mud inhabited by immense numbers of crabs of several species, and sometimes cluster in dense "mangrove swamps." Anyone venturing among them must cling to the trunks of the mangroves to avoid sinking in the mud, which is almost as treacherous as quicksand.

In spite of the difficulty of wading around in such an area, scientists do— because mud flats and mangrove swamps are of considerable biological interest. Several species of the marine wood-boring mollusks called shipworms are found in mangrove roots, and usually if not always in dead roots; it is not quite clear whether the roots died because the shipworms invaded them, or whether the shipworms invaded after the roots were dead.

Crabs of various species live among the mangroves or in the mud beneath them. One of the most common is the fiddler crab, so named because the male has one immense claw and one small one, the larger claw somewhat resembling a violin. This claw is used in fighting, the males being very pugnacious and wrestling each other around with great energy at the slightest opportunity. In some species the claw is highly colored and is considered by some biologists to be a kind of banner to attract the female. Probably its most important use is to block the burrow against intruders, for the fiddlers burrow in the mud, and a claw that is approximately as large as the body must make a very effective door behind which to take refuge.

Fiddler crabs are not restricted to the tropics; one species occurs as far north as New England. But the greatest number of species and of individuals occur in the tropics, and they are regarded as animals of tropical mud flats and mangrove swamps.

The term "soldier crab" is sometimes applied to fiddler crabs, either because of their pugnacity or because their abundance on the mud flats suggests an army; but the term is better applied to crabs that perform long marches in single line. This habit is characteristic of crabs that have abandoned the sea and become more or less completely terrestrial in habit, but which return to the edge of the sea to lay their eggs. One group of these is related to the fiddler crabs, another group to the hermit crabs, those curious creatures that back into any unoccupied shell and carry the shell around with them. I have seen relatives of the fiddler crab marching in single file toward the sea in columns at least a mile long.

A relative of the hermit crab that has become almost completely adapted to land is the coconut crab of the South Pacific. This crab, which lives on coconuts and even climbs trees to get them, has given up the habit of living in abandoned shells of snails and whelks, possibly because it is a foot or more in diameter and cannot find any shell that is large enough. It has developed shelly plates to protect its otherwise vulnerable abdomen, but it still retains an atavistic habit; if it finds a broken coconut shell of suitable size, it will back into this and carry it around just as a hermit crab carries a seashell.

One would not expect to find fish in a mangrove swamp or on a tropical mud flat, but there are fish to whom this is home. They are the mudskippers, of which *Periophthalmus* is the principal genus. They live half in and half

41. Coral heads seen beneath the rippled waters of a reef channel off Tahiti. Surf pounds on the outer reef at upper left. (Jack Fields)

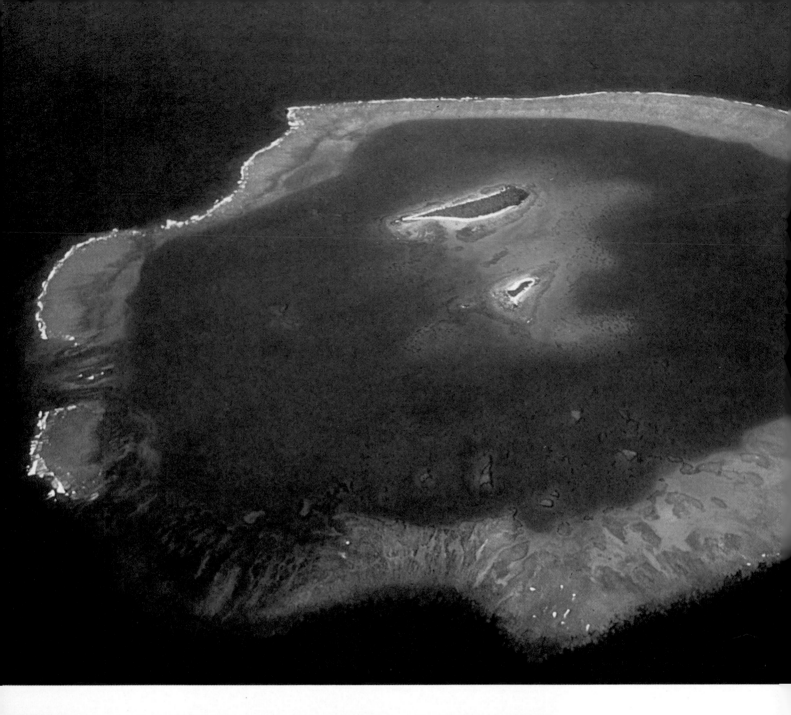

42. Above: Atolls such as this one in the Fiji Islands are seldom symmetrical because the coral grows less rapidly on the leeward side of the island. (Jack Fields)

43. Left: Some species of reef-dwelling clams of the genus *Tridacna* burrow into the coral and, like those shown here, would scarcely be visible except for the colorful edges of the mantle. (Allan Power)

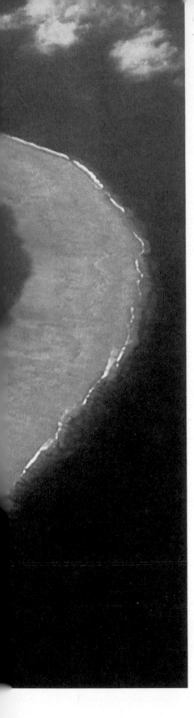

44. Right: A school of blueheads *(Thalassoma bifasciatum)*—the yellow fish are the young—seen against a Florida reef. The branching structures are gorgonians, sometimes called "false corals." In the foreground are true corals. (Robert Stenuit)

45.   Upper left: This moray eel off La Paz, Mexico, is as vicious as it looks, but tolerates the four tiny gobies acting as "cleaners" at the rear of its body. (Al Giddings)

46.   Lower left: Vaselike sponges and colorful royal grammas *(Gramma loreto)* off Yucatan Peninsula at a depth of 60 feet. (Al Giddings)

47.   Right: Reef fishes often blend into their colorful environment, as demonstrated by these Australian cardinal fish *(Apogon* sp.). (Allan Power)

48. Left: Feather-duster worms (tube-dwelling annelids) protrude from a coral head off the coast of British Honduras. The fish are two purple-and-yellow royal grammas *(Gramma loreto)* and a blue chromis *(Chromis cyaneus).* (Al Giddings)

49. Upper right: A peppermint-striped squirrel fish momentarily provides a background for a bright blue cleaner fish in Teavanui Harbor, Bora Bora. (Douglas Faulkner)

50. Lower right: As demonstrated by this imperial angelfish *(Pomacanthus imperator),* the shape of reef fishes can be as bizarre as their color schemes. (Allan Power)

out of the water; they even climb up among the mangrove stems. When the tide is out, they skitter over the mud so fast that it is extremely difficult to catch them. They leave a curious track, which looks like a diagram of a monorail railroad, the pectoral fins by which they propel themselves leaving marks that suggest cross-ties, while the body leaves a line in the middle.

These fish enjoy being out of water and will even climb up among the mangrove roots. In a public aquarium they have to be provided with a means of getting out of the water, such as a rock or a mudbank. When they climb out of the water—to the amazement of visitors—they are merely repeating the cycle to which they are accustomed—submerging at high tide and out of water at low tide. If kept continually under water, they will drown!

HOW ISLANDS GROW FROM REEFS

In discussing atolls, we may seem to have assumed that, whether land or ocean levels are rising or sinking, coral reefs will build up and coral islands emerge if there is a submarine platform at the proper level. This may in general be true, but the process is far from simple.

Coral grows up to only about the level of low tide. Islands have to be above the level of high tide to be habitable either by land plants or by men. How, then, does a coral reef become an island?

We have mentioned some of the guests of coral organisms, which the corals entertain possibly to the advantage of both host and guest. But corals also entertain, or are subjected to, a great variety of organisms—worms, mollusks, sea urchins, sponges, and algae—that bore into them. Some of these, like the mollusks and sea urchins, bore by mechanical action of shell or spines; others apparently bore by chemical means since limestone is easily dissolved by even very weak acids. This does not require any great specialization or ingenuity on the part of the borers, as evidenced by the fact that immense caverns are often excavated in limestone rock by the simple solvent action of fresh water.

It is not uncommon to see a coral reef studded with boring sea urchins or boring tridacnids, smaller relatives of the giant clam, which itself—like a genial giant—lives on the reefs without seeming to harm them. By action of the numerous organisms that do attack the reef, it becomes eroded and weakened, and its outer edges are broken up into larger or smaller blocks by the pounding surf. Some of these sink down as talus along the outer slope; others are washed up over and inside the reef. It is the latter that form the coral islets.

Some of the blocks become cemented together by the overgrowth of coralline algae. Others are ground by wave action into coral sand. Lastly, the coral sand is worked over by many organisms—various species of worms, and especially sea cucumbers, which range in size from a few inches to two feet in length, and occur in great abundance on the reefs. They are soft-bodied and look like large slugs, but are actually related to starfish and sea urchins. Although they look unappealing, they are edible and, under the French name *bêche-de-mer* or the name trepang (taken from their Malayan name), they have long been commercially important in the

51. A sea lily *(Crinoidea)* with delicate curling arms, on a growth of branching staghorn coral, near Cozumel Island, Yucatan. The pink organisms with hollow centers are vaselike sponges. (Al Giddings)

South Seas, being dried and shipped to China and other places. The sea cucumbers feed on coral sand, which is not itself nutritious but contains remains of algae and other organic matter that the sea cucumber extracts as the sand passes through its digestive tract. In this process, coarse sand is reduced to finer sand or mud.

Several species of reef fishes with powerful jaws and durable teeth break off and eat fragments of the coral, which are likely to be carried to a new location by the time they have passed through the digestive tract. Tooth marks are often found on the coral, and one investigator has suggested that gnawing and scraping by fishes may be an important factor in producing and transporting coral sediments.

Thus, through the interaction of various agencies, reefs may create low-lying islands, composed basically of coral rocks but with at least patches of soil consisting of coral sand or coral mud. The islands are now ready for the arrival of plants, which constitutes another fascinating story.

Coconut palms are undoubtedly one of the most widely distributed trees on tropical islands in every part of the world. Their place of origin is presumed to be the West Indies, and there has been considerable debate about how they became world-wide in distribution. Because coconuts are a useful product, yielding both food and drink and various commercially valuable fibers and substances, they have been carried by man and planted in various parts of the tropical world; one school of thought maintained that this is the

A species of requiem shark *(Carcharhinus)* common in all tropical seas. (Peter Stackpole)

reason for their wide distribution. But the palms are also found in uninhabited islands, where they are not likely to have been planted by man. It is thus probable that they have frequently been distributed by natural means.

When they fall from the trees, coconuts are covered by a thick husk which enables them to float for months without being soaked through by salt water. There is one record of a coconut, complete with husk, that having presumably drifted from the West Indies in the Gulf Stream, washed up on the coast of Norway. When planted in a greenhouse, it sprouted and grew!

When the island of Krakatoa in the East Indies exploded in 1883 in the greatest volcanic eruption of recorded history, all of the vegetation of the island was destroyed. Nevertheless, by 1906 Krakatoa had a good growth of coconut palms along its shore, with smaller trees three feet high representing a second generation.

Mangroves, more widespread in the tropics but of less immediate importance to man, have a curious method of reproduction. They give rise not to seeds but to seedlings, which can float in salt water for as long as six months and still take root in a new locality. The result is that the only tropical isles that do not have mangroves are those few whose soil is not suitable for their growth.

Certain plants have seeds that can survive for long periods in salt water. Outstanding among these—aside from the mangroves—are the pandanus, a widespread tropical plant of many uses, and the shoreside legumes, members of the bean and pea family. In addition, seeds that have hooks or adhesive properties may be carried from island to island on the feathers of birds. Thus plants get around, and any suitable island will in the course of time have a considerable and varied vegetation.

Certainly, once an island becomes available, it will be occupied by plants, and if large enough, will sooner or later be occupied by man. If he is Polynesian or Micronesian man, he will bring with him his domestic plants—taro, sweet potato, breadfruit, and sugar cane—and his domestic animals—the pig, the chicken and the dog. He already knows how to fish. Thus we see how self-sufficient communities have been set up on just about every island in the tropical Pacific that is habitable for man.

Yet these charming islands, crowned with palms that sway in the trade winds, are, with the exception of large volcanic islands such as Hawaii, Samoa, and Tahiti, only small, slightly elevated portions of much larger reefs. As Marston Bates and Donald Abbott have put it in their book, *Coral Island, Portrait of an Atoll:*

"We stood and looked, first to one side, then the other, then back again. There it was, a ring of reef, about the same width on either side. To the windward the ring bore islets on . . . well, on the reef flat, really. To the leeward the corresponding region of the flat was broad and empty.

"Marston gave a surprised exclamation: 'Why, the islets are just incidents on the reef!'

"And so they were: just piles of sand and coral, the rubble of the reef, swept inward by a broom of wind and wave, deposited on the flats where the force that carried it was spent. Here, in a shallow heap, it formed the land. This was no new idea, but Marston had put it well, I thought. The reef was the real Ifaluk; the islets that were the homes of men were—just incidents on the reef."

11
The Open Sea

To the landsman the sea is a wilderness of water fraught with danger. To the seaman it is a highway to all the continents and islands of the world. To the sea lover it is a place of vast and lonely beauty. To the biologist it is an underwater world teeming with plants and animals of such infinite variety that even in a lifetime he can hope to make himself familiar with only a small fraction of them.

The fact that as one goes out from shore the water gets deeper is absurdly simple, yet it leads to an immense number of complexities. To mention only a few, as the sea gets deeper, the bottom water becomes colder, denser, more saline, and darker, because light is rapidly filtered out in the surface layers. There is also a rapid increase in pressure because of the weight of the layers of water above. The surface waters also have a character of their own, and are populated by an immense variety of organisms never seen by the landsman unless they drift ashore or—as occasionally happens in some unknown marine accident—become piled up in impressive and sometimes smelly windrows on the shore.

Marine organisms, whether plant or animal, are placed in several broad categories according to the nature of their habitat. Forms that live on or in the bottom are collectively known as benthos. The term applies to forms that are attached to the bottom, such as seaweeds and corals; those that creep about, like snails and starfish; those that walk or even run, like some rather active crabs; and to forms that burrow in mud or bore in rock.

In contrast to the bottom dwellers, we have two groups that live at various levels of the water itself. These are known as nekton (the Greek word for "swimming") and plankton (the Greek word for "drifting"). The nekton are animals that are able to swim strongly enough to go where they will: for example, whales, porpoises, seals, and a majority of fishes. Plankton are organisms that swim either feebly or not at all, and thus are carried hither and yon by ocean currents. It is to be noted that the benthos and the plankton include both plants and animals. Plants may live on the bottom, or they may float at the surface or at some intermediate depth, but they do not swim actively. Some microscopic forms have swimming organs, such as beating flagella, but these merely keep them from sinking and do not propel them anywhere.

An organism in one category may shift to another. Thus a very young fish

A jellyfish, *Rhizostoma pulmo,* of the Mediterranean and eastern Atlantic. A simple animal, the jellyfish consists of about 99 percent water. It moves through rhythmic contractions of the umbrella. (A. Schuhmacher)

belongs to the plankton, but as soon as it becomes large enough to swim actively it graduates into the nekton. A crab larva drifts around in the plankton, but as soon as it settles to the bottom and becomes a young adult, it is a member of the benthos.

It would be a mistake to think of all plankton as being microscopic or even small. Jellyfishes, for example, belong to the plankton because they swim only very feebly and are carried along by currents; but most of them are easily visible, and a few species grow as big as a washtub. But most plankton organisms are small, and a majority are microscopic.

MICROSCOPIC PLANT LIFE OF THE SEA

If one takes a bucket of sea water from almost any sea in the world and strains it through a handkerchief, a brownish sediment will remain on the cloth. If this is examined under a microscope it will prove to be alive with hundreds or even thousands of individuals. It would be more practical to use a small conical net made of silk bolting cloth, which comes in various degrees of fineness, such as a No. 10 cloth, which has 11,881 meshes to the square inch, or a No. 15, which has 22,500 meshes per square inch. The investigator uses a mesh corresponding to the size of the organisms he wishes to study. It is also customary to tie a small bottle or a test tube to the lower end of the net to collect the captured plants and animals. With large plankton nets, metal cylinders with fine wire sieves may be used as the collecting vessel.

In any such collection, the most prominent organisms are likely to be one-celled plants called diatoms. These abound in fresh and salt water and, containing chlorophyll, have the capacity to produce carbohydrates from carbon dioxide and water with the energy provided by sunlight. They serve the same function in the sea that grass and other green plants do on land.

Diatoms have siliceous skeletons, generally in the form of a two-piece capsule. Diatom capsules, known as frustules, are of almost infinite variety in shape and form; many of them are extremely beautiful. Because the frustules are made of silica, they are very durable, and are useful to geologists as indicators of the age of marine sediments and sedimentary rocks.

Most diatoms have no individual motion; they simply drift with the current. In many cases they have long spines, which take advantage of the viscosity of the water to prevent sinking to the bottom. A few diatoms actually move under their own power; by osmosis they take in water at one end and let it out at the other—an elementary and leisurely method of jet-propulsion. A common genus, *Navicula* (meaning a little boat), is so named because it is pointed at both ends and moves slowly but steadily across the field of the microscope by the method described; but its movement is on a microscopic scale.

Another group of extremely interesting organisms of diverse shapes found abundantly in almost every plankton sample is the dinoflagellates. These have two motile hairlike appendages, one winding around the body in a spiral groove, the other longitudinal and usually trailing behind. It has long been debated whether these organisms belong to the plant or the animal kingdom, botany textbooks describing them as plants and zoology textbooks

Top row, left to right: Larva of a burrowing sea cucumber, *Labidoflax digitata* (magnified 50 times).

Larva of *Owenia fusiformis,* a tube-building worm (magnified 40 times).

Living dinoflagellates, *Ceratium tripos,* with two small chains of diatoms (magnified 60 times).

Middle row, left to right: Living zooplankton (magnified 14 times). In the center is the larva of a crab. Diagonally below it is an arrowworm, *Sagitta,* and to the left a fish egg with embryo visible inside. The rest are copepods, with a tiny jellyfish at center bottom.

Larva of a marine snail, *Nassarius incrassatus* (magnified 36 times).

Bottom row, left to right: Larva of a starfish (magnified 25 times), remarkable in its ballet-skirted beauty.

Larva of a sea-urchin, *Psammechinus miliaris* (magnified 45 times).

Pelagic tunicates, *Doliolum* (magnified 15 times), related to the salps. (All photographs by D. P. Wilson)

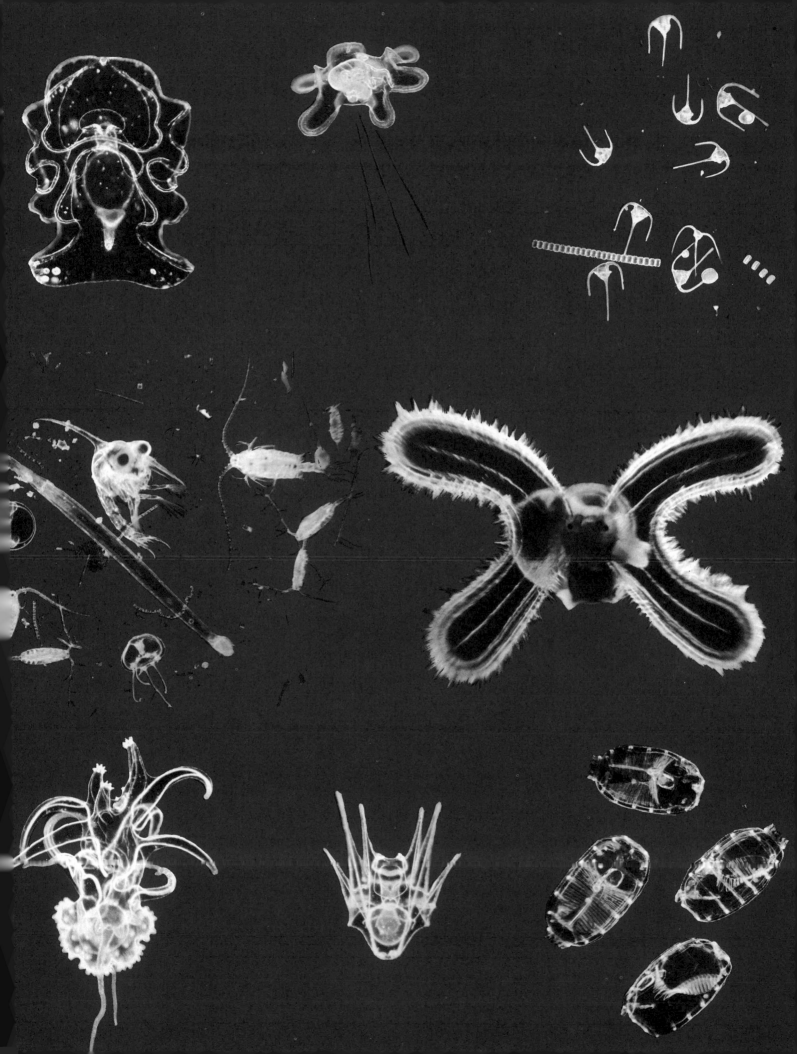

Dinoflagellates, *Gonyaulax,* one of a species responsible for much "red-water," fish poisoning, and indirectly for mussel-poisoning in man. (Kofoid, Univ. Calif. Publ. Zool., Vol. 8)

Silicoflagellates are among the most minute of plankton organisms having a siliceous skeleton. These are fossil forms, but closely related species still survive. (G. D. Hanna)

treating them as animals. When they have shells or skeletons, these consist of cellulose and are less durable in the fossil record than diatoms. In the living state they contain pigment bodies, which function like the chlorophyll of plants in producing carbohydrates from carbon dioxide and water. Thus in the ecology of the sea they function as plants, although most of the monographs on them have been written by zoologists.

A few kinds of dinoflagellates are poisonous, and when abundant enough they may cause extensive killing of fish. The famous "red tides" that were mentioned earlier, which result in the death of great numbers of fish, are due to dinoflagellates that occur in sufficient abundance to discolor the water. Another and more insidious effect of poisonous dinoflagellates occurs when they are eaten by shellfish, particularly sea mussels, but also at times by various clams; while apparently not harming the bivalve itself, they render its flesh poisonous to humans. Departments of public health in seaside areas often put a quarantine on mussels during the warmer months of the year. The dinoflagellate generally responsible for mussel poisoning is *Gonyaulax.*

Very few of the dinoflagellates, however, fall into this dangerous category. While red water is to be regarded with suspicion, it is not by any means always poisonous. The large dinoflagellate *Noctiluca,* which occurs practically all over the world, often gives water the appearance of tomato soup, yet it is nonpoisonous. Indeed, the Red Sea derives its name from a nonpoisonous alga, *Trichodesmium erythrythaeum,* which periodically occurs in such immense numbers as to give the water a red or red-brown color.

Many of the dinoflagellates become luminous in the dark when stimulated by contact with other organisms or objects or simply by the movement of the water. There are many other luminous organisms in the sea, including species of jellyfish and a number of the true fishes; but because of their abundance, the dinoflagellates are the major cause of luminescence in the water. The best-known luminous form is *Noctiluca,* perhaps because it is considerably larger than most one-celled organisms. But many other common dinoflagellates contribute to producing the glow, often quite bright, that can be seen in the wake of a ship or even on the crests of waves when the sea is slightly rough. The luminosity varies according to the number of light-producing organisms present, which is more or less seasonal, usually being greatest in summer and autumn. Fishermen are often able to detect schools of fish by the trail of light they produce in the water as they agitate the dinoflagellates around them. Certain fisheries, such as the California sardine and anchovy fisheries, are conducted only in the dark of the moon, when the luminescence in the water outlines the schools of fish. An experienced fisherman can distinguish different species of fish by the trail of light they produce; it is easy, for example, to tell a school of sardines from a school of mackerel; the latter, being larger fish, leave more clearly marked trails.

Dinoflagellates, with their motile flagella, are more active than diatoms. Some of them, like *Noctiluca,* eat smaller organisms; but most of them are nourished primarily by photosynthesis, the process of combining water and carbon dioxide that forms carbohydrates, that is synthesizing food and giving off excess oxygen in the process. Thus they function as plants, and even zoologists agree that in the ecology of the sea they act as plants. In the aggregate, the diatoms and dinoflagellates, together with some smaller and less important groups, are called phytoplankton, and are regarded as the basic plant life of the sea.

A very common marine diatom, *Coscinodiscus* (magnified 200 times). (G. D. Hanna)

THE SMALLEST PLANTS

It is frustrating to the biologist to know that the most abundant organisms in the sea are those that escape through the meshes of his plankton net, the bacteria. Bacteria are undoubtedly as abundant and important in the sea as they are on land, and they perform the same useful functions. It is a mistake to think that bacteria are generally harmful; a majority are not only useful but necessary.

An authority in marine microbiology, a field that is still in a pioneering stage, has estimated that the number of bacteria in a cubic centimeter of sea water may range from one to one million. In general, bacteria are not abundant in the water itself, but live on the surface of various plants and animals and on rocks or wood immersed in water. Their greatest concentration occurs at the sea bottom. Bacteria are indispensable in the cycle of life in the sea. Without their activity, the bodies of dead plants and animals that continually drop down into the ocean depths would accumulate on the bottom, not only constituting a vast morgue, but robbing the water of substances necessary for organic life. Bacteria prevent the sea bottom from becoming a charnel house, and also return to the ocean the substances of which plants and animals are composed, which are thus used over and over again in the unending cycle of organic life.

Bacteria also form an important item in the food of many larger but still minute unicellular organisms. Since bacteria are not, like the one-celled algae, dependent upon light, they provide a food supply at times and places where food might otherwise be lacking.

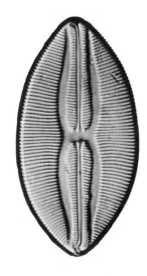

A diatom, *Navicula* (magnified 400 times). (W. M. Grant)

Larger than bacteria but still too small to be captured by the finest plankton net is a group of numerous organisms known as the nannoplankton (from the Greek word *nannos,* meaning dwarf). They seldom exceed one thousandth of an inch in size, and may be as small as one ten-thousandth of an inch. Often referred to collectively because of their minute size, they belong to several different groups. All or most of them are flagellated; but some, called silicoflagellates, have a siliceous skeleton, others, the coccolithophores, have a calcareous skeleton made up of tiny rounded plates known as coccoliths, and still others have no skeleton at all.

The organisms comprising the nannoplankton are difficult to collect and study. In many cases their structure can be determined only by use of the electron microscope. They can be concentrated by centrifuging samples of sea water from which the larger organisms have been strained out. In the sea they are also concentrated by certain larger organisms, species of tunicates, that feed upon them; an investigator can thus obtain them, as it were, at second hand.

Much remains to be learned about the nannoplankton; but those who have studied it believe that, notwithstanding the minute size of the individual organisms, its total bulk is astonishing—sufficient to give it a major role in the sea.

A triangular diatom (magnified 250 times), is named *Triceratium,* meaning "three-horned." (G. D. Hanna)

THE ANIMAL PLANKTON

In contrast to the phytoplankton we have the animal plankton or zoo-plankton, made up of organisms distinguished by the fact that they cannot synthesize food like the green plants nor absorb it like fungi and other nonpigmented plants—they must eat. They usually eat phytoplankton, though some of them eat other, smaller animals in the zooplankton. The amateur microscopist can generally recognize the zooplankton by the fact that its members wiggle, swim, or dart about, moving so actively that it is difficult to keep them in the field of the microscope. Their movements, of course, are on a microscopic scale, leaving them still at the mercy of the currents as to where they go in the ocean.

There are two groups of zooplankton organisms that neither swim nor wiggle but whose only movements consist of pushing out strands of proto-plasm for the capture of food. They are related to the ameba, from which they differ in having skeletons, often of great complexity and beauty. These are the Foraminifera and Radiolaria. They are usually taken in the open sea, where they sometimes occur in great abundance.

The Foraminifera form their skeletons of calcium carbonate, adding successively larger chambers as they grow. Some take the form of a flattened helix, resembling a tiny snail or, if we take account of the successive increments, a miniature chambered nautilus. Others start out with a minute globular skeleton and, as new additions are made, assume roughly the form of a spiral made up of increasingly larger globules. Their calcareous skele-tons are perforated by numerous tiny holes (Latin "foramen," a hole), form-ing a sieve through which protoplasmic processes can extend outward in quest of food. The typical genus of this group is *Globigerina,* which, as mentioned in an earlier chapter, occurs in such abundance that its remains predominate in an important sea-bottom deposit known as globigerina ooze.

The Radiolaria build siliceous skeletons remarkable for their symmetry and fragile beauty. As they grow, some form a series of perforated capsules, one outside of another, which Professor Alister Hardy has compared to the concentric ivory spheres that the Chinese are so fond of carving. Several species have their radiating spines composed of strontium sulphate, as if nature had engaged in some curious chemical experiment. Radiolaria are

Newly shed egg of the pilchard (magnified 43 times). An oil glob-ule seen at the top gives buoyancy. The developing embryo is discernible around the underside of the yolk. The embryo fish with the oil globule still plain, is ready to hatch. Newly hatched larva of the pilchard (mag-nified 25 times), still kept afloat, albeit upside down, by its oil globule. Yolk sack and oil globule absorbed, the tiny fish swims right side up. It is now on its own. (Sequence by D. P. Wilson)

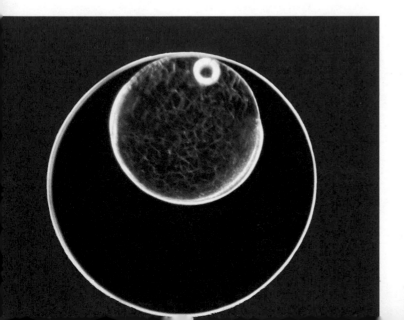
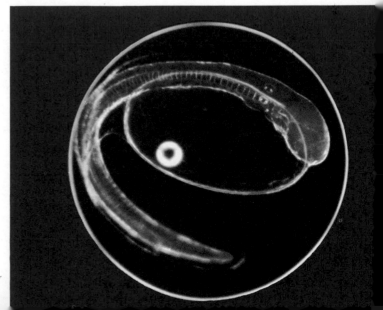

particularly characteristic of tropical waters, in part because there they have few competitors among the microplankton. Their remains form the radiolarian ooze found over limited areas of the bottom of tropical seas. Some occur also in temperate waters, but there they tend to be obscured by the abundance of other plankton.

Most conspicuous in the microplankton of temperate waters are likely to be the copepods, a very large group of small crustaceans, easily recognized by their large antennae and tapering bodies. They eat the phytoplankton, and in turn are eaten by nearly every kind of small fish, including the young stages of larger fish. Copepods lead energetic, hazardous and brief lives.

Other animal organisms in the sea are amphipods, which resemble very small shrimps; ostracods, which have bivalve shells from which they thrust out antennae and feet as if to prove that they are really crustaceans and not mollusks; and the grotesque larvae of crabs, barnacles, and other crustaceans. There will also be a large number of small animals with rapidly beating cilia, short, hairlike structures that collectively serve as tiny propellers. Some of these ciliated forms will be tintinnids, one-celled animals usually having a tubular papery shell, pointed at one end and open at the other, from which a crown of cilia protrudes; some will be rotifers, also having a crown of cilia but lacking a shell and having a trace of segmentation; some will be the ciliated larvae of marine organisms too numerous to mention. Nearly all marine organisms that are fixed or sedentary as adults—sponges, annelid worms, mollusks, starfish, and so forth—have free-swimming larvae that occur in the plankton; this is the way the species are distributed from place to place.

Even a small plankton sample is likely to contain some larger forms easily visible to the naked eye; for example, the long, slender, nearly transparent arrowworm; a pulsing jellyfish, or a comb jelly moving by means of its rows of rhythmically beating iridescent swimming plates; pastel-colored pteropods (from the Greek for "wing foot"), sometimes called sea butterflies, curious pelagic mollusks that swim by means of winglike extensions of the edge of the foot; and mysids and euphausids, which are pelagic crustaceans many times larger than the microscopic forms we have been discussing, and known to fishermen as "feed" and to whalers as "krill." In contrast to the nannoplankton and the microplankton, those drifting or

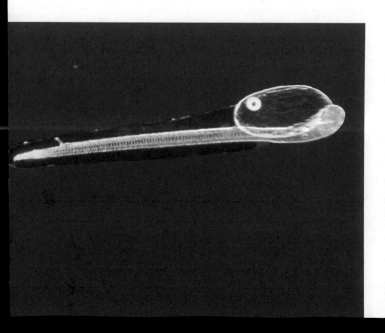
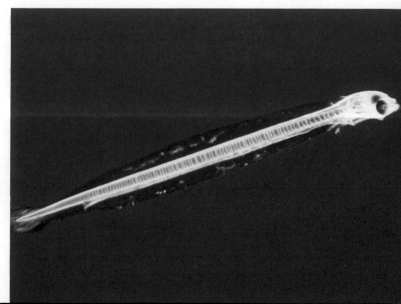

feebly swimming forms that can be readily seen with the naked eye are known collectively as the macroplankton (from Greek *"macros,"* meaning large).

HOW PLANKTON IS STUDIED

Because plankton is the basic food supply in the sea, it is important to know how much and what kind is present in a given body of water. And because the individual members of the plankton may range in size and bulk from the smallest flagellate to the largest jellyfish—a range of from one ten-thousandth of an inch to two or three feet in maximum dimension—a quantitative study presents obvious difficulties.

The small silk plankton net will yield enough different kinds of organisms to provide a lifetime of study. But such methods produce only the vaguest notion of the actual and relative abundance of plankton organisms in the surface waters, and no knowledge at all of their occurrence at greater depths.

To ascertain the quantity of plankton present in the water, various methods have been devised. One was to lower a weighted plankton net to a given depth, then draw it up vertically. This was supposed to give a measure of the plankton in a column of water having the diameter of the plankton net. But it was found that as the net came up its meshes became clogged with organisms, so that it lost its efficiency as a filter. To remedy this, a reverse canvas cone was placed at its mouth to reduce the diameter of the column of water to be strained, and by a well-known physical principle, that of the Bernoulli cone, increase the flow of water into the net. Even so the net

Simplified diagram of two food chains, one in or near the surface waters (top row), the other coming up from the depths (bottom row). In both chains, each organism feeds on the one to the right of it. Top: left to right: false killer whale, tuna, mackerel, anchovy, phytoplankton; bottom: gulper eel, viperfish, lantern fish, bristle-mouth, euphausid, phytoplankton.

212

sometimes became clogged, and there was no guarantee that the amount of water passing through was uniform. This was remedied by introducing in the mouth of the net a small propeller geared to a recording meter, and calibrated to the net so as to give a record of the actual amount of water passing through it.

A quantitative plankton sample obtained in this way is subjected to a number of toilsome operations. Occasionally there is time for a cursory examination of material in the living state; only thus can the true structure and beauty of many of the more delicate organisms be observed. More commonly the whole sample is placed in a jar and preserved in a weak solution of formaldehyde for future study. In due course, the larger organisms—jellyfish, arrowworms, and the like—are picked out by hand and counted. Then the microplankton is shaken up to insure uniform distribution, and the organisms in a measured sample are painstakingly identified and counted under the microscope.

Some short cuts have been devised. A measured sample of the plankton may be dried, weighed, and then incinerated; the difference between the dry weight and that of the ash gives a fair measure of the organic matter originally present. Determination of the amount of chlorophyll in a sample will indicate photosynthetic capacity of the living material. But there is no real substitute for identification and counting of the organisms.

The vertical plankton haul gives a fair idea of the amount of plankton in a column of water from, say, three hundred feet to the surface, but it discloses nothing about the distribution of the organisms at various depths. A simple method of getting such information is a net that can be lowered to a desired depth, towed horizontally for a distance, and then closed by sending a metal

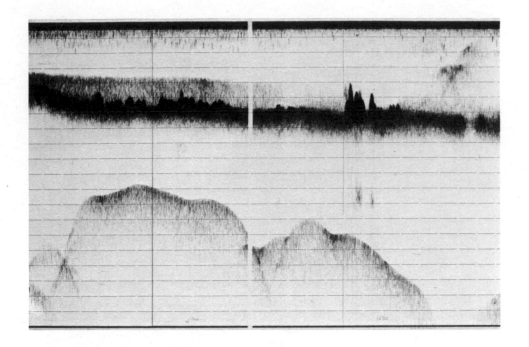

Echogram of the so-called deep scattering layer, off Cape Lagaro, west coast of Mexico, March, 1963. The heavy dark line at top represents the outgoing signal. The small blips immediately below are probably individual fish or patches of plankton near the surface. The undulating line nearest the lower edge is the actual profile of the bottom, which went off scale at lower right, and was picked up again near the upper right by shifting to a deeper scale (1900–2000 fathoms). The heavy dark line between is the "false bottom" or deep scattering layer. The peaks are probably schools of fish. (Official Photograph, U. S. Navy)

rider known as a "messenger" down the cable to actuate the closing mechanism.

One of the most ingenious devices of all is the Hardy continuous plankton recorder which consists basically of a torpedo-shaped metal box containing a long strip of silk gauze which winds from one roller onto another like the film on a camera. As the device is towed from a ship, water entering from an aperture at the front of the box is filtered through the silk gauze, on which the plankton is retained. The rollers are activated by a propeller which rotates as the plankton recorder is towed through the water, so the amount of silk gauze passing through the machine is directly related to the distance traveled and hence to the amount of water filtered. The strip of collecting gauze is ruled transversely into numbered areas, and at the end of a run of say two hundred miles the spool of gauze may be removed and the record of the plankton filtered by the gauze may be studied mile by mile under a special microscope. The spool may also be preserved in formalin for future study.

Notwithstanding all the methods that have been devised, the study of plankton is still a time-consuming process requiring both wide knowledge and endless patience on the part of the investigator.

VERTICAL DISTRIBUTION OF PLANKTON

Plants in the sea, like those on land, require light; therefore, the phytoplankton is concentrated in the upper layers of the sea. But there is an optimum illumination for photosynthesis; too much light can be detrimental. For this reason the greatest concentration of phytoplankton is ordinarily found not at the surface, but at a depth of from six to thirty feet. Below this there is a gradual diminution to a depth of two hundred fifty or three hundred feet, beyond which the only phytoplankton organisms are those that have drifted down from above. Although some light may penetrate to a depth of half a mile or more, below three hundred feet it is too weak to enable plants to function effectively. The depth at which photosynthesis ceases cannot be set absolutely, because it varies with latitude, time of day, and clarity of the water. The phytoplankton itself affects the clarity because it can in a sense get in its own light; the more abundant it is in the upper layers, the less the depth to which light can penetrate.

Early students of plankton were puzzled by the fact that their largest catches of zooplankton in the upper layers of the water were made at night. It seemed unlikely that animals unable to swim effectively against a rather leisurely ocean current should be able to make extensive vertical migrations. Yet, after careful investigations and especially after invention of the closing plankton net, this proved to be exactly what was occurring. Organisms whose movements were considered to be on a microscopic scale were moving up from a depth of around three hundred feet to the surface waters at night, and returning to their original depth by day.

Laboratory experiments on several species of copepods showed that they could swim upward at a rate of around fifty feet an hour, and downward at a faster rate. Microscopists had been misled by the fact that, under the microscope, the jerky movements of these organisms appeared to be random but always in a horizontal direction; they did this, it was found, because in the film of water in a microscope slide there was nothing else they could do. It now appears that in nature they generally swim up or down according to

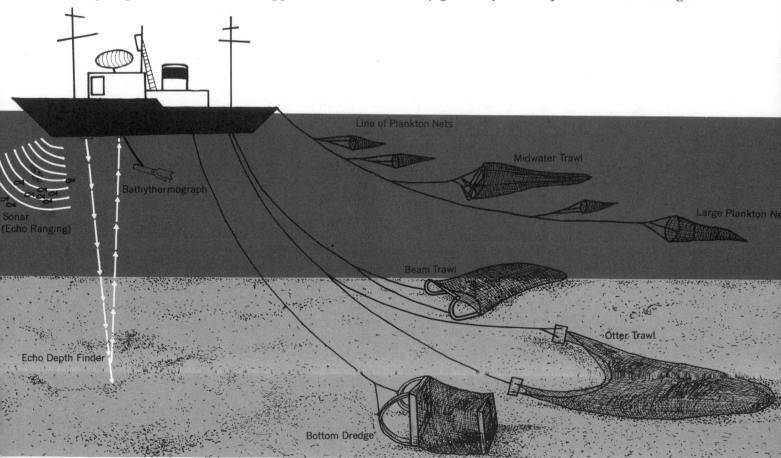

Types of oceanographic gear used when ship is under way. Only one or two cables can be out at a time because of the danger of their becoming tangled.

Sonar (Echo Ranging)

Bathythermograph

Line of Plankton Nets

Midwater Trawl

Large Plankton Net

Beam Trawl

Otter Trawl

Echo Depth Finder

Bottom Dredge

the time of day or night. Moreover, all zooplankton organisms, or the great majority of them, make similar or even more extensive vertical diurnal migrations.

It is easy to understand why the zooplankton comes to the surface at night; that is where the food is. But why does it move to lower levels by day? So many theories have been advanced to explain this that in a recent book one oceanographer devoted eighteen pages to reviewing them. One of the more convincing theories is that because the phytoplankton is most abundant on the surface, the zooplankton comes to the top at night to feed on it. The zooplankton then retreats to the darker depths during the daylight hours, when its presence near the surface would render it easily visible to predators. Opposed to this is the fact that many zooplankton organisms are highly luminescent; they can hardly gain protection from darkness if they are shining like little lamps.

Another explanation is that, since surface and subsurface currents move in different directions, the organisms manage, through vertical migration to drift first one way and then another thus gaining wider dispersal in the sea. Opposed to this is a theory that if they are carried in one direction by a surface current, then in an opposite direction by a subsurface current, they will remain in approximately the same place.

There is at present no generally accepted theory of the reason for vertical migration of the zooplankton. But it is such a widespread phenomenon that there undoubtedly *is* a reason, and it can confidently be predicted that the reason will be found out. This is one of the numerous unsolved problems that make oceanography fascinating.

THE FOOD CHAIN IN THE SEA

It is not uncommon to refer to the phytoplankton as constituting the pastures of the sea, for the vegetable plankton in the upper layers of the sea serves the same purpose as vegetation on land—manufacturing carbohydrates out of water and carbon dioxide and, during the day, giving off oxygen for respiration of both plants and animals and providing a source of food for animals to consume by day or night. Because there is so much more sea than land, the pastures of the sea are correspondingly larger. Phytoplankton, therefore, represents the largest basic food supply on our planet.

Like grass, clover, vetch, alfalfa, and other forage crops, however, this food becomes available for human beings only after various intermediate steps. Man eats some vegetable products, such as fruits, potatoes, and green vegetables, but he does not eat grass. He does eat cattle that eat grass, and thus consumes his grass at second hand. This is a satisfactory arrangement— at least to man—but it is not highly efficient. It has been roughly estimated that one thousand pounds of grass contributes one hundred pounds of weight to cattle or sheep, and that this in turn yields one pound of weight to man, the ultimate consumer. On the face of it this appears a very wasteful process, but no satisfactory short cut has been found. Man cannot live on grass or hay because he is not equipped to digest it. He has only one stomach, in contrast to which a cow has four, each serving a function in the successive processing of grass into milk or steak.

216

52. Right: A jellyfish *(Chironex)* of the waters north of Australia, one of a group known as sea wasps because of their sting. (Keith Gillett)

A pelagic nudibranch mollusk, *Glaucus marinus,* widely distributed in tropical seas, but rarely seen. (Charles E. Lane)

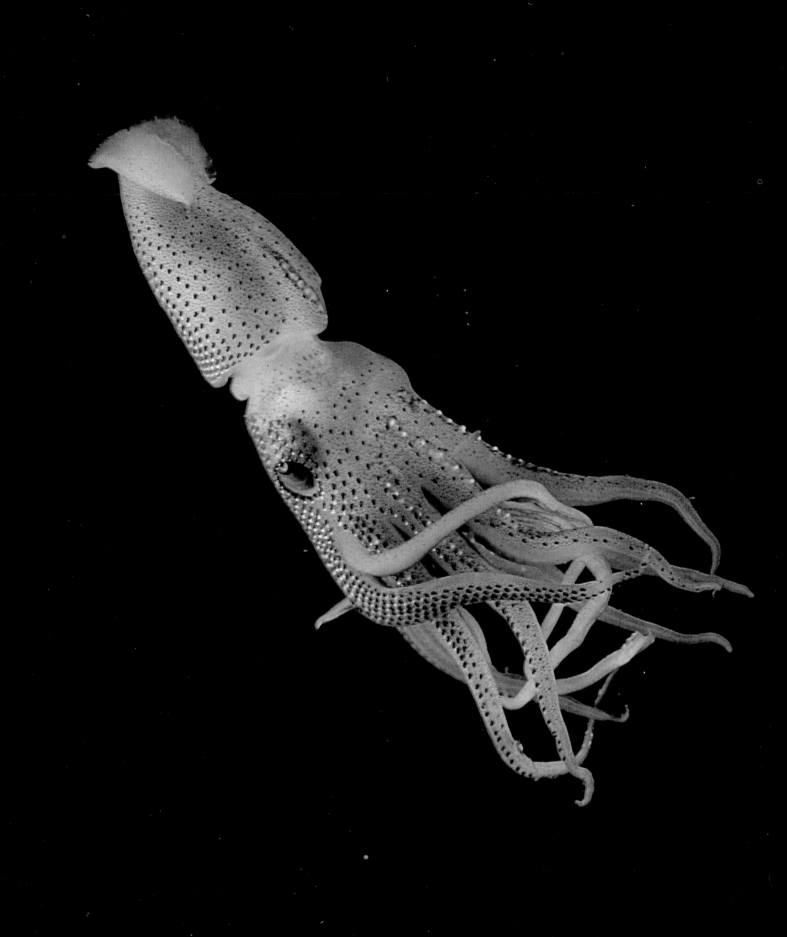

53. Left: A small squid
(Calliteuthus sp.) closely
related to the cuttlefish.
Its luminous organs, seen
here as spots, are doubtless
for recognition purposes,
and to keep a group
together. (Peter David)

54. Right: The remora or
shark sucker attaches
itself, by a suction disk on
top of the head, to sharks
and other fishes, or even
to the hull of boats.
(Douglas Faulkner)

55. Below: A scale worm
(Polychaete annelid).
Some species are found
among rocks in the inter-
tidal zone, others at much
greater depths.
(Noel Monkman)

56. Lower right: Angler
fish *(Melanocetus* sp.)
with luminescent
fishing lure. More than
100 species of this group
range in depth from
around 1000 to several
thousand feet. (Peter
David)

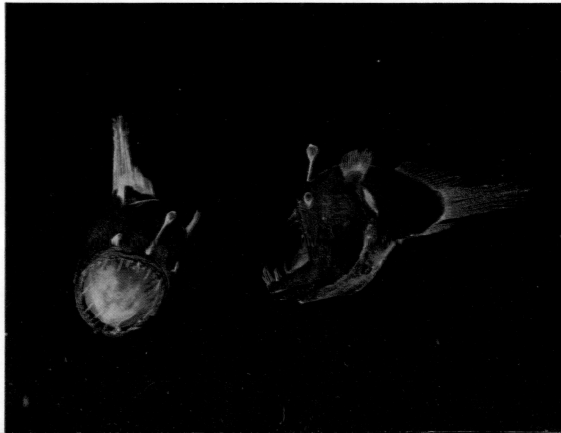

57.   Above: An aggre-
gation of foot-wide
jellyfish *(Chrysasora)*
washed ashore at Point
Barrow, Alaska, during
the short summer
period, demonstrates
the richness of Arctic
seas. (G. D. and
M. M. Hanna)

58.   Lower right:
A chain of salps, pelagic
tunicates related to the
vertebrates. (Robert
Ames)

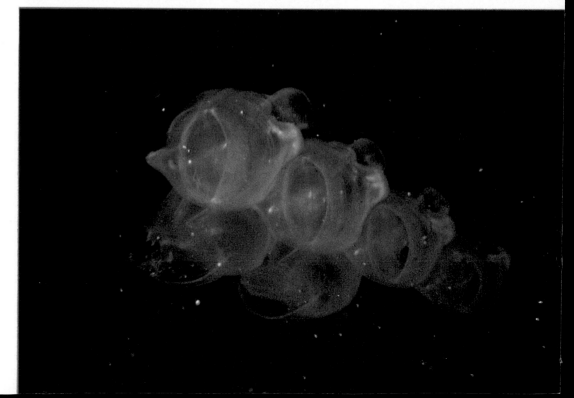

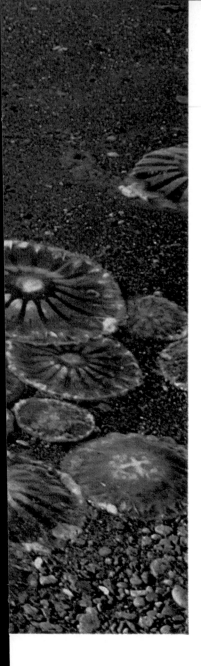

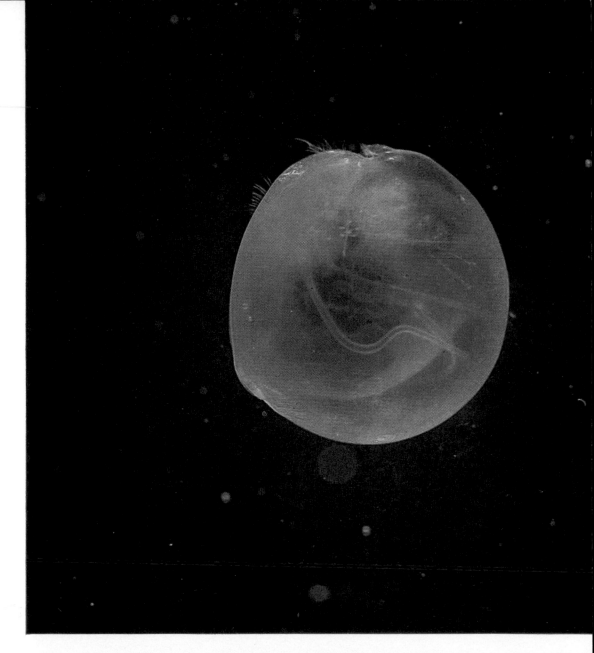

59. Upper right: Most ostracods (crustaceans enclosed in a bivalve shell) are microscopic, but the genus *Giganto-cypris* contains species as large as a man's thumbnail.
(Peter David)

60. Right: Bubble shell *(Hydatina physis)* is a marine snail found off northern Australia and in the Indo-Pacific region. It creeps about in intertidal areas and is sometimes found among eel grass, on rocky shores or on coral reefs. (Keith Gillett)

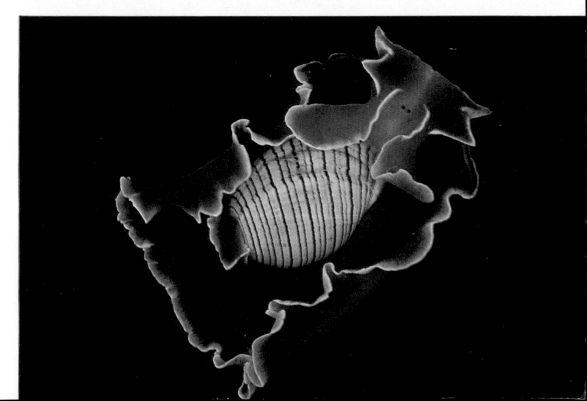

61. Upper left: Plankton larva of a shrimp, probably of the genus *Hoplophorus,* about 6 times natural size. (Peter David)

62. Lower left: The sargassum fish *(Histrio),* with its bizarre colors and shape, is barely distinguishable amid the floating sargassum weed of the Sargasso Sea. (Douglas Faulkner)

63. Right: A shrimp of the genus *Sergestes,* which lives at a depth of 200 to 400 fathoms during the day, but migrates upward to about 25 fathoms at night. (Peter David)

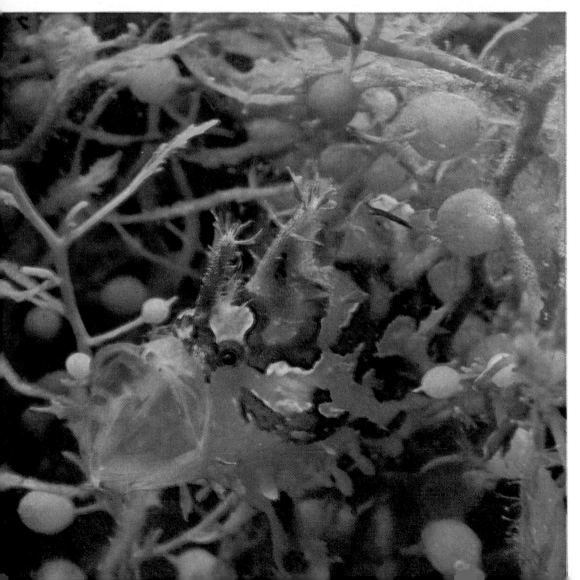

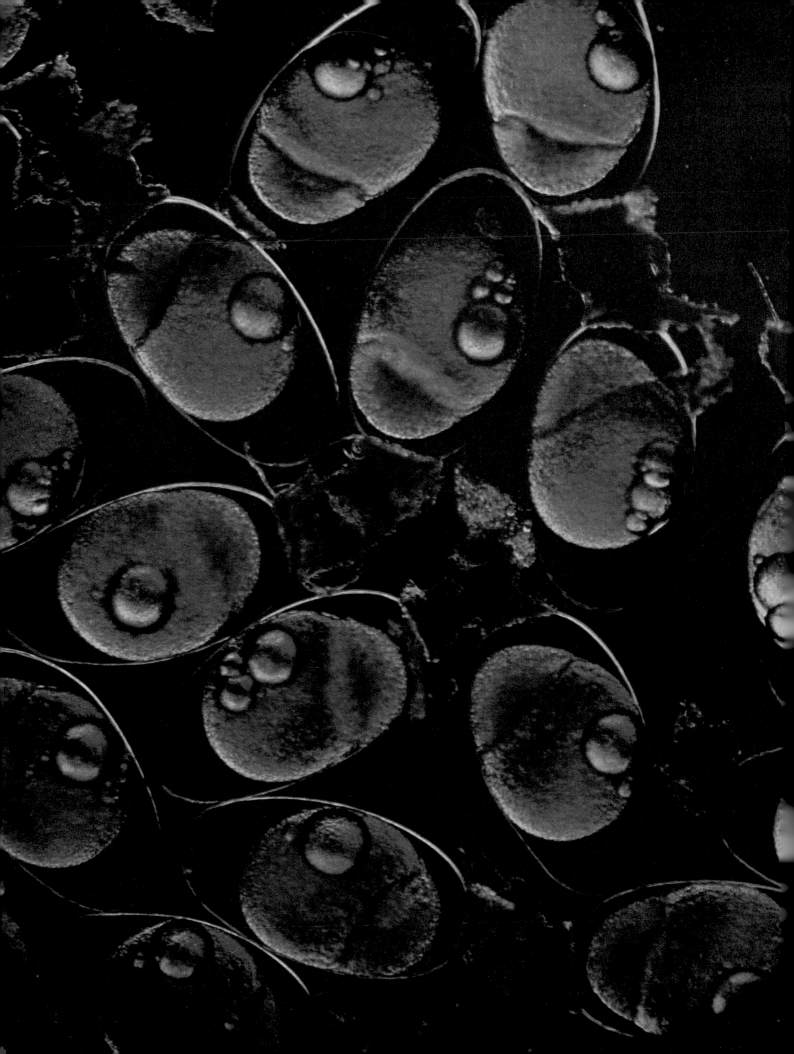

The food chain in the sea is more complex, with more intermediate stages. The phytoplankton is eaten by small crustaceans—copepods, ostracods, amphipods and the like. These in turn are eaten by fish, particularly small fish such as sardines, anchovies, herring and smelt, and by the young of some larger fishes. All of the small fishes provide food for larger fishes, including cod, salmon, tuna, marlin, sailfish, and a great variety of other species.

It is estimated that it requires ten thousand pounds of phytoplankton to produce one thousand pounds of zooplankton, which in turn produces one hundred pounds of herring, sardines, anchovies, and other plankton-feeding fish. These in turn are fed upon by larger fish, and by seals, sea lions, porpoises, and so forth, one hundred pounds of plankton-feeding fish yielding ten pounds of body weight in the larger carnivorous fish and animals. These figures are only very rough approximations: the point is that at each step in the food chain there is a large loss of energy. Continuing these assumptions, when man comes at last into this picture, ten pounds of salmon or tuna or cod will provide him with one pound of body weight. He does to some extent cut into the food chain at a lower level: if he eats a pound of herring or anchovy, he is doing perhaps ten times as well in the economy of nature as if he eats a pound of salmon. This does not mean that little fish are more nutritious than big fish, but only that there are vastly more of them. A given population of herring would feed a great many more people if eaten directly by man than if the salmon ate the herring and man in turn ate the salmon. But man may prefer salmon or find it easier to catch.

When we compare the food chain on land with that in the sea, on the basis of the above assumptions, it takes only one thousand pounds of grass to produce one pound of body weight in man, whereas in the sea it may take ten times that amount of phytoplankton to yield him the same amount of nourishment. On land the relationship between basic food supply and end product may be quite simple and direct—grass, cows, people. In the sea it is considerably more complicated—vegetable plankton, animal plankton, little fishes, big fishes, the larger carnivores, including sharks, seals and sea lions, porpoises and killer whales, all of which are better equipped than man for getting a living from the ocean.

Can man then really successfully compete in this apparently unequal contest? The answer is that he can and does, and furthermore that the sea is a food resource that has barely been tapped.

EXPLORING THE DEPTHS

Until well into the twentieth century the principal tools for investigating the sea bottom were the sounding lead, the dredge, and the trawl. The sounding lead, used to determine depth, also yielded information concerning the bottom. A tube could be sent down with the sounding lead in the hope of bringing up a sample of the bottom or, in the simplest case, a shallow depression in the lower end of the lead weight was filled with tallow to which—with luck—particles of sand, shell, or other bottom materials might adhere. Two or more types of "bottom grab" were also

64. Developing eggs (magnified 125 times) of the damsel fish (*Amphripion* sp.) are attached to rocks, shells or coral reefs. Cell division is in progress, some showing only one or two cells, others more. (Noel Monkman)

Wrasse being "cleaned" of parasites by two large isopods, which benefit the fish while obtaining food for themselves—an example of mutualism. (Jacques Hérissé)

used to bring up larger samples; if nothing came up, it was assumed that the bottom was rock. Sounding with a lead has now been entirely replaced by echo sounding.

The dredge is a device for scraping the bottom, generally in order to bring up bottom-dwelling organisms. Normally it consists of a reinforced shrimp-net bag with an iron frame. It is drawn by a bridle attached to each side, with a "breaking link" on one side, which is weaker than the cable itself; if the dredge gets caught on a rock, this link will break, allowing the dredge to slide around the rock and be pulled up by the remaining piece of the bridle. A device constructed something like a badly made mop, and called a "tangle," is frequently attached to the dredge to capture such animals as will grab anything that comes their way. For geological investigation a cylindrical dredge made entirely of iron is dragged along a rocky bottom expressly to break off pieces of rock. A heavy iron frame with a network of link chain is also used for this purpose.

Trawls are of several types, most of them considerably larger than dredges. Their purpose is to skim over the bottom or, in certain cases, to fish at intermediate depths. The common types are the beam trawl, a net held open by a rigid beam along the upper edge; and the otter trawl, a net held open by two so-called "otter boards" at the edges that act like kites spreading the net as it is towed forward, the pressure of the water against the boards forcing them apart. Beam trawls are used on the bottom to fish for shrimps, scallops, and bottom-living fish, principally sand-dabs, soles, and flounders. The otter trawl may be used either on the bottom or at intermediate depths. In recent years several types of mid-water trawls have been designed to collect organisms at any desired depth.

The dredge, which was first seriously used for study of bottom-dwelling organisms by the Manx naturalist Edward Forbes between 1832 and 1849, is still important in marine research. Trawls usually must fish in the position for which they were designed, but the dredge can turn over and over as it goes toward the bottom and fish either side up. A dredge moreover is cheap and easily replaced. One disadvantage is that it covers a relatively small area of the bottom. Forbes, perhaps through inadequate length of towing rope, concluded that no life existed in the ocean below about three hundred fathoms. This was rapidly found to be a misconception: the *Challenger* expedition (1872–1875) found living invertebrates at the greatest depths it was able to dredge, about three thousand fathoms. Dredging to this depth was a remarkable achievement, considering that the dredge line was only a heavy hemp rope. Wire rope was not used for this purpose until about 1877.

Whether animal life existed at depths greater than those explored by the *Challenger* was not certainly known for three-quarters of a century. In 1950 the Danish research vessel *Galathea* set out to explore the ocean depths beyond eighteen thousand feet. The vessel was equipped with a wire cable 7 ½ miles long and weighing about ten tons. On the night of July 22, 1951, a successful haul was made from a depth of 33,463 feet in the Philippine Trench, using a sledge trawl and two small dredges. The haul contained several rocks, grayish clay and gravel, attached to or among

Pacific sailfish leaping.
(Frank Kucherchuk)

which were found twenty-five sea anemones, about seventy-five sea cucumbers, five bivalve mollusks, one amphipod and one annelid worm. It was thus proved that living animals can exist at depths from which they were hitherto unknown. The best evidence indicates that the ocean is inhabited by animal life at its very greatest depths.

A blue shark in the Catalina Channel off California looks dangerous, and sometimes is. (Peter Stackpole)

ECHO SOUNDING

The sonic depth-finder, described in an earlier chapter, has not only immensely speeded up the mapping of the ocean bottom, giving a continuous record of the depth as a ship moves along; it has provided useful and even commercially important information regarding the inhabitants of the ocean. Basically, echo sounding consists of sending a sound from the hull of a ship to the bottom and recording the time it takes for the echo to return. At first there were some unexpected echoes: a large whale underneath the ship would give a firm echo that might be mistaken for a sunken rock. Schools of fish would also return an echo; this was soon turned to good account, leading to a device that would range laterally as well as down and thus locate schools of fish. We now have sound-ranging equipment (known as sonar) that can determine depth, locate schools of fish, submarines or submerged mines, and be used for underwater communication.

In the development of sonar, two sets of biological factors had to be taken into consideration. One was the echoes from whales or schools of fish or from other inhabitants of the ocean; the other was the noise made by marine animals themselves. The development of sound-ranging equipment required listening to underwater sounds with hydrophones; and when scientists began listening, they were both amazed and confused. They were accustomed to a great deal of sound at the surface of the ocean—the whistle of the wind, the splash of waves, the roar of surf—but they had casually assumed that the world below the surface of the sea was one of relative calm and quiet. They discovered that, on the contrary, the ocean is a very noisy place. They were gradually able to sort out the gruntings of gruntfish, the croaking of croakers and the drumming of their close relatives, the drumfishes, the snapping of the abundant and widely distributed snapping shrimps and, more unexpectedly, the high-pitched squeals of whales and porpoises.

What function these noises serve is not completely known. That they serve some useful purpose to the fishes—perhaps as a primitive form of communication—is indicated by the elaborate mechanisms that fishes have developed for producing and amplifying sound. It is surmised that the sounds produced by whales and porpoises are a form of communication: at least one careful investigator, Dr. John C. Lilly, considers that these animals have a language, and he has been trying to talk things over with them. It is definitely known that the sound-producing equipment of the animals is a form of sonar and that the animals can detect objects at a distance by giving off a sound and receiving the echo from it. It has been shown that a blindfolded porpoise in an aquarium pool can unerringly locate an object as small as six inches in diameter by echo alone.

Dr. Thomas C. Poulter of the Stanford Research Institute has shown that sea lions also have sound-ranging equipment. He repeatedly found California sea lions on Año Nuevo Island that were completely blind; yet they were well-nourished and apparently took to the ocean whenever they were hungry and caught all the fish they needed. Underwater recordings demonstrated that, in addition to their well-known noisy barking when at the surface of the water or on land, sea lions produce sounds in a wide range of frequencies; these are almost certainly used for echo ranging to warn them of obstacles and to guide them toward prey.

Fishermen are now catching up with their animal competitors in locating fish. Sound-ranging devices have become standard equipment on commercial fishing vessels; these indicate the size and location of schools of fish and sometimes, it is claimed, even the species. This last claim may be slightly exaggerated, but it is certainly possible to tell big fish from little fish, and in an area where the dominant species are known, a sonar operator might well be able to distinguish a school of albacore from a school of mackerel, and mackerel from anchovies or sardines; to tell the last two apart would be largely guesswork.

MYSTERY OF THE DEEP SCATTERING LAYERS

As echo sounding came into general use, some puzzling facts emerged. In deep water, almost around the entire earth, there showed up on the sonic

recordings a kind of false bottom at a depth of between two hundred and four hundred fathoms—a phenomenon that might be compared to "ghosts" on a television screen resulting from reflection from a nearby hillside or a tall building. Obviously something at an intermediate depth was scattering and echoing back the sonic impulses; this mysterious factor was termed "the deep scattering layer."

It is deepest in the daytime and moves toward the surface at night, corresponding with the vertical migration of plankton discussed elsewhere; but the echo is sharper than would be expected from plankton organisms of average size. Physicists have surmised that discontinuities in the water might be responsible; that is, the sonic impulse might be reflected back if it struck a layer of water that was denser by reason of greater salinity or lower temperature. But this could hardly explain why the layer goes up and down regularly with night and day. Its behavior strongly suggests that it is a phenomenon of biological origin.

Students of plankton thought that a group of crustaceans, the euphausids, were abundant enough to give back a firm echo. Numerous efforts have been made to "catch" the deep scattering layer by coordinating nets with echo sounding, or to photograph it with underwater cameras; but the results have never been entirely satisfying. Among prime suspects are the lantern fishes, small (one to six inches), extremely abundant, bright silvery fishes that during the day live in the twilight zone between deep-blue dusk and total darkness at a depth of as much as half a mile, and that regularly come to the surface at night. Lantern fishes *and* euphausids have been the most abundant animals taken in attempts to identify the cause of a scattering layer. It has in fact become increasingly clear that no single kind of organism is responsible for the phenomenon of deep scattering. Two or more such layers are sometimes found at different depths in the same locality, and occasionally one layer will remain at a fixed depth while others are travelling up or down. The term deep scattering layers is therefore generally used in the plural; meanwhile the attempt to solve the mystery goes on.

DEPTH AND POPULATION DENSITY

The greatest concentration of plankton, as we have said, is found just below the surface of the sea. It is not found at the surface because the light there is too strong and plankton, like human beings, can get a bad and even deadly burn from the sun. It is generally assumed that the greatest concentration of living organisms is in the upper layers of the sea, that is, in the photic zone, but there is some evidence to the contrary.

In 1954 William Beebe, in his famous bathysphere, descended to a depth of more than half a mile, deeper than anyone had ever gone before. He reported a remarkable abundance of organisms at that depth, especially hatchet fishes—those small, silvery, shining fish almost as flat as a silver dollar—the odd pelagic mollusks known as pteropods, and various other forms of life. This has been confirmed by Captain Jacques-Yves Cousteau and his associates in deep sea diving. Captain Cousteau has declared that he cannot find anything like a deep scattering layer, but only a great bowl of living soup that gets thicker as one goes deeper.

Sir Alister Hardy, English biologist, puzzling over these contradictions along with the accepted fact that most of the biological activity in the ocean occurs in the upper layers with energy provided by the sun, has suggested that the "living soup" that seems to get thicker with increasing depth may consist chiefly of the remains of organisms drifting down from above. Copepods, a main constituent of plankton, are encased in chitinous armor and can grow only by shedding this casing at frequent intervals. For each of the countless billions of adult copepods in the upper layers of the ocean, there may be half-a-dozen shed skins, ghosts of its former self, settling slowly toward the bottom. Mingled with sinking diatom frustules and remains of other plankton organisms, these may account for what seems to be an increasing density of organic life with depth. This is one of the numerous problems of oceanography waiting to be solved.

STRANGE CREATURES OF THE DEEP

No fishes have yet been taken at the greatest depths, but a number of species have been taken at depths of from one thousand to three thousand fathoms. Living in perpetual darkness, they have developed various adaptations to their environment. Some are blind, depending on their other senses for survival in a world of eternal night. Others have developed light-producing organs, which, while not strong, may serve to inform other fishes of their presence or to attract prey, as in the terrestrial world a candle lures moths.

Most interesting and most abundant are the angler fishes, which have a luminous organ at the end of a tentacle in front of the mouth. The mouth is immense, and the fish is able to swallow organisms at least as large as itself. The slender, pointed teeth are turned backward, so that a victim once seized

cannot escape. This could be a hazard to the angler fish itself as well as to its victim, because if it gets hold of a fish too large to handle, it is unable to let go.

We know as much as we do about the habits of the deep sea angler fishes because in shallower water they have relatives, known also as angler fishes, or because of the large mouth, as frog fishes. The forms found in shallower water have a fleshy lure at the end of a tentacle in front of the mouth but no luminescence, and Dr. Douglas Wilson of the famous biological laboratory at Plymouth, England, has observed these fish in an aquarium definitely using this appendage for fishing, moving the lure back and forth until a victim approaches, then suddenly gulping the prey. There is little doubt that the deep-water species use their luminous lure in the same way in the darkness. Another species of angler, with a forked light organ *inside* the cavernous mouth, was discovered by the *Galathea* expedition.

Some species of angler fish have solved in a curious way the problem of locating a mate in the darkness of the deep sea. When a male, which is much smaller than the female, finds a mate, he becomes very much attached to her; in fact, he literally becomes a permanent appendage of the female, ceasing to eat or fend for himself and being nourished through the blood stream of his spouse. Regardless of how we may look on such a union, it insures the presence of the male when the eggs need to be fertilized, and thus contributes to the preservation of the species.

Most people consider angler fishes rarities, and of course the deep sea forms are. But there is one species, the goosefish, living on the bottom in the shallower waters of the Atlantic Ocean, which is abundant enough to be a fairly important food fish, yielding a harvest of around two thousand tons a year. A related species is found off the coast of Japan.

SEA SERPENTS

Since earliest times man has imagined the ocean as peopled with legendary creatures—mermaids, and sirens, along with less attractive characters such as Scylla and Charybdis and miscellaneous monsters. Among the most

The common cuttlefish or squid *(Sepia officinalis)* has ten arms. When disturbed, it gives off an inky secretion that clouds the water and covers the squid's escape. This pigment has been used to make a brown drawing ink known as sepia. (A. Schuhmacher)

The cuttlefish can swim slowly by waving the flap-like edges of its body, or rapidly by "jet propulsion"—squirting water from its siphon. When it swims, it holds its arms close, streamlining itself. (A. Schuhmacher)

232

persistent of such tales are those of a giant sea serpent that according to the more colorful accounts could destroy ships and devour their crews. Olaus Magnus, a fourteenth-century historian and cartographer, has left us a vivid drawing of a horrendous sea serpent enveloping a two-masted sailing ship in its coils. Another artist of the same period has left us a more detailed picture showing a great serpent devouring the crew headfirst, in the manner of a reptile.

But legends are often founded on fact, embroidered with imagination. For example, Charybdis, which was said to be a monster lying in wait for sailors, was a whirlpool on the Sicilian coast, while Scylla, thought to be a six-headed monster occupying a cave on the opposite Italian coast, was apparently pure invention. The legend of the mermaid probably originated from the fact that the female of such marine mammals as the dugong and the manatee holds its young in her flipper while it suckles at her breast. Zoologists with a wry sense of humor have named this order of mammals Sirenia, although its members are in fact very unprepossessing and are popularly known as sea cows.

On the theory that tall tales often have some basis in fact, scientists have given considerable thought to the sea serpent tradition. Many accounts of sea serpents are doubtless based on faulty observation. A school of porpoises swimming in line and coming to the surface one after another can appear to be different sections of a single long serpentine animal. Sea lions also behave in this manner, which is sometimes referred to as "porpoising."

It seems significant that no zoologist or oceanographer has ever reported a sea serpent; most sea-going scientists, however, will agree that they have on occasion seen something that could be mistaken for a sea serpent.

It has been suggested that somewhere in the vastness of the ocean, a few plesiosaurs, giant aquatic reptiles that were abundant during the Mesozoic period, may survive. In support of this it is pointed out that in recent years coelacanth fishes, representatives of a group previously known only as fossils and believed to have become extinct some sixty million years ago, were discovered off the African coast. But the cases are not comparable. Coelacanths are bottom dwellers and thus more easily escape detection. Plesiosaurs were air-breathing; it seems improbable that a plesiosaur could be splashing around in the surface waters anywhere in the world without having come to scientific notice. The same reasoning applies to the suggestion that primitive species of whale, supposedly long extinct, may still be living undiscovered somewhere in the ocean.

Somewhat more probable than live plesiosaurs or primitive whales is the possible existence of giant eels. This was a view held by the late Dr. Anton Bruun, leader of the *Galathea* expedition. He did not announce a search for the sea serpent as one of the official objectives of the expedition, but acknowledged in conversation and lectures his hope of catching such an eel. Behind this expectation is a very interesting story.

Plankton hauls in the North Atlantic often brought up a transparent, leaflike organism that was obviously a fish and ranged in length from about one quarter of an inch to three inches. It was described as a new species, *Leptocephalus brevirostris*. Two Italian biologists who kept some of these little fish in an aquarium were astonished to discover that they developed into elvers of the common fresh-water eel of Europe and eastern North

America. Subsequently the Danish zoologist Johannes Schmidt, in a remarkable piece of scientific detective work, uncovered the strange life history of the common eel. The young elvers enter fresh-water streams and grow for a period of eight to twelve years (longer in the case of the females than the males). Then they return to salt water and migrate to a spawning ground in the area of the Sargasso Sea. Here they spawn, and presumably die, because they are never seen again. The floating eggs hatch into larvae that because of the original error in naming them are known as leptocephali, which swim and drift with the Gulf Stream back to the shores of Europe, where they transform into elvers and go back up the rivers. It is much like the life story of the salmon but in reverse.

Now, the largest leptocephalus ever seen, taken on the *Dana* expedition of 1928–1930, measured over five feet in length. The adult form is not known; but it has been reasoned that, if a three-inch leptocephalus of the fresh-water eel can grow to a five-foot adult, might not a five-foot leptocephalus grow to a one-hundred-foot adult? This is sound arithmetic, but the conlusion does not necessarily follow. There is no fixed ratio between the sizes of young and adults; human infants are considerably larger at birth than the offspring of Alaska brown bears. No giant eels corresponding to this oversized leptocephalus have ever been found, and their existence remains in the realm of conjecture.

Giant squids *(Archeteuthis* spp.) are fearsome-looking creatures with two very long, sinuous tentacles and eight shorter ones. They are known to reach an overall length of more than fifty feet, and such a specimen would undoubtedly pass for a sea serpent in the eyes of persons unacquainted with the existence of such enormous squids. But these animals remain at a fair

The stargazer *(Urolophus),* one of a group of bottom-dwelling fishes, commonly lies half-buried in sand or mud, with eyes directed upward, watching for passing prey. Some species have a worm-like lure attached to the mouth; some have electric organs for paralyzing prey. (A. Schuhmacher)

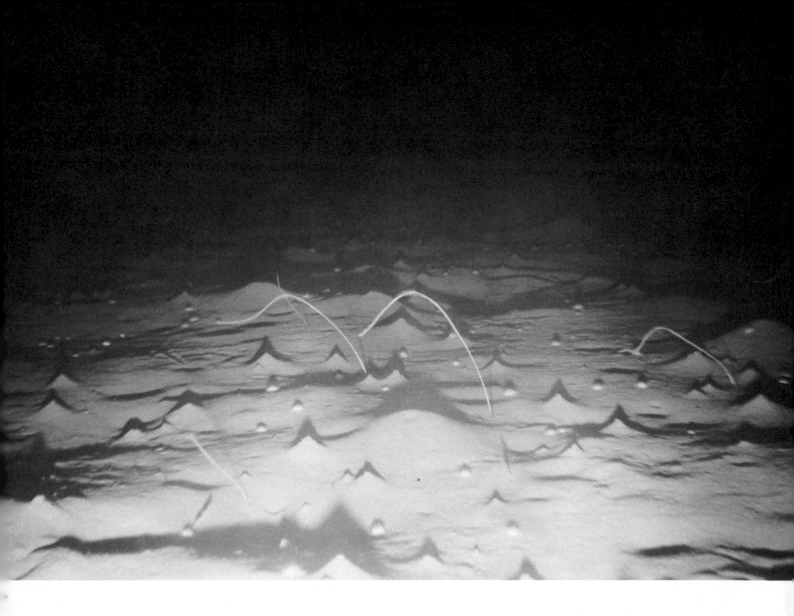

Sea floor (295 feet down) near Catalina Island, photographed by a "benthograph," an unmanned camera. The long curved rods are sea-whips, and the spherical objects are sea urchins. The conical piles have probably been made by burrowing worms. (K. O. Emery, by permission of John Wiley & Sons, Inc.)

depth and would not be seen at the surface except under unusual conditions. Sperm whales feed upon them; it is easy to imagine the turmoil of an underwater struggle between a fifty-foot squid and a fifty-foot whale. Apparently the whale always wins. Sir John Murray mentions a whale, taken off Iceland, which bore numerous circular scars as big as dinner plates evidently made by the suckers of a giant squid; inside the whale's mouth, he found a good-sized piece of a squid arm, and the whalers told him that in its death throes the whale had disgorged a squid tentacle nearly twenty feet long.

In combat with a squid, the whale, being an air-breathing animal, would have to surface at intervals. It is barely possible that seafarers have seen such a whale with the tentacles of a squid wrapped around it and have drawn awesome conclusions about a sea serpent, although the whale was merely coming up for air while devouring a squid.

One of the lesser-known but more plausible candidates for the honor of being the great sea serpent is the giant oarfish *(Regalecus glesne),* a somewhat rare but widely distributed species which in both appearance and size is one of the most unusual fish that scientists know. It is long and slender, so flat in shape that it is sometimes called a ribbonfish. It swims with an undulating, serpentine motion.

235

The size an oarfish may reach has been a matter of debate. Conservative scientists suggest eleven or twelve feet. But there is a well-authenticated record of a twenty-two-foot specimen taken at Newport Beach, California, in 1901. The late J. R. Norman of the British Museum believed a length of fifty feet or even more to be probable. The reason for this uncertainty is that the fish is uncommon, and that the largest reported specimens are those which have died and washed ashore, and have either disintegrated or been disposed of before a scientist has had a chance to examine them.

The giant oarfish has a bright-red dorsal fin extending the whole length of the body from the head to the long, tapering tail. The forward end of this fin has long spines, which can be elevated into a rather tall red crest when the fish is disturbed. This would seem to take care at least of the tales of sea serpents with bright red hair.

Morays prefer the shelter of rocks and reefs, but sometimes venture into the open; they bite viciously if provoked. (A. Schuhmacher)

12

Seafaring Man

There is abundant archeological evidence that primitive man was, at least in many cases, a beachcomber. Kitchen middens—great heaps of shells along the seashore mingled with human artifacts and sometimes the bones of terrestrial animals, dating from prehistory—are found in various parts of the world such as Denmark, Britain, Brazil, Japan, and the Pacific Coast of North America. This is proof that in prehistoric times many peoples lived along the sea and gained much of their living from it.

Sir Alister Hardy, who is both an oceanographer and a professor of anatomy at Oxford University, has suggested that the evolution of man was at least in part a consequence of residence by the sea. He does not dispute the commonly accepted theory that man developed from tree-dwelling ancestors, but thinks that the divergence between simians and prehumans occurred considerably farther back than is usually assumed. He surmises that the group ancestral to man took to the seashore where, as we know today, food was abundant. In his further quest for food, man ventured farther from shore and found that the water supported him; he developed an upright posture, partly to keep his head above water. He also learned to swim, thus becoming semiamphibious.

In support of his view of man's evolution along the seashore, Professor Hardy points out that man's bodily form is more streamlined than that of the more clumsily built higher apes, and that the hair, shed before birth, with which all human embryos are covered, differs in pattern from that of the apes and is more like that of an animal adapted to swimming. He also points out that man, unlike the apes, has a layer of subcutaneous fat similar to that of the marine mammals such as whales and porpoises, which gives his body buoyancy and insulates him against the colder surrounding water.

Various arguments can of course be advanced against Professor Hardy's view. One is that almost all animals swim better than man when plunged suddenly into water without previous experience. Horses, cattle, dogs, pigs—even cats—can swim considerable distances, but a man who has not learned to swim merely thrashes around in the water and generally drowns. On the other hand, men who have learned to swim are much more at home in the water than most other terrestrial mammals. It is well known to anyone who has visited the South Sea Islands that Polynesians are practi-

Oriental naval vessel as depicted in bas-relief on the temple of Bayon, Angkor, Cambodia, late twelfth century. (Pierre Pittet)

cally amphibious. They venture far out to sea and swim for hours without tiring. Prince Tangi of Tonga has been quoted as saying, "I am really more at home in the sea than on the land."

Professor Hardy admits as a drawback to his theory that no human or prehuman remains have been found on submerged shorelines and suggests that a search for them be made. Certainly if such remains were found it would provide strong evidence; but considering all the changes in shoreline that are known to have occurred even in recent geologic time, the absence of such evidence is not in itself significant.

The question of whether man became differentiated from his other simian relatives by reason of his onetime residence along the seashore may always remain a matter of conjecture. But whatever the merits of Professor Hardy's theory, there is no doubt that man has for many thousands of years been a creature of the land.

THE ART OF SEAMANSHIP

Seamanship is one of the great achievements of the human race, comparable with the conquest of the air and the penetration of outer space. It enabled land-based man to extend his horizons and to explore his world. It led him to astonishing feats of ingenuity, courage, and endurance; and even today,

239

after centuries of accumulated knowledge and experience, it is a venturesome and often heroic pursuit.

Seamanship developed independently among different peoples. Its origins are lost in the mists of antiquity—indeed of prehistory. We may imagine that the earliest craft was a floating log, which primitive man discovered he could use to keep himself afloat. From this it was a simple step to lash two or more logs together to form a raft. The flattened paddle for propulsion and steering was such an obvious development that it is found in every part of the world. A raft was cumbersome and hard to maneuver; an alternative was the dugout canoe. This required more ingenuity to design and make; nevertheless it was invented separately by many different peoples, for example, the Swiss lake dwellers, American Indians, and various African tribes.

It may be debated which came first, the dugout or the canoe consisting of a frame covered with bark or the skins of animals. It is quite possible that they developed concurrently. The Haida Indians of Northwestern America, for example, made war canoes sixty feet or more in length hewn out of a single log, while at the same time the Alaskan Eskimos, with no large timber available, made sea-going boats—umiaks—up to twenty-five feet long out of driftwood frames covered with walrus hide. To take another case, among the Polynesians the New Zealand Maoris made large hand-hewn canoes, while the Samoans, lacking the forest resources of New Zealand, *built* their canoes out of smaller timbers, calked the cracks with coconut fibers, and waterproofed the hulls with gum from the bark of the breadfruit tree. In each case human ingenuity, taking the materials at hand, made seagoing vessels that would do the job to be done.

In considering the influence of circumstance and available materials, it is worthy of note that the only people who ever developed rafts into respectable seagoing vessels were the Peruvians. They had balsa wood, which is lighter than cork but without the structural strength to be shaped into canoes. Accordingly they built rafts, which could carry a dozen or a score of men and cargo, and which used sails to take advantage of the wind.

Thor Heyerdahl's Kon-Tiki adventure, a successful drifting across the South Pacific to mid-Pacific islands, was a colorful and courageous undertaking. But it proved little except that such a voyage can be made on a balsawood raft. It did not prove that ancient Peruvians actually made such voyages from Peru to Polynesia, any more than Columbus' crossing of the Atlantic proves that it had been done before by, say, Phoenician or Egyptian seamen. In fairness to Heyerdahl, it should be added that he claims archeological and ethnological evidence of early east-west voyages in the South Pacific, and does not base his views solely on his own voyage. With no reflection upon his courageous voyage nor upon his right to dissent, we shall present here the view of migrations in the Pacific that is still most widely accepted among anthropologists.

PRIMITIVE NAVIGATORS IN THE PACIFIC

It is customary to begin accounts of the history of navigation with the Egyptians, Phoenicians, Greeks, Romans, and Vikings. This is probably

Odysseus and the Sirens. Early Grecian boat as depicted on a Greek vase.

chronologically correct, but it overlooks one of the great chapters in the history of navigation. While western ships were undergoing a slow development—at least a thousand years before Columbus ventured out across the Atlantic—Stone Age men had sailed all over the vast reaches of the central and South Pacific and had colonized all of its habitable islands.

The Polynesian people are believed to have lived in southeastern Asia a few centuries before the Christian era. They have a rich legendary history and an elaborate genealogy, which is carefully passed on from generation to generation. A Rarotongan genealogy of ninety-two generations would carry them back to the fourth or fifth century B.C. in a land to the west that some suppose is India. This is perhaps pressing a legendary history too far; but many if not most anthropologists would agree that the Polynesians set out from some point in southeast Asia, probably Malaya or Indonesia, at least as early as the second century B.C. Whether driven by population pressure, enemies, or simply love of the sea and adventure, they began exploratory voyages to the east, discovering, one after another, island bases that could be used for further discovery.

Their narrow dugout canoes could not cope with conditions in the open sea, so they invented the outrigger and the double canoe. The outrigger is a float lashed to the gunwale of the canoe by two supporting members that are long enough to keep the canoe from capsizing. In the double canoe, a second canoe serves as the outrigger. Although the outrigger is very widely used in southeast Asia and in Polynesia, it is likely that the double canoe was used for long voyages of exploration and colonization. According to Polynesian tradition, some of these canoes were a hundred feet long. The area between the two canoes was decked over and often carried a small deckhouse. This type of craft could carry fifty or sixty men and women, together with their supplies, domestic animals—dogs, pigs, and fowl—and fruits and vegetables for planting in a new environment.

The canoes were propelled by paddles and usually by a triangular sail or sometimes two sails of matting woven from pandanus fibers. Navigation was by sun and stars, by the direction and pattern of swells, by knowledge of prevailing winds, and by following the direction taken by birds that were known to rest on land. If several canoes were traveling together they would fan out to increase the possibility of sighting atolls, islands, or birds.

Seamen of the Marshall Islands even used sailing charts of a sort, made of pandanus or other fibers tied together in various patterns and dotted with cowrie shells. Exactly how these charts were used is still debated; but they are known to have covered specific areas, and they probably were constructed by the navigator to remind himself of features of the seascape observed on previous voyages.

Recent investigations have indicated that navigation by sun and stars was much more highly developed among the Polynesians than was previously supposed. Latitude was determined by the brightest fixed stars. Sailors were aware that the stars we know as planets were different from

Primitive anchor of stone and wood, for a balsa wood craft, Brazil. (James R. Simon)

Polynesian double
canoes, used for long
voyages, as they looked
to early European
explorers of the Tonga
Islands. (Bernice P.
Bishop Museum)

the fixed stars, and not to be relied on for navigation. One of the ancient
Hawaiian names for Venus, Naholoholo, means "running to and fro."
Sirius, the "dog star," the brightest star in the sky, other than the planets,
passes almost directly above the islands of Tahiti and Raiatea. Another
bright star, Arcturus, passes directly across the Hawaiian Islands. The conclusion seems almost inescapable that Polynesian navigators used these stars
in determining their approach to these islands.

There is also evidence that early Polynesian navigators knew the great
circles that we describe as the Tropic of Cancer and the Tropic of Capricorn.
Stars within the tropics were regarded as "inside stars" and those beyond
the tropics as "outside stars." It is believed that a good Polynesian navigator
was familiar with at least 150 stars and the places of their rising and setting.

Thus by methods that were primitive but very precise, these intrepid seafarers not only accomplished considerable feats of island hopping, but made
remarkable voyages across wide expanses of open sea. It is believed that by
the end of the fifth century A.D. they had occupied all of the major island
groups—Samoa, Tahiti, Hawaii, Tonga, and the Cook Islands. Thereafter
there was considerable voyaging among these and other islands, including a
second wave of immigrants from southeast Asia, whose cultures sometimes
overwhelmed that of the original adventurers.

According to legend, New Zealand was discovered in the tenth century
by a voyager who accurately described it as "a land inhabited only by
birds." Some Polynesian settlement was effected there at intervals over the
next four hundred years. The last wave of migration went from central
Polynesia to New Zealand in 1350, giving rise to the Maori culture. This was

163 years before Balboa crossed the Isthmus of Panama and became, in European eyes, the "discoverer" of the Pacific.

ORIGINS OF WESTERN SHIPPING

Other than the dugout canoe, which, as we have seen, can be traced back to the Stone Age in Swiss lakes, the oldest craft of which we have any record were boats used in the Nile Valley before the time of the Pharaohs. Such boats are depicted on vases, in funerary paintings, and in carvings considered to be predynastic. These tell us that they are older than 3500 B.C., but not how much older. If we take the most conservative dating, these pictures are five or six thousand years old, yet they show us rather advanced vessels with high bows and sterns, figureheads, and numerous oars. One clearly shows a steering oar, another a square sail. It is possible that these boats were made of papyrus stalks; papyrus boats of somewhat similar form are still used on the Nile today.

Wooden ships were in use in Egypt certainly by the Fourth Dynasty (2600–2500 B.C.) and probably much earlier. Because of the lack of large timber in the Nile Valley, there was no tradition of the dugout canoe; the early ships were built of planks fastened with wooden pegs and with quite effective hourglass-shaped joiners. Soon ships more than one hundred feet in length were being built for use in the eastern Mediterranean in trade and commerce and sometimes for war. A carved mural in the tomb of Ramses III provides the first known picture of a naval battle (around 1200 B.C.).

Earlier naval engagements had undoubtedly taken place, but the records

Boy with boat made of reeds, north coast of Peru. (Foto Fee Schlapper)

Arab dhows have for ages plied the Indian Ocean between ports in Africa, Arabia and India. (R. C. Miller)

are obscure. The half-legendary King Minos of Crete is reputed to have been the first monarch to develop sea power as an instrument of conquest. He conquered the Athenians and exacted tribute from them and is said to have rid the Aegean Sea of pirates—which in itself indicates that sea-borne commerce must already have been well-developed. Successors to the Minoans and the Egyptians in dominating the Mediterranean were the Phoenicians, who were by far the greatest seamen of antiquity. They occupied a narrow strip of coast at the eastern end of the Mediterranean, in what is modern Syria. So great was the reputation of the Phoenician seamen in the tenth century B.C. that King Solomon found it wise to make

The gufa, a large round wicker basket covered with skins and water-proofed with bitumen, was described by Herodotus in the fifth century B. C., and is still used on the Tigris River. (Ewing Galloway)

an alliance with the Phoenician King Hiram of Tyre. Between them they supported an expedition to the still unidentified land of Ophir (possibly India or East Africa); and a passage in the Bible *(I Kings* 10:22) indicates that a number of such voyages were made. The Greek historian Herodotus says that the Phoenicians had circumnavigated Africa, starting out from the Red Sea and returning via the Mediterranean. The Biblical account is not incompatible with this.

The Phoenicians invented the bireme—a vessel propelled by two banks of oars—and this was elaborated into the trireme, which also came into wide use among the Greeks and Romans. The final battles between the Romans and the Carthaginians seem to have been fought with quinqueremes—ships propelled by five banks of oars. The Romans finally won, partly because of a very simple invention—a kind of supergangplank that, when a Roman ship came to grips with a Carthaginian ship, could be lowered, allowing the Roman infantrymen to rush across to the enemy deck and engage in the hand-to-hand combat with which they were familiar. This proved more decisive than ramming, Greek fire, or other early methods of naval combat.

A Mediterranean galley of the classical period was designed to be propelled by galley slaves toiling at the oars; it had an auxiliary sail to take advantage of a favorable wind. It took many centuries—no one knows how long—for man to learn that he could sail against the wind. Galleys propelled by oars gradually gave way to ships propelled entirely by sail; but even these still depended much on favorable winds. One of the complaints of Columbus' sailors as his little fleet moved steadily westward was that they would never be able to return home against the prevailing wind. Undoubtedly Columbus himself knew how to tack and make headway against an adverse wind; but his sailors still believed that it took a favorable wind to get a ship to its destination.

The lateen sail ("lateen" is a corruption of "Latin"), a triangular sail better adapted than the square sail for sailing close to the wind, was introduced to the Mediterranean sometime between Roman and medieval days. It possibly came to the Mediterranean from the Arabs, who have used this sail time out of mind to get their dhows from Arabian ports to Zanzibar and East Africa and back. It is also possible that the lateen sail developed independently in the Mediterranean, for men are ingenious and, faced with the same problems in different places, they are likely to come up with the same answers. The Polynesians learned to use a lateen sail and to sail close to the wind, and it is unlikely that they learned this from the Arabs.

It is a common assumption, too, that the Vikings—who made almost incredible voyages in open boats in the roughest seas and developed a tradition of seamanship that has lasted to this day—acquired their knowledge of

An early fourteenth-century artist's impression of Magellan being killed by natives on the island of Mactan.

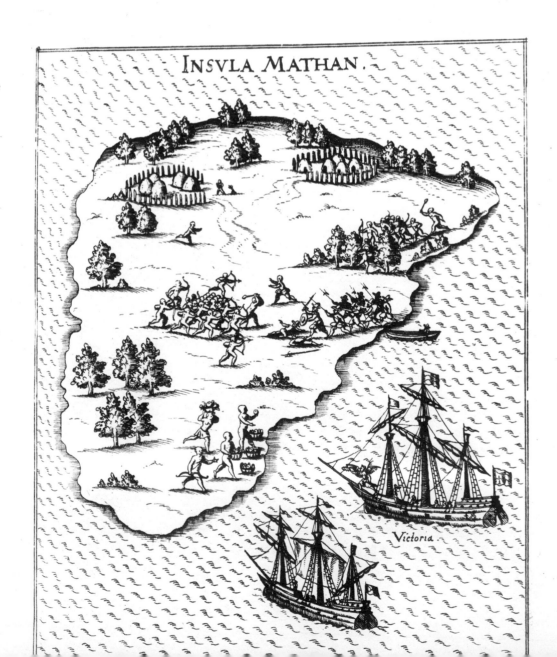

seafaring at second hand from Mediterranean sources. On the contrary, there is abundant evidence that it was a development indigenous to their time and place. In the sense that they used oars as a primary means of propulsion, with a square sail to assist when running before the wind, their practice resembled the Mediterranean one. But their ships were clinker-built—that is, each plank was overlapped by the one above it—and they always had a steering oar on the right side, which thus came to be known as the starboard (steerboard) side of the ship. The clinker-built hull is a sturdy hull, still highly esteemed for whaleboats and dories; and the familiar term starboard is a remembrance of the old Viking steering oar.

VOYAGES OF DISCOVERY

It seems likely that the first European to land in America, Leif Erikson, reached the shores of northeastern America somewhere around A. D. 1000. He called it Vinland (vine land)—perhaps with the same sense of euphemism that had led his father to apply the name Greenland to one of the most inhospitable places in the Northern Hemisphere. The Norsemen left no permanent settlements on the American coast, but there is almost indisputable evidence that they were here. This in no wise diminishes the stature of Columbus, who with his little fleet reached the West Indies in 1492. The earlier Viking voyages in the North Atlantic were almost incredible feats of seamanship and daring, but—apart from the establishment of settlements in Iceland and Greenland—they had little impact on history. The voyage of Columbus changed the history of the world. It is ironic that North and South America should have been named after a later and lesser voyager, Amerigo Vespucci, who explored the northern coast of South America in 1499.

Columbus' discovery of the New World came at a crucial moment. Western Europe was in a ferment of expansion of maritime trade, commerce, and competition for the treasures of distant lands, which led in turn to exploration, discovery, colonization and conquest. The year after Columbus' first voyage he was back over the same course with seventeen ships and fifteen hundred people, and he established two settlements on the island of Haiti. Colonization and exploitation were under way. Columbus died completely unaware that he had discovered two new continents but convinced that he had reached some part of Asia. Hence comes the confusing practice of calling the American aborigines Indians, and the Caribbean islands the West Indies. In the meantime, however, the real Indies had been reached by a different route.

In 1498 the Portuguese navigator Vasco da Gama, with a fleet of four ships, rounded the Cape of Good Hope and set out acros the Indian Ocean. It is said that when his captains began murmuring and threatened to turn back, da Gama called them aboard the flagship for a conference and in the meantime had their navigating instruments seized and thrown into the sea. Thereafter they had to follow him because they had no other means of finding their way. He was successful in reaching the coast of India and thus opened up the sea route between Europe and the Orient that was to be used until the Suez Canal was completed in 1869.

248

Drake's "Plate of Brasse," with which he marked his landing on the west coast of North America, claiming the land for England and calling it New Albion. (Bancroft Library, University of California)

AROUND THE WORLD IN THREE YEARS

The most remarkable voyages of the sixteenth century were two circumnavigations of the world, the first by Ferdinand Magellan in 1519–1522, the second by Sir Francis Drake in 1577–1580. Magellan, a Portuguese navigator in the service of Spain, set out to achieve the objective of Columbus—to reach Asia by sailing west. It had become pretty well known that the Americas were in the way, so Magellan proposed to find a route either through or around South America. He thought he might have to go as far as 75° S.—which, had he done so, would have carried him into the Antarctic Continent—but in fact he discovered a way through the tortuous Strait of Magellan at a little more than 52° S. He discovered and named the Patagonians, and Tierra del Fuego, and set out on a seemingly endless voyage across the Pacific, which he also named. By chance he missed all of the islands where he might have obtained food and water, and after ninety-eight days—his crew decimated by hunger, thirst and scurvy—he arrived at the island of Guam. He was able to replenish his supplies here and to proceed to the Philippines, which were already under Spanish influence; there he was killed in a fight with some of the islanders.

Magellan had started out with five ships and 240 men. When he arrived in the Philippines he had only three ships remaining, and of these only one, the *Vittoria,* with thirty-one men aboard, finally arrived back in Spain, the first ship to have sailed around the world. As a younger man Magellan himself had followed the Indian Ocean trade route opened up by Vasco da Gama and had been at least as far as the Moluccas. So when he met his untimely end in the Philippines he had already passed the longitude reached on his earlier voyage east, and thus he was, in fact, the first man to circumnavigate the globe—accomplishing a feat not repeated for more than half a century.

This was a time when Portugal, Spain, and England were all striving for mastery of the sea and the colonization of foreign lands. In 1577 Sir Francis Drake persuaded Queen Elizabeth I to support an expedition into the South Seas. He left England in December of 1577, sailed across the South Atlantic, passed through the Strait of Magellan, and proceeded up the west coast of South America. Here he became what might be called a licensed pirate, attacking and plundering every Spanish ship he could find until his own ship, the *Golden Hind,* was laden with treasure. Then he began to consider how to get home. If he went back over the route by which he had come, Spanish ships of war would be waiting for him in force. Sir Francis was a courageous but also a prudent man. He decided that the safest way home was the longest way round—that is, around the world.

He beached the *Golden Hind* to repair damage to its hull by shipworms. He established friendly relations with the Indians and took formal possession of the land for England, calling it New Albion. He marked his landing with a crudely inscribed "plate of brasse," which was discovered in 1936 a few miles north of San Francisco. Then he set sail across the Pacific and Indian Oceans, touching at the Moluccas and elsewhere for water and supplies, and reached England in September, 1579—the first man to have sailed around the world in command of the same ship in which he had started. The voyage took almost three years.

Octant, used in determining latitude by measuring the altitude of a celestial body, usually the sun, above the horizon. It has a scale of 45 degrees, as compared to the 60 degrees of a sextant. (Cranbrook Foundation)

THE MANILA GALLEONS

There is no more stirring—or less known—chapter in maritime history than the story of the Manila galleons that, starting in 1565, for two and a half centuries plied the Pacific between Spanish possessions in the Orient and those on the west coast of America. With a regularity comparable in their time and place to the great steamship lines of modern times, these colorful Spanish merchant ships served between Manila and Acapulco on the west coast of Mexico, bringing to the isolated Spanish garrisons in the new land the treasures of the Orient, and returning with the wealth of America in the form of silver ingots.

Beset by such obstacles as raging storms and dead calms, which left their sails hanging idly from the masts, these ships carried on. Some were lost at sea, some were taken by pirates, for whom the ships held tempting prizes. The captains of these galleons learned the currents and the prevailing winds of the Pacific. Their sailing charts were really a map of ocean currents. (Compare the chart of their voyages with the oceanic circulation in the North Pacific shown in the drawing on page 124.) The Manila galleons— like the earlier Viking ships and the later New England whalers and Yankee clippers—wrote one of the great sagas in the history of seafaring.

NAVIGATING INSTRUMENTS

The magnitude of the achievements of these early navigators can be judged from the crudity of their navigating instruments, if indeed they had any at all. They sailed by sun and stars and prevailing winds, augmented by

The astrolabe, a forerunner of the sextant and octant. The navigator suspended it in a vertical position and then adjusted the arm until he could sight the sun through peepholes in the two short uprights. (Cranbrook Foundation)

human ingenuity and a "feeling" for the sea. The first Polynesian discoverer of New Zealand left such sailing directions as: in November and December a little to the left of the setting sun. Subsequent voyagers, following these directions handed down by word of mouth, had little difficulty in finding New Zealand. Arab dhows plied—and still ply—between Arabia and East Africa, sailing before the wind—southwest monsoon in summer, northeast monsoon in winter. It is hard to miss an entire continent if one is sailing even approximately in the right direction; and to the early traders it probably made little difference what port they arrived in making a landfall. But the Arabs were good navigators who, from tradition and experience, generally knew where they were going and how to get there. Vasco da Gama was fortunate to pick up an Arab pilot in East Africa on his first voyage to India.

The first improvement on sailing by stars and by knowledge of winds and currents was the mariner's compass; its origin is almost completely lost in rumor and legend. The fact that a sliver of loadstone (a magnetic oxide of iron) will, if permitted to move freely, consistently orient in a certain direction must have been discovered at several times and places. There are legends attributing an extremely ancient discovery of the compass to the Chinese in 2600 B.C., but the first reliable account of a Chinese marine compass was in A.D. 1297, and a magnetic compass of sorts was in use in Europe and also among the Arabs at least a century before this. The Chinese compass needle has always been delicately pivoted on an upright support, while the early Arab and European compasses consisted of a magnetic needle attached to a straw or a sliver of wood floating in a vessel of water and thus free to rotate.

The mariner's compass was much improved through time, and was a mainstay of navigation for more than five hundred years. But it always has had one drawback. It does not point toward the north pole but toward the earth's north magnetic pole, which is in northern Canada about 30° of latitude "off center," and which, moreover, slowly changes its position. Thus, except for a few places in the world where the magnetic compass points due north, a correction, which is indicated on sailing charts, must always be made. The magnetic compass can also be affected by the proximity of other metals, such as the steel hull of a ship.

These difficulties have been overcome by the modern gyrocompass, the core of which is a universally mounted rapidly spinning wheel, which maintains its position relative to the rotation of the earth and thus constantly indicates true north. It is not affected by magnetic influences, since its principle is the same as that that keeps the stars in their courses and the spinning earth in its path around the sun. But the mariner out of sight of land needs to know not only in what direction he is going, but where he is. Earlier navigators had to guess their position by the number of days they had sailed in a given direction, and whether the wind was in their favor. Modern sea captains would shudder to think of trying to determine their position at sea by such methods.

It was not until the early sixteen hundreds that a means was devised to determine the speed of a ship. This was the common log or chip log, the use of which may be roughly compared to flying a kite in the water. The device consisted of a triangular board, the log chip, which was weighted at one edge and rigged in such a way as to remain upright in the water at the end of a line. The board offered sufficient resistance to the water to keep it in nearly the same place as long as the log line was paid out freely from the moving ship. Markers (originally knots) were placed on the line at measured intervals, and count was kept of the number of knots paid out in a length of time as measured by a sandglass. A ratio was established such that the number of knots paid out by the time the sandglass was emptied would give the speed of the vessel in nautical miles per hour. Hence we have the terms "knots" for the speed of a ship and "log" for the book in which the observations were written down. The taffrail log came into use around 1875.

But currents could carry a ship miles off course. Dead reckoning was never expected to be exactly right, and could sometimes be dead wrong. More precise methods had to be developed for ascertaining latitude and longitude. The cross-staff, the astrolabe, and the sextant were successively invented as instruments of increasing refinement for determining the angle between the horizon and the sun or some other celestial body. Columbus and Vasco da Gama were believed to have had the cross-staff and the astrolabe. The sextant was not invented until 1731.

At first these instruments could be used only for determining latitude. Time changes with longitude; for example, there is five hours' difference in time between London and New York. Thus longitude could not be determined from the sun without an accurate means of measuring time. This came about with the development of the chronometer, which is commonly attributed to John Harrison; in 1765 he received an award amounting to £20,000 from the British government for producing a seagoing clock that proved accurate within three seconds a day over a voyage of several weeks. Many people, however, contributed to the development of the chronometer both before and after Harrison. Good modern chronometers will run month after month with a variation of no more than one second a day.

Modern adjuncts of navigation are radio, which permits ships to communicate with each other and with stations on land and to receive weather reports and accurate time signals every day; and radio direction finding, by which a ship can fix its position at the intersection of two lines determined by signals from stations on shore. Echo sounding gives a quick and accurate measure of the depth of the water, and radar makes it possible to "see" rocks, other ships, or icebergs through darkness or fog. But while these things are a great convenience to the navigator and increase safety at sea, it was the development of the compass, the log, the sextant, and the chronometer that gave him the basic tools of his trade, and made navigation a reasonably exact science.

By the first quarter of the nineteenth century man had explored substantially every part of the world that can be reached by ships. He was now ready to begin the more difficult and challenging exploration of the world beneath the sea.

13

Harvest of the Sea

The ingenuity shown by primitive man in catching fish has led more than one historian to assert that there has been no essential improvement in fishing techniques in five thousand years. This generalization is too sweeping, but certainly the basic equipment—hand lines with baited hooks, fish traps of various kinds, and nets adapted to different types of fishing such as shore seining or fishing from boats—seems to be at least as old as recorded history. This statement is based partly on archeological evidence, and partly on the aboriginal fishing methods of Polynesians, North American Indians, and Eskimos, all of whom were Stone Age people at the time of their first contact with western man.

The simplest and perhaps the earliest fishhook was the gorge hook, a small piece of bone sharpened at both ends, with the line attached in the middle. The bait was wrapped around the hook, and when a fish swallowed it a jerk on the line would turn the hook crosswise so that it would be caught fast in the fish's gullet. Hooks of this type have been found in Stone Age caches in Europe, and they were used by American Indians.

Egyptian fishhooks of the early Dynastic period, some five thousand years ago, were barbed and resembled a modern fishhook except in being made of bronze instead of steel, and in lacking an eye through which to thread a line. This latter difference meant merely that an Egyptian fisherman had to tie a better knot than his modern counterpart to make the hook fast to his line.

Fishing with artificial lures instead of bait was practiced by the Eskimos, who carved and decorated colorful, beetlelike lures which they used to attract shallow-water fish, and then jig them by suddenly drawing up the hook while the fish were investigating the lure. Natives of Polynesia and Melanesia used shining, leaping pearl-shell lures and spinners.

The Indians of the northwest coast of America made a curved wooden hook to which they lashed a barb of ivory or bone. The hooks were baited with squid, and weighted with a stone sinker to float a few feet off the bottom. How did the Indian know that he should float his bait a few feet off the bottom? How did he know in the first place that the halibut were there, living on the bottom of a rough and stormy sea?

Men of the Caroline Islands in Micronesia fished for the escolar, or oilfish, a fish that weighs from sixty to one hundred pounds and lives at depths

Fishing with cormorants on the Nagara River, Gifu, Japan. After flares have attracted the fish, the cormorants catch them, but a ring around each bird's neck prevents it from swallowing the catch. (Japan Tourist Association)

of from one hundred to four hundred fathoms. To catch it, the Caroline Islanders designed a large wooden hook, which is carried down rapidly by a heavy coral sinker to prevent sharks from stealing the bait. The sinker is attached by a light line, so that when a fish is hooked the sinker will drop off as the fish is pulled in. How did the fishermen ever become aware that there were fish to be caught at a depth of nearly half a mile?

We can, for the most part, only surmise the development of fishing techniques, but we may assume that the methods developed in logical stages, with an occasional breakthrough now and then. We have stated in a previous chapter that primitive man living along the sea was first of all a beachcomber. He collected mussels and limpets off rocks and found that they were edible; he broke open sea urchins and ate the eggs; he dug clams where he saw little spurts of water as he walked along a beach; he nibbled at seaweeds and found that they were rather tasty and did him no harm. He could not have known as we do that they did him good, that they contained iodine, potassium and vitamins; but he was hungry and ate anything that was nonpoisonous.

He found small fish in tide pools. Some of them he could catch with his hands. Many got away, but he found a way to control that; he wove baskets in the shape of a truncated cone, which could be suddenly thrust down on a group of fish in a tide pool to prevent their escape, while a hole near the top large enough to admit a human hand and arm allowed him to retrieve his catch. He became aware, either by gazing into deep, still pools or by beachcombing after a storm, that there were larger fish in deeper water, and he devised ways to catch them with baited hooks or artificial lures or woven nets of various design.

Of course major improvements have been made. The beam trawl was an improvement on the shore seine; the otter trawl was an improvement on the beam trawl; and the purse seine was, for its purpose, an improvement on the otter trawl. But the basic principles are older than recorded human history; indeed the gill net or drift net, which entangles fish as they swim into it and is widely used today, is hardly different from that invented by primitive man.

65. Kasumiga Ura, a lake northeast of Tokyo, connected with the sea, has runs of smelt, eels, and other fish. Picturesque fishing boats, propelled by colorful sails, are used to pull trawls, especially on the windy days of autumn and winter. (Orion)

SELECTIVE FISHING

It may be assumed that the earliest fishermen ate everything they were able to catch, unless they found it distasteful or poisonous. This is still true in such areas as the coasts of Asia and Africa, where food is scarce. But it early became evident that some fishes are more desirable than others, either because of better flavor or texture, or because they have more flesh in relation to the number of bones. It was also found that certain fish can be caught in greater quantities and with less effort than others. Thus selective fishing developed and has been practiced increasingly over the centuries. Fishermen set out to catch particular kinds of fish, using boats and gear designed for that specific purpose.

The great fisheries of the world have come to be those for the cod and its relatives (including haddock, pollack, whiting, and hake); for flatfish (sole, flounders, halibut, plaice); for salmon; for sea bass; for various species of

66.   Left: Ocean swell
in the China sea, after-
math of a distant storm.
(Pierre Pittet)

67.   Upper right:
Native canoe with out-
rigger, Bougainville
Island, Papua Ter-
ritory, New Guinea.
(Eric Read)

68.   Lower right: In his
kayak, a frame covered
with sealskin, the
Eskimo hunter wears a
waterproof garment
tied about his face and
wrists, and attached to
the deck of the kayak.
He can turn completely
over and come up
smiling. Point Barrow,
Alaska.
(William Bacon)

69.   Overleaf: In this
Japanese oyster farm,
shells of scallops or
oysters are strung on
bamboo frames to pro-
vide a surface on which
the oyster larvae can
settle. Later the shells
are spaced out to
permit growth of the
young oysters. (Orion)

70. Upper left:
Portuguese fishing boats
unloading seaweed which
will be used as fertilizer.
(Nancy Flowers, Nancy
Palmer Agency)

71. Left: Zanzibar,
dugout canoes with double
outriggers. (Victor Glas-
stone)

72. Upper right:
Women cleaning sardines
at Nazaré, Portugal.
(M. R. Bull)

73. Right: Fish being
dried, Aberdeen, Hong
Kong. (Bill Homan)

rockfish; and for the pelagic fishes that travel in schools, such as the mackerels, tunas, and the herring and its relatives, including sardines, anchovies, menhaden, and shad. The members of the herring group are of particular interest because they are plankton feeders that are eaten by larger fish; thus, as we have said, they are one step farther down in the food chain, and they provide the most abundant fisheries in the world. Unfortunately herring and most of the herringlike fishes fluctuate rather violently in numbers for reasons not yet completely understood, and often disappear with little warning from regions where they have been taken for long periods in great abundance.

It has often been pointed out that the federation of North German cities in the thirteenth to the fifteenth centuries known as the Hanseatic League owed much of its prosperity to the herring fishery in the Baltic Sea. When the fishery suddenly went into a decline, the wealth and power of the Hanseatic cities also declined. Certainly other factors contributed to the dissolution of the Hanseatic League, but the failure of the herring fishery was doubtless one of the causes. It was assumed that the herring had moved out of the Baltic and gone westward into the North Sea or even to the vicinity of Iceland. But it is now known that the Baltic herring was a particular race of herring not found elsewhere; at that period its numbers simply decreased, for reasons that are still unknown.

The decline of a fishery may bring disaster to one area, but is likely to lead to the development of new fisheries elsewhere. Following the failure of the Baltic herring fishery, the Dutch began to exploit the herring of the North Sea, and for nearly four hundred years, from the fifteenth through the eighteenth century, Holland was the leading fishing nation of the world. She also built up a large merchant fleet for the export of herring pickled in brine. Then England, Scotland, and Norway began to exploit the North Sea herring fishery, to the extent that each of them obtained a larger annual catch than Holland. In the early years of the present century, the United Kingdom ranked first, Norway second, Holland third, and Germany fourth in the catching of herring.

Naturally the competition led to many disputes, and to one war, that of 1652–1654, which grew out of the attempt by England to impose a tax on Dutch ships fishing in British waters. But it became evident to all concerned that the fisheries of the North Sea were a resource that must be shared by the nations adjacent to it and also conserved to prevent depletion. This led to the formation of the International Council for the Study of the Sea in 1902, with headquarters in Copenhagen. In the years immediately following, the North Sea came to be the most intensely studied body of water in the world.

Two world wars, which stopped fishing in the North Sea and at least curtailed it in various other portions of the world, have resulted in a complete realignment of the pattern of world fisheries. Those nations that quit fishing lost their market, and have seldom been able to regain it; thus the British herring fishery has never regained the leadership it held in 1913.

The fact that the loss of a fishery in one locality is likely to be compensated by development of a new fishery in another is well illustrated by the brief history of the California sardine (also called pilchard). In 1928 the total catch of this fish was less than fifty thousand tons. The catch increased

74. Fish weirs at Dahomey, western Africa, are made of upright stakes wattled together with twisted strands of vegetation. The canoe is a pirogue or dugout. (Pierre Pittet)

until in 1937 it reached a record high of seven hundred and ninety-one thousand tons. It was then the greatest single fishery in the world; more than one-fourth of all the fish landed in the United States, including the Atlantic, Pacific, and Gulf coasts, were Pacific sardines. They were caught in considerable numbers as far north as the coast of British Columbia, where they constituted an important fishery. Then came a sudden decline, which continued year after year. The total California catch in 1963 was one thousand and fifty tons, and no sardines at all were taken farther north. The Pacific sardine had, in about thirty-five years, risen to the status of the world's largest fishery, and then declined to one of minimal importance. This was as catastrophic and as difficult to explain as the decline of the Baltic herring. In the meantime, the South African pilchard fishery has increased to the extent that it now exceeds the highest production ever attained by the California fishery.

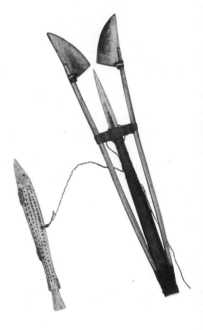

From these examples it will be seen that selective fishing has the advantage that the fisherman, pursuing a particular kind of fish and knowing its habits, can use boats and gear adapted to catching the largest quantity of that fish with the minimum of effort. But it has the drawback that, if the supply fails, as so often happens, the fisherman is caught with a large investment in his vessel and equipment which he cannot divert to other purposes. Two or three years of poor fishing may well mean bankruptcy.

Selective fishing is also wasteful. Any trawler will take, in addition to the main catch, considerable numbers of "trash fish" for which there is no market whatever. These he tosses back in the ocean. Moreover, if he is fishing for flatfish, he is likely to toss back any pollock or hake that may come into his net; the wholesaler to whom he sells deals with one or a very few species, and so does not want them, and the fisherman has no convenient way of getting them to market. If the fish that are tossed back survived, there would be no waste; but the majority probably die in the course of netting and handling.

Eskimo fishing spear and carved ivory minnow lure.

Primitive fishing hooks (from top to bottom): Egyptian fish hook of the Bronze Age, Polynesian hook for catching deep-living oilfish *(Ruvetta),* Eskimo "beetle" fishing lure, Tlinget Indian halibut hook. (Margaret d'Hamer, courtesy Lowie Museum of Anthropology)

Much if not all of this waste could be avoided by developing uses for "trash fish," such as converting them to fish meal and oil, or educating the public to their edibility. Fish meal is widely used as a desirable protein additive to poultry and other animal foods. The better grades of fish oil are used in the manufacture of paints and varnishes, printer's ink, and soap. Fish glues serve in a variety of industries, from wood-joining to photo-engraving. However, converting people to eating fish with which they are unfamiliar is extremely difficult. Fresh tuna is among the most delicious fish in the world, yet it sells poorly in fish markets partly because most consumers are used to buying their tuna in cans and are unaccustomed to a fresh tuna. The average housewife is familiar with perhaps three or four kinds of fresh fish, which she will prefer to some fish she has never seen before.

The first time I saw a ling cod—it was on the coast of British Columbia—a fisherman said, almost contemptuously, "Nobody eats that." A few years later I saw on a restaurant menu the words, "king cod." I asked the proprietor if the ling cod was meant. He replied: "If I labeled it ling cod nobody would order it." But the ling cod has gradually become established as an important food fish on the west coast of North America, and can now be found on restaurant menus under its correct name.

The best measure for fish conservation is to create a demand for fishes not now being utilized. This would reduce the pressure on the more heavily fished stocks and thus provide a more equable use of the fish resources of the sea.

MAN AS A PREDATOR

One of the unanswered questions of fisheries science is whether man's fisheries can exterminate a fish. Whenever a fishery resource begins to decline, the usual explanation is "overfishing." But the fish taken by the fisherman are only a small fraction of those taken by other predators, such as fish that eat eggs and larvae, larger fish that eat smaller fish, and marine mammals and birds that get their entire living from the sea. How important is man in this relationship? His take is certainly very much smaller than that of the predators that precede him; the question really is whether predation by man is "the straw that breaks the camel's back."

There is no certain answer. Fish are immensely prolific. Each female, with very few exceptions, produces anywhere from fifty thousand to several hundred thousand eggs a year. The general theory of biologists is that this results in a surplus of fish that may safely be taken by man. Nobody has found a reliable way of estimating how large this surplus is.

What happens rather commonly is that a fishery is worked to a point where further fishing becomes uneconomical. Ordinarily this results in the end of the fishery, and the species has a chance to rehabilitate itself. There are exceptions to this in areas where food is scarce: along sections of the coast of Asia, for example, fisheries have been carried to a point of minimal return, yet the people still fish because they have no other livelihood. There is no record of a marine fishery being carried on until the species disappeared.

The ability of a depleted fishery to rehabilitate itself is graphically illustrated by the tilefish of the western Atlantic. About 1879 this fish was discovered by fishermen who were fishing for cod on Nantucket Shoals southeast of Massachusetts. It was found to be a new species, unknown to fishermen or scientists. It was a colorful fish weighing from ten to a maximum of about fifty pounds, and it found a ready market over the next two or three years. Then a catastrophe occurred. Dead tilefish were found floating at the surface over a large area of ocean; one sea captain estimated that the area exceeded five thousand square miles, and the number of dead fish were of the order of one billion. No explanation of this disaster ever was found. For several years no tilefish were seen, and the species was thought to be extinct. But ten years after the catastrophe a few specimens were taken, and the fishery thereafter returned to a fair measure of abundance; the catch in 1961 exceeded three-quarters of a million pounds.

The case of the tilefish should not be taken too definitely as proof that a marine fishery is indestructible. There were no statistics available on the population of the fish prior to its discovery in 1879; it is also now known that the species is not limited to the banks where it was first discovered, but occurs all the way from New England to the Gulf of Mexico, so that its destruction in one area would not extirpate the species. But the tilefish does provide evidence that a marine fish can survive catastrophic destruction and reestablish itself in substantial numbers.

We also have the reassuring case of the fish of the genus *Latimeria,* which created a sensation when it was discovered along the southeast coast of Africa in 1938. This fish belongs to the coelacanths, which were known only as fossils and were supposed to have become extinct some sixty million years ago. Yet here it was living in a remote part of the Indian Ocean and was found, to the embarrassment of scientists, to be well known to the native fishermen as a food fish.

CAN FISHERIES BE MANAGED?

This optimistic view of the durability of marine fish populations does not apply to fishes such as salmon, striped bass, and shad, which are anadromous, that is, spend most of their life at sea but move into rivers to spawn. Nor does it apply to those, such as the common eel of Europe and eastern North America, that are catadromous, spending most of their life in fresh water but returning to the sea to spawn. A fish that spends any part of its life in fresh water is subject to the hazards of sewage and industrial pollution, and to the obstacles presented by dams for power and irrigation. Though eels seem in no immediate danger, the once abundant Atlantic salmon has all but disappeared, and the several species of Pacific salmon are seriously depleted. Notwithstanding the fish ladders designed to enable the salmon to bypass dams and the efforts to transplant the fish to undammed streams as well as to reduce stream pollution, the outlook for salmon is not bright.

Purse-seining for salmon, off Kodiak Island, Alaska. The seine is run around a school of salmon, then is "pursed up" by pulling on a line, thus trapping the fish. (E. P. Haddon)

A biologist has several advantages in dealing with an anadromous fish. Because the salmon return to the streams in which they were spawned, he can determine the size of the stock, count the fish quite accurately, tell whether their numbers are increasing or decreasing, and predict the size of the "run" in future years. He can also transplant fish stocks to new localities by simply placing newly spawned eggs or the young fry where he wants them. Transplanted to a suitable stream, young salmon will in due course proceed downstream to the sea and after three or four years of growth in salt water will return as adult fish to streams in which they were planted, there to repeat the cycle.

The biologist can also conduct breeding experiments, which is almost or entirely impossible with an exclusively marine fish. By selective breeding, for example, it is possible to produce salmon that grow faster and reach a larger adult size. Survival of the salmon has accordingly become a sort of contest between the biological advantages and disadvantages of the homing instinct that brings the fish back from the ocean to their fresh-water spawning grounds.

Marine fish face other hazards. Notwithstanding the unlikelihood of a marine fish's being exterminated by overfishing, heavy fishing can reduce a stock, perhaps even to the point where further fishing is uneconomical. The most heavily fished areas in the world have been the North Sea and the Grand Banks off Newfoundland. Fisheries are still carried on there, and profitably; but depletion has been a cause of concern. It was noted that after each of two world wars, during which fishing had to be suspended, the stocks of fish improved substantially, demonstrating that fishing had been a factor in their decline.

The objective of fisheries management is to regulate the catch so as to produce the maximum sustainable yield and to enable a fishery to be carried on profitably year after year without depletion of the stock. This may seem a utopian ideal; but there is some evidence that it can be a achieved in spite of tremendous difficulties. Ocean fisheries are for the most part carried on in international waters, and regulations require international agreement. It would obviously be futile for one nation to try to conserve a fishery if some other nation were to carry on unrestricted fishing in the same area.

There is at the present time no general agreement on the limits of territorial waters, that is, the distance seaward over which a maritime nation can claim jurisdiction. The United States still adheres to the three-mile limit, which has been traditional for centuries. Iceland asserts a twelve-mile limit, and more recently Canada and Russia have done the same. Ecuador and Peru claim jurisdiction two hundred miles out from their coasts.

The three-mile limit is said to have been adopted when that was the distance a cannon could be fired from shore, and hence was the zone that could be defended by land-based fortifications. It is justifiably claimed that this concept is obsolete; but nothing has been found to take its place. If one were to take the continental shelf as a basis, this would work to the advantage of areas with a wide continental shelf, as on the eastern and Gulf coasts of the United States, but to the disadvantage of Japan and other countries with a narrow continental shelf. A claim has been made that a country has a vested interest in a fishery that its own nationals developed; but what about the North Sea and the Grand Banks and the Mediterranean,

which have been fished for centuries by many countries?

The only solution appears to be a new set of ground rules adopted by international agreement. Difficult as this may appear, it has been achieved in limited areas. Canada and the United States have long had a treaty governing their joint interest in the sockeye salmon run of the Fraser River, and a treaty regulating the halibut catch in the eastern North Pacific. All nations carrying on whaling in the Antarctic have subscribed to an agreement governing that activity. The International Tropical Tuna Commission, while without regulatory powers, is investigating the tuna resources of the eastern tropical Pacific, with a view to recommending regulations for their conservation.

A classical example of a successfully managed marine fishery is the halibut fishery of the northeastern Pacific. This valuable fishery was pursued by fishermen of the United States and Canada with such intensity that between 1910 and 1920 the catch seriously declined. Under a treaty between

Alaska king crabs, sometimes weighing as much as 12 pounds and measuring 4 feet from tip to tip, have become a large industry. After the crabs have been shelled, they will be frozen or canned. (Information Office, Consulate General of Japan)

270

the two countries, the International Fisheries Commission set catch limits for the stock, and in a few years the fishery was restored to its original abundance. It is still carefully regulated, so that the annual catch does not exceed the rate of replacement. The halibut, being a large, bottom-dwelling fish of somewhat sedentary habits, is easier to keep track of than rapidly swimming pelagic fishes. But the success of this pioneer undertaking points the way to what may be accomplished by scientific management under international agreement.

WORLD FISHERIES TODAY

It is the concensus of marine biologists that, while some areas of the ocean and some species of fish have been overexploited, the fisheries resources of the world have barely been touched. Vast areas of the ocean are scarcely fished at all. Although the greater part of the water in the world is in the Southern Hemisphere, as recently as fifteen years ago only two per cent of the world's total catch of fish came from south of the equator!

This situation is rapidly changing, and the change has been in the direction of a more balanced utilization of the resources of the sea. Between 1957 and 1962 the total world catch of fisheries increased forty-four per cent; the largest increase was in the herringlike fishes, which doubled in this five year period, and the greater part of this increase was in the Southern Hemisphere. In 1966 and for several years thereafter, the Peruvian anchovy fishery was the largest in the world, reaching a maximum of some 12 million metric tons in 1970. In 1971 it declined to about 10 million metric tons, in 1972 took a sharp drop to less than 4.5 million metric tons, and today the fishery is practically nonexistent. This has been attributed both to overfishing and to a change in ocean climate—in this case, a lowering of the temperature of water. (Such changes often occur and may persist for several years.) But in 1973, for the first time in recent history, the total world catch of fisheries declined slightly instead of increasing. This was due essentially to the decline of the Peruvian anchovy fishery, but it may be an ominous sign.

Japan is, according to latest statistics, the leading fisheries nation of the world, with the U.S.S.R. second, China third (although statistics from this area are partly an estimate), Peru fourth, Norway fifth, and the United States sixth. These six nations catch well over half the world's supply of fish.

Fishing is still mainly concentrated along the coasts, or on well-known fishing banks; but the improvement of refrigeration, and the increased use of "mother ships" and floating canneries serviced by fleets of fishing vessels have made it possible to fish effectively almost anywhere in the world. Improved methods of fishing also increase the catch. Schools of fish can be located by sonar, and the position of the net with relation to a school can be "seen" by electronic devices. Or schools located by sonar can simply be pumped aboard by a "fish pump," eliminating the net entirely. An American fisheries scientist who recently visited Russia reports seeing such an operation in the Caspian Sea. Anchovies were pumped aboard and automatically frozen into blocks of convenient size for handling and shipment, while the fishermen sat on deck and played chess.

Many species of fish when subjected to an electrical field will by some strange compulsion swim toward the positive pole. It requires less current to affect large fish than small ones. Theoretically one could herd the larger fish toward a net or a fish pump while allowing the small ones to escape. This has been demonstrated in laboratory experiments, but has not yet proved to be of much use at sea, chiefly because of the difficulty of providing a suitable electrical field. This problem can conceivably be solved.

These improved methods have given rise to fears that we are in danger of fishing out the entire ocean, which has led to some careful estimates of the potential of the sea. In 1938 the world catch of marine fishes was just short of twenty million metric tons. (A metric ton is 2204.62 pounds, roughly ten per cent greater than the American ton of two thousand pounds.) In 1948, following the substantial suspension of fishing during the war, the world catch had reached practically the same figure (19.6 million tons). Fifteen years later, in 1963, the figure had risen to forty-six million tons. Professor Milner B. Schaefer, Director of the Institute of Marine Resources of the University of California, estimates that on the basis of present knowledge and techniques, "an increase of the harvest to two hundred million tons a year is not unreasonable and is probably conservative."

The rate of increase of fisheries products has for some years past been more than twice that of the increase of agricultural products. In a world in which millions of people go to bed hungry every night, the ocean seems to be our most promising resource. However, if the above mentioned figure of two hundred million tons is reached in the next fifteen or twenty years, we might be approaching the danger point.

Salted codfish being dried in Sweden. (Toni Schneiders)

CAN MAN INCREASE THE PRODUCTIVITY OF THE SEA?

The phytoplankton has already been referred to as constituting "the pastures of the sea." It is on the basis of this concept that biologists estimate the maximum sustainable yield of marine fisheries, much as a farmer decides how many cows he can pasture on forty acres of land. In the sea the conditions are more complicated and less well known, but it has been stated on good authority that, acre for acre, productivity of the sea is about the same as that of the land.

Increasing the productivity of the sea is not simply a matter of improving the methods of harvesting, but of actually increasing the crop available to be harvested. The farmer can think of ways of improving his pasture, as by irrigation or the use of artificial fertilizers, so that he can sustain a larger number of cattle on the same area. The fisheries biologist looks enviously at these methods, which are hardly available to him; the sea is already wet enough, and artificial fertilization presents an awesome problem, although it might possibly be managed in limited, partially landlocked areas.

Natural fertilization of the surface waters of the sea occurs from upwelling of bottom water, rich in nutrients from the dissolution of organisms that have died and sunk to the bottom. Upwelling occurs wherever surface currents swing away from the land owing to Coriolis force, as discussed in chapter 3; in such areas the surface water is replaced by water from the depths. Upwelling also occurs on shoals where deep currents are forced to the surface by the topography of the sea bottom; this explains the fertility

of many well-known "fishing banks" frequented by commercial fishermen.

Methods of increasing upwelling have been proposed, such as the introduction of baffles in the path of subsurface currents, or by placing on the sea bottom atomic reactors that would send thermal currents to the surface. It has even been suggested that judicious placement of atomic power plants along the seashore might increase the growth rate of fishes, since it is well known that fishes subjected to seasonal changes of temperature grow more rapidly during the warmer months of the year. All programs involving atomic energy must of course take into consideration the difficulty of controlling the escape of radioactivity into the water. Yet, these suggestions, however impractical at the moment, should not be wholly discounted.

In the meantime fisheries biologists are pursuing methods that may be feasible right now. One is transplantation of marine fishes to new localities where they seem likely to survive; the other is application to marine species of artificial hatchery techniques that have proved successful with fresh-water fishes. Anadromous fishes, those which spend most of their life-span in the sea but go up fresh-water streams to spawn, are, as we have said, quite easily transplanted.

By this procedure striped bass and shad from the Atlantic coast of North America have been successfully introduced to the American Pacific coast, where they have become the basis of important sport fisheries and have even at times supported a commercial fishery. The Atlantic salmon and two species of Pacific salmon have been transplanted to New Zealand; it is interesting to note that the Atlantic salmon has changed its habits in New Zealand and spends its entire life in freshwater instead of going out to sea. This is not without precedent, for there are several races of Pacific salmon that do not have a sea run and live entirely in inland waters. In such cases, the adults are smaller than normal. Apparently the pastures of the sea are richer than those of lakes and streams. It seems likely that anadromous species that have been successfully transplanted could be introduced to still other areas, wherever the stream and oceanic environments seem favorable.

Purely marine species have been more difficult to transplant. In the late 1950s sardines from the Marquesas Islands were imported to Hawaii in the hope of establishing a new bait fishery there since sardines are excellent bait fish for tuna and there are no native sardines in the Hawaiian Islands. After about ten years the Marquesan sardine appears definitely to have become established in Hawaii, although not yet in sufficient numbers to constitute an important bait fishery.

Fish hatchery techniques, which have been used extensively and successfully for the propagation of freshwater fish—especially trout—for the restocking of streams and lakes depleted by overfishing, have been tried out with marine fishes. Experiments in this direction were started in Norway as early as 1866 and were seriously taken up in America in 1871. In 1885 the first hatchery for propagating marine fishes on a commercial scale was built at Woods Hole, Massachusetts, under the auspices of the United States Fish Commission. By 1917 the production from hatcheries on the American Atlantic seaboard had risen to more than three billion young fish a year, including haddock, cod, pollock, and flounder. But in 1952 the United States program was terminated in the belief that the marine hatcheries had not significantly increased the catch available to fishermen. Experiments have

An octopus catch hangs high on the island of Thasos in the Aegean Sea. (Toni Schneiders)

274

Oyster culture along the Bay of Biscay, near Marennes, France. Young oysters, 18 to 24 months old, are brought in from nearby Arcachon and placed in small fenced-in areas to protect them from starfish and rays. (Walter Othmar)

continued in Norway, Britain, New Zealand and elsewhere. British investigators have been concentrating on the plaice, a flatfish of the North Sea highly esteemed as food. They have been successful in rearing substantial numbers of young plaice in special tanks, to the stage where they could be released into the sea. Now plaice are being reared in saltwater ponds under conditions that can be controlled. Dr. J. E. Shelbourne of the Fisheries Laboratory at Lowestoft, England, reports that in 1961 35,000,000 plaice were caught in the North Sea by British vessels. If, in pond culture, one square foot of bottom were allowed for each fish, the entire British catch for a year could be reared in an area of one and one-fourth square miles. A medium-sized female plaice may produce 100,000 eggs. Thus, allowing for a mortality of 50 percent during rearing, twenty females could provide enough eggs to yield a million hatchery-reared or pond-reared fish. If the water could be maintained at an optimum temperature for their growth, the fish might well mature in two years instead of the usual five. And the crop could be harvested without the use of nets or boats by simply draining the ponds and picking up the fish! While this view may be overoptimistic, it does point to the possibilities of scientific fish farming as opposed to the present haphazard harvesting of marine species. About five acres of shallow salt water have been set aside along the Ardnamurchan peninsula on the west coast of Scotland and is presently being used for reasonably large-scale experiments to determine the relative advantage of rearing the fish to adult size in ponds or sheltered inlets rather than releasing the young fry to complete their growth in the ocean.

SHELLFISH

Shellfish is a term rather loosely applied to two groups of marine animals that are not at all closely related zoologically: mollusks, such as clams,

Dried kelp is piled in large ricks on the coast of Portugal. (E. Aubert de la Rue)

oysters, abalones, and whelks; and crustaceans, such as crabs, lobsters and shrimps. Both groups as a rule have a shell on the outside of the body, but the difference is obvious to the most casual observer. To put it very simply, lobsters have legs while oysters do not; the body and legs of a lobster, moreover, are jointed to permit flexibility of movement, while the shell of a mollusk is solid, consisting either of one piece, as in a whelk or abalone, or of two pieces (valves) joined together by a hinge, as in a clam or oyster.

There are of course exceptions to this. There are a number of mollusks with a reduced or vestigial shell; the squid, for example, has an internal shell which is the cuttlebone of commerce, commonly placed in canary cages to allow the birds both to exercise their bills and to get calcium in their diet. The squid has ten limblike appendages, and the octopus eight; these are generally called tentacles or arms rather than legs, but the point is that they are not jointed as in the crab or the lobster. Lacking external shells, both the squid and the octopus are nevertheless mollusks and hence "shellfish" in the wide sense of the term.

Shellfish provide the basis of an industry that is of interest to those who relish seafood, and of considerable commercial value. The catch averages more than eight hundred thousand tons a year in the United States alone, and undoubtedly reaches comparable figures in other parts of the world. France is said to have a shellfish catch of one hundred and fifty thousand tons, and Spain, one hundred and forty-four thousand tons. Accurate statistics are difficult to arrive at because of differences in the basis of reporting in different parts of the industry and in different parts of the world. Clams and oysters, for example, may be reported in bushels or in weight, with or without shells, or in numbers sold in the market. The increase in importance of the canning industry for shellfish products also results in statistics based on the number and size of cans. On any basis, however, the shellfish industry is important in the economy of maritime states.

Crabs and lobsters are taken in baited traps, commonly referred to as "pots." A picturesque feature of the waterfront scene in lobster-fishing areas is the piles of lobster pots on the docks. For conservation purposes, laws have been passed to prevent the taking of young crabs or lobsters below a certain size. A crab trap has been devised with an escape hatch that permits undersized crabs to escape while the larger crabs are retained.

Shrimps are taken in bottom trawls, usually of the otter trawl type, that is, with otter boards that act as kites to hold the trawl open as it is pulled forward. A good many shrimps are taken in beam trawls, but this is incidental to the main purpose of the trawls, which is catching bottom-dwelling fish. There are many species of shrimp, and they vary considerably in size, with the larger species often being called prawns.

Clams for the most part have to be harvested by the laborious process of digging them out of the sand or mud. Shallow-dwelling species such as the edible cockle are usually harvested with short-handled rakes; in some European coastal areas they are located by the interesting method of feeling for them in the sand with bare feet. Along the New England coast the little-neck clam *(Venus mercenaria),* which is also shallow-dwelling, may be obtained by dredging the bottom with a heavy chain-link dredge. Scallops, which are free-living on the bottom instead of burrowing, are fished for with beam trawls or dredges.

Oysters are in another category; although they may be pried off rocks at low tide or obtained from the bottom in shallow water by the use of oyster rakes or tongs, they have been widely cultivated by man. Clams have been successfully cultivated in Japan and to some extent along the coasts of both Europe and America. But oyster culture has on the whole been much more successful than clam culture and considerably more profitable. Cultivation of oysters was probably started in the Orient many centuries before the Christian era. In the western world, it was developed by the Romans, doubtless independently, and is still carried on in Italy.

The greatest center of oyster culture in Europe is the Bay of Arcachon, southwest of Bordeaux. There were originally large natural beds of oysters here, which became seriously depleted by overharvesting during the first half of the nineteenth century. This led to efforts to introduce artificial culture which, after many initial difficulties, proved successful. At the present time about five hundred million oysters are marketed every year from this nearly landlocked bay of about thirty-seven thousand acres. Oyster culture in the Gulf of Morbihan, some two hundred miles to the north of Arcachon, was the theme of perhaps the only popular book ever written on the industry, *The Oysters of Locmariaquer* by Eleanor Clark. These oysters, a different and slightly smaller species from that cultivated at Arcachon, are highly esteemed by epicures.

Oyster culture has been practiced in the United States for somewhat more than a century, where it has become a large and flourishing industry on both the Atlantic and Pacific coasts. Dr. Paul S. Galtsoff of the United States Fish and Wildlife Service has said that the returns for oyster farming often exceed the best returns from farming on land. The success of cultivation of oysters is based on their fecundity—an adult oyster may produce several million eggs in a single season—and on the fact that oyster larvae, which are free-swimming, microscopic plankton organisms for a week or more

Tortoise-catching is a man-sized job in the Ryukyu Islands, Japan. (Yashinobu Nakamura, Orion)

after hatching, require a solid surface on which to settle down and grow. Oyster growers need only provide suitable materials at the right time and place in order to get an abundant catch of young oysters, which are then known as spat. In American oyster culture the most common material used to obtain spatting is old oyster shells. Other materials are used, too—such as broken drain tiles, slag, or cardboard egg-crates dipped in a mixture of cement and sand. The young oysters are not particular; they are merely looking for a place to light.

In Japan, the young oysters are cultivated on strings of shells suspended from bamboo stakes, or from rafts. In Australia, stones or mangrove stalks are used. In France the favorite material for obtaining spat consists of roof tiles, which are stacked criss-cross in wooden cratelike structures, providing a large surface for the young oysters to occupy. The following year, the spat is carefully removed and planted out. They are marketable size when about four or five years old.

The process of spatting young oysters on movable objects makes it easily possible to transport them to new locations and stock areas that have become depleted, or even new areas where oysters have not been known before, if conditions are suitable for their growth. This all sounds quite simple and easy. But oysters have many enemies, such as crabs, starfish, skates and rays, and the oyster drill, a snail-like mollusk that bores through the shells. Oysters are also very susceptible to silt in the water. All in all, oyster growers have about as many problems as farmers of the land. But they manage nevertheless to keep a lively and productive industry going.

THE PEARL INDUSTRY

Although the pearl industry is a byproduct of the shellfish industry, it seems important enough to warrant separate attention. Oysters produce pearls and so do many other mollusks. The inner layer of a molluscan shell is smooth and often shiny, being made of a substance called nacre, or mother-of-pearl, and in certain species is beautifully iridescent. The optical reason for this is known—iridescence is produced by the play of light on very thin layers or films, as on a soap bubble.

Of a number of species of mollusks that produce an iridescent inner layer of the shell, only a few kinds, known as pearl oysters, produce the pearls of commerce. They are found chiefly along the borders of the Indian Ocean (such as the Red Sea, Gulf of Persia, Ceylon, the East Indies, and the north coast of Australia), but they also occur in Japan and in parts of tropical America, including the Gulf of California, Panama, and Venezuela.

Pearls are produced by any irritating substance that gets inside the oyster and lodges between the mantle, which secretes the nacre, and the shell. This irritant may be a small parasite, or even a grain of sand. The oyster protects itself by surrounding the irritant with nacre, thus walling it off. If the irritant is attached to the shell, the result will be a "blister pearl"; but if the irritant is not so attached, it may become completely surrounded by nacre and thus form the nucleus of a true pearl. As the oyster adds additional layers to the interior of its shell, it at the same time builds a pearl. The value of such a pearl to man depends on its size, shape, color and perfection.

A huddle of unmated or "bachelor" guano birds on Macabi Island, northwestern Peru. (R. C. Murphy)

In earlier days pearl oysters were harvested by skindivers who, by long practice, had learned to hold their breath for a minute or more. Some are said to have been able to stay under water as long as five or six minutes, but this seems improbable. The divers were in danger of attack by sharks and were exposed to other hazards. In recent times more modern methods have been utilized, including helmeted divers and an air supply. But at best the industry is not so profitable as one might think. Perhaps not more than one oyster out of a thousand contains a pearl, and of those that are found, many are irregular, misshapen, or for other reasons not of gem quality. The oysters that do not contain pearls are not a total loss; they may be used in the manufacture of pearl buttons. The Australian fishery for pearl oysters is carried on chiefly with this in view, the actual pearls being almost a byproduct.

A great many kinds of mollusks, as we have said, may produce pearls, but only a few have the lustrous inner nacre necessary for pearls to be commercially valuable. There are a number of freshwater mollusks found in lakes and streams, some of which produce pearls of considerable beauty. (It should be added that shells of freshwater mollusks are also used extensively in manufacturing pearl buttons.) Many centuries ago the Chinese developed a method of producing artificial pearls from freshwater clams. They inserted a small carved image of Buddha between the valves of the mollusk and in a few months recovered the image of Buddha neatly covered with pearl.

In 1891, Kiyuoshi Mikimoto, then an obscure noodle salesman in Japan, conceived the idea of culturing pearls in native pearl oysters. He was finally able by a complex technique to produce pearls hardly distinguishable from natural pearls. This has become a large industry in Japan, and even experts cannot tell cultured pearls from natural pearls by their outward appearance; the only way to tell them apart is by an X-ray that reveals what is inside. Japanese cultured pearls are now raised in large quantities in Ago Bay. They are still harvested by primitive methods by women divers. But this old practice is being replaced by more efficient methods.

SEAWEEDS

As everyone who has visited the seashore knows, seaweeds often cover the rocks at low tide. Some float offshore and are known as kelps. All seaweeds grow on or are anchored to the bottom by rootlike structures known as "holdfasts," because that describes their function. As land plants obtain water and minerals from the soil, so seaweeds get the same substances from the sea. From the sun they get the energy which enables them to carry on photosynthesis.

Seaweeds have been used by man from earliest times. They have been used as food, and still are, particularly in the Orient, but also in other parts of the world, as indicated, for example, by the term "Irish moss" for a well-known seaweed of commerce. Seaweeds are rich in vitamins and in at least a score of minerals useful in human nutrition. The stalks or stipes of the larger kelps may be sixty feet long; they are extremely tough and have been used as ropes by primitive peoples. Alaskan tribes formerly used them for fishing lines and would tie several lengths together to reach the bottom in fishing for halibut.

One of the most important uses of algae has been in the manufacture of agar, a gelatinous substance used throughout the world for studying bacterial cultures, and made principally from the genus *Gelidium*. For a long time Japan had a monopoly of this product; when the Second World War cut off this source, various species of *Gelidium* along the coasts of America were brought into use. However, when the war made America's need mandatory, suitable species of algae were found on both the Atlantic and Pacific coasts and the shortage of agar was solved.

Seaweed has also been widely used as fertilizer in China, Japan, France, the British Isles, and elsewhere. It contains all the nutrients required for vegetable growth, and is especially valuable for potatoes, which require more potash than most other crops. Its use has made agriculture possible on barren, rocky islands such as the Isle of Aran off the Irish coast.

An important substance derived from the large kelps is algin, a gelatinous material that can be treated chemically to provide compounds known as alginates. These are used as "stabilizers" in the manufacture of dairy products, in puddings, salad dressings and various bakery and confectionery products. The purpose is to give body and texture to substances that might otherwise be inconveniently soft. Alginates are also used in toothpaste, shaving cream, hand lotions, and pharmaceutical emulsions, and in many other ways.

It is obvious that a product as versatile as kelp is in great demand, and kelp cutting is an important industry along the west coast of Europe and on both Atlantic and Pacific coasts of North America. The cutting was formerly done by hand at low tide, or by the use of grappling hooks from small boats a short distance offshore. But cutting has now become mechanized through the invention of an undersea mowing machine mounted on a barge, the kelp being hoisted aboard by a conveyor belt. Some of these barges can hold several hundred tons of kelp.

For a time it was feared that mechanical cutting on such a scale would deplete the supply, or have an adverse effect on fish life. But it has been found that the kelp beds quickly recuperate, and little or no effect on the fish population has been observed. The industry is, however, usually regulated by law to prevent this valuable resource from being overexploited.

In Japan, the collecting and drying of edible seaweeds forms the basis of a considerable industry. One type of red alga *(Porphyra)* is actually farmed, and in a manner not too different from the cultivation of oysters previously described. Algae reproduce by spores, of which a great many more are produced than find a surface for attachment and growth. Bamboo brush, or pieces of hemp net strung between stakes in the intertidal zone, become covered with small algae which man can then conveniently harvest when they grow to suitable size.

Of many other minor uses of algae, one of the more surprising occurs on Kamchatka, where the natives have learned to make an alcoholic beverage from seaweed.

14

Man in the Underwater World

The history of oceanography has been in large measure a history of the development of devices and techniques for exploring the ocean depths. For a long time scientists had to work from the surface, using nets, dredges, trawls, water bottles, thermometers, bottom-grabs, and similar equipment, in an attempt to find out about an unseen world. Such exploration of the sea bottom has been compared to exploring the earth from a space ship in the stratosphere, and in recent years there has been a major effort to explore the ocean depths by direct observation. The idea itself is ancient. Alexander the Great is said to have had a diving bell constructed in which he could be lowered into the sea to observe the underwater world. Since Alexander was a pupil of Aristotle, one of the greatest scientists of antiquity, the tale is not completely improbable.

One of the first successful inventions for staying under water longer than a man could hold his breath was devised about 1715. It consisted of a watertight leather suit, permitting movement of arms and legs; the head and body were encased in a barrel-like helmet of wood that had a face plate and contained "about half a hogshead" of air. The device operated well enough to be used for salvage work and the like, and it is said to have made its inventor John Lethbridge, an Englishman, a fortune. The next major advance came in the early nineteenth century: the diver was encased in a heavy rubber suit, with lead weights on his shoes to keep him right side up. A cumbersome helmet supplied him with air pumped down through a hose that might become entangled with anything from seaweeds and corals to octopi.

The first scientist to use diving equipment for exploration of the world beneath the sea is believed to be the Belgian-born French zoologist, Henri Milne-Edwards, who in 1844 went beneath the sea with some primitive equipment invented by the Paris fire department for investigating flooded basements. His adventure was successful, and he not only brought up specimens for scientific investigation but had the unique experience of seeing these organisms in their original habitat.

Although there were some early experiments in breathing under water through a tube, somewhat like the modern "snorkel," and in pumping air to a diver with a bellows, the diving helmet, with attached hose and air pump, seems to have been invented in England by Augustus Siebe in 1819.

A diver removes large black coral at a depth of two hundred feet off Mokumano Island, Hawaii. (Ron Church)

Siebe's diving helmet was partially successful and enabled divers to remain under water for long periods; but it had one serious drawback: if the diver stooped over or fell, his helmet would fill with water and he might drown. About ten years later the inventor introduced the completely closed diving suit, with valves to regulate the inflow and outflow of air. This has been the basis of most commercial diving equipment ever since, although many improvements have been made, including the development of diving armor, which helps protect the wearer from water pressure and enables him to work at greater depths. Salvage operations have been carried out in diving armor to depths of more than three hundred, and in one case to a depth of four hundred thirty-eight, feet.

The problem of deep diving is not actually so much one of pressure on the human body—animals of various kinds live at depths of six to seven miles—as it is the effect on the human respiratory system. Air consists mainly of a mixture of one part oxygen with four parts nitrogen. When a diver is subjected to the heavy pressure of water at even a few fathoms under the sea, nitrogen along with oxygen is forced into his blood. Nitrogen is an "inert" gas—that is, it does not readily enter into combination with other substances. If the diver comes up suddenly, the nitrogen forms bubbles in the bloodstream, causing difficulty in respiration, excruciating pain, and even death. The result of such sudden decompression is "the bends"; and in bringing divers up from even moderate depths, it is not unusual to put them in a decompression chamber in which the nitrogen can gradually be released from the blood without forming bubbles. Physiologists have also discovered that under the extreme pressures of deep dives, an artificial atmosphere of oxygen and helium is much better than a normal atmosphere of oxygen and nitrogen.

When Jules Verne in 1869 published his famous *Twenty Thousand Leagues Under the Sea,* it was assumed to be like his *Voyage to the Moon* and *Voyage to the Center of the Earth,* a work of pure imagination; but he had in this case a much firmer basis in fact. Siebe's diving equipment was in wide use, and more than one workable submarine had already been devised.

During the American Revolution, David Bushnell invented and built a one-man submarine, operated solely by human muscle-power. Manned by an intrepid sergeant named Ezra Lee, it maneuvered amid the British fleet in New York harbor; although it failed in its objective of sinking the British flagship, it did explode a torpedo in open water and caused consternation among the British vessels. Most remarkable of all, Sergeant Lee got himself and his submarine back to his home base intact; the Bushnell one-man submarine of 1776 deserves more recognition than it has generally received.

In 1800–1803 Robert Fulton, generally credited with the invention of the steamboat, tried to sell a submarine to Napoleon Bonaparte for use in the war with England; but the Little General, while interested, was more at home with military activities on land and did not buy the idea of submarine warfare. Thereupon Fulton tried to sell his submarine to William Pitt and the British Admiralty for use against the French; but submarines were outside their thinking too. There is rather good evidence that Fulton's submarine, the *Nautilus,* was workable. But failing to get any substantial support, he abandoned the idea.

Diving bell probably used in searching for the sunken ship *Vasa* in the 1660's. At a depth of 100 feet the air in it was compressed to one-fourth of the volume of the bell, so that the water rose up to the divers' necks. Drawing by Francesco Negri, Padua, 1700. (A.B.P.A. Norstedt and Söner, Publishers, Stockholm)

A modern replica of the seventeenth-century diving bell made for the *Vasa* exhibit in Stockholm. (Pressens Bild)

Here we are concerned with submarines only to the extent to which they have contributed to oceanographical research. In the 1930s the Dutch physicist, F. A. Vening Meinesz, used a submarine for a series of measurements of the earth's gravity. This required observations of the movement of a delicate pendulum, which could not be used on a vessel rocking on the surface waters of the sea but did operate very successfully in the calm depths of the ocean. In 1931 Captain Sir Hubert Wilkins attempted to reach the North Pole under the ice in an antiquated military submarine, refitted and renamed the *Nautilus*. The submarine broke down before reaching its objective; but valuable information was obtained by the distinguished oceanographer Harald U. Sverdrup, a member of the expedition. In 1958, after the untimely death of both of these pioneer undersea polar explorers, the undertaking was completed by the atomic submarine *Nautilus,* which reached the North Pole August 3 of that year, and by the rendezvous of two United States nuclear submarines, the *Sea Dragon* and the *Skate,* at the North Pole in 1962.

Reaching the North Pole by submarine was of minor consequence; but the submarines also took soundings over much of the Arctic Ocean, gathered plankton samples, and made a great number of other observations. They proved the feasibility of traversing the Arctic Ocean underneath the ice, and opened the way to the possible use of atomic-powered submarine freighters that can use the Arctic Ocean all year round and cut thousands of miles off present routes between seaports in the North Atlantic and the North Pacific.

SMALL SUBMARINES AND FREE-DIVING EQUIPMENT

About 1926 the zoologist William Beebe proposed to build a metal cylinder in which he could dive a mile into the sea. Working with an engineer named Otis Barton, who persuaded Beebe that a sphere would be better than a cylinder, they built the bathysphere; after some preliminary trials and errors, they descended in 1934 to the greatest depth reached by man up to that time, 3,084 feet.

Beebe has described in graphic detail the descent of the bathysphere, how the luminous green waters of the surface changed into a blue that turned deeper and deeper until it became the perpetual night of the ocean depths. But it was a night illuminated by stars! Phosphorescent organisms shone brightly against the dark, and occasionally one would shine with a brilliance that Beebe could only describe as an "explosion." Many of the organisms he immediately recognized; but many were unknown to him, and some had never before been seen by man.

What could be seen through the small quartz windows of the bathysphere was wonderful to behold; but it was frustrating to be able merely to observe strange fish and other organisms swim rapidly in and out of the field of vision. Some method had to be found to collect these organisms. Beebe turned his attention to other matters but Barton persisted, and, in 1948, descended to a depth of 4,500 feet in his "benthoscope," a version of the bathysphere with a window in the bottom.

In the meantime Auguste Piccard, the Swiss physicist who had originally gained fame by ascending to record heights in a balloon, became interested in a deep descent into the ocean. He devised a "bathyscaphe," a small submarine; designed by a balloonist, it is a kind of undersea balloon resembling a blimp, except that the cabin, accommodating two men, is designed to resist

Captain Cousteau's diving saucer probing the ocean floor. (Official Photograph, U.S. Navy)

Two marine technicians installing a long-period wave-recording instrument in 65 feet of water off Barbers Point, Hawaii. The cinder blocks anchor the instrument in the crevice. (Ron Church)

the pressure of great depths. The craft consists mostly of a relatively thin shell filled with liquid so that it does not collapse under the pressure of the water. The liquid is lighter than water to enable the craft to surface when ballast is dropped. Such a liquid is gasoline; it corresponds to the hydrogen used in early dirigibles and like hydrogen has the disadvantage of high flammability, but no disasters have yet occurred. All bathyscaphes thus far built have dived and surfaced successfully.

Auguste Piccard and his son Jacques reached a depth of 10,395 feet in 1953. On November 15, 1959, the bathyscape *Trieste,* under the auspices of the United States Navy, in a dive conducted by Jacques Piccard and the American biologist Andreas P. Rechnitzer, reached a depth of 18,150 feet in the Mariana Trench in the western Pacific, and on January 23 the *Trieste,* with Jacques Piccard and Lieutenant Don Walsh, U. S. N., aboard, reached a depth of 35,800 feet in the same area. This is the farthest that man has penetrated into the ocean depths and may be close to the bottom of the deepest sea.

In the meantime, the French bathyscaphe, designed according to Professor Piccard's principles, in August of 1962 reached a depth of 30,511 feet in the Japan Deep south of Tokyo. Getting to the bottom of the Japan Deep or the Mariana Trench is more than a stunt. It has provided information from direct observation at these great depths and has opened the way for future, more intensive, investigations. But at the moment the most important developments in undersea investigation are those in shallower water on the continental shelf.

This has come about through the invention of free-diving equipment in which the diver takes his own air supply with him and thus may go where he will, without a cumbersome hose for breathing and a tender up above to pull him to the surface. During World War II, Captain Jacques-Yves Cousteau, now director of the Oceanographic Institute at Monaco, and Emile Gagnan, developed the aqualung, a tank of compressed air that can be strapped to a diver's back, enabling him to remain under water for a considerable period of time. Originally this was used simply with a diving mask with face plate. A diver thus equipped and wearing swim-fins on his feet could spend a considerable time under water, go where he wished, and surface before his air supply became exhausted. Known as skindiving, this has become a popular aquatic sport everywhere.

The aqualung was soon applied to more important uses than recreation. As a diver descends, the water becomes chilled, even in the tropics. A rubber suit has been developed that enables an aqualung diver to work in really frigid water. Navy divers using this equipment, "frogmen," are able to work successfully even under Arctic conditions. Thus at Point Barrow, Alaska, where it is possible to bring in supply ships only during the brief summer, it is standard practice for frogmen to precede the ships and find a suitable channel.

Aqualung diving is thus no longer "skindiving," and has come to be known as "scuba" diving, the letters of "scuba" standing for "self-contained underwater breathing apparatus." This equipment can be used to depths of two hundred feet or more and is being improved by the use of a suitable mixture of gases, such as oxygen and helium, for work at greater depths.

Gold Cross with seven emeralds recovered in 1955 from a Spanish galleon wrecked on a reef west of Bermuda about 1595. Its crudeness suggests that it was probably made by Indians under Spanish supervision. (Peter Stackpole)

LIVING AND WORKING UNDER THE SEA

Competent scientists have visualized man in the future living and working on the continental shelf and even at greater depths down the continental slope. Thus Sir Alister Hardy of Oxford University suggests the possibility of farming the sea much as land is farmed. He believes that divers working in short shifts may drive tractors over the sea bottom, hauling nets where they can obtain the maximum catch of fish. He also thinks that they may, as a farmer removes weeds on land, remove starfish and other predatory organisms from the sea bottom in order to help more desirable species.

Dr. Columbus Iselin, retired director of the Wood's Hole Oceanographic Laboratory, has suggested fertilizing the upper layers of the ocean by placing underwater baffles in the Gulf Stream or other areas where major ocean currents run. This would deflect the water upward and bring to the surface the fertilizing substances needed to produce a rich plankton content in the water, resulting in the abundance of fish that is found wherever an upwelling of nutrient-rich water occurs. Another suggestion is that of placing atomic energy sources at strategic points on the sea bottom, which

would cause an upwelling of deep water with its rich nutrient materials, thus increasing the productivity of the sea. But all these present unsolved difficulties.

The most interesting experiments in these directions have been carried out by Captain Cousteau, who thinks that men can live and work under the sea for lengthy periods of time. He has put this idea to extensive and rigorous tests. On expedition "Conshelf I"—so called because it was carried out on the continental shelf—in September 1962, two men lived for a week in a seventeen-by-eighteen-foot steel cylinder at a depth of thirty-three feet in the Mediterranean Sea off Marseilles. Cousteau devised a small two-man submarine, which has been termed the "diving saucer"; easily maneuvered, it is available for undersea studies to a depth of one thousand feet. The diving saucer has a device, manipulated from within, for collecting specimens on the bottom and a container in which specimens can be brought up to the surface. He is now designing a similar submarine, "Deep Star," that will withstand pressures to a depth of twelve thousand feet.

In the summer of 1963 Captain Cousteau set up on the continental shelf in the Red Sea what was very close to being an underwater village. Thirty-six feet beneath the surface of the water he established a residence consisting of four connected chambers. Two contained sleeping quarters, one showers and other conveniences, while the fourth provided kitchen facilities, a laboratory, and a darkroom. In the center were the living and dining room, and the control and the communication facilities.

Because he wished to go considerably deeper than this base of operations, he established a "Deep Cabin" at a depth of ninety feet, and there two men lived a week, making deeper and deeper sorties until they finally reached three hundred and sixty-three feet.

The four-chamber main undersea dwelling, called Starfish House, functioned perfectly: a regular crew lived in it for an entire month. People came and went at will from two surface ships. There were, of course, certain hazards. An iron grille was provided to afford protection from attacks by sharks as personnel were entering or leaving the undersea station.

The two men in the Deep Cabin had a less comfortable time. There was supposed to be sufficient pressure to keep the water out, but because of a leak somewhere, the water rose every night and the men were almost afraid to go to sleep. At length they discovered that helium, a very light gas, was leaking out through the telephone cable leading to the surface ship. New packing around the telephone cable corrected this and the inhabitants of Deep Cabin had no further trouble. Captain Cousteau also built an undersea hangar for his diving saucer so that it would be continually ready for deeper explorations.

This was to that time the most successful undersea venture of this kind. Captain Cousteau believes he has opened the way for man to live under the sea for considerable periods, carrying out operations that have previously been accomplished at a distance, as in drilling for oil from surface rigs, or by methods in which the diver, supplied with air by hoses from the surface, could work only a few hours at a time.

About a year later than Captain Cousteau's experiment in underwater living, Jon Lindbergh and Robert Sténuit spent forty-nine hours at a depth of four hundred and thirty-two feet near the Bahama Islands in an inflatable

Old drawing of raising a sunken ship by means of pontoons, with ropes passed under the sunken vessel by divers. Woodcut from Olaus Magnus, 1755. (A.B.P.A. Norstedt and Söner, Publishers, Stockholm)

"igloo" designed by the American inventor Edwin Link. They went deeper than Cousteau and his associates, but did not stay so long, and they had to spend four days in a decompression chamber before returning to normal surface living.

The problems of decompression, especially the time required after a deep dive, have long been a hindrance to work at any considerable depth. For example, when the submarine SQUALUS was sunk in 240 feet of water in 1929, the rescue and salvage operations required 640 dives, with an average working time of only ten minutes at the bottom for each dive, although many hours were spent in descending, ascending, and decompression.

Impressed by the inefficiency of this kind of operation, Captain George F. Bond, a medical officer of the United States Navy, conceived the idea that, once a diver's blood has become saturated with breathing gases at a given depth, decompression time is related only to the depth, and not to the length of time the diver remains there. Thus, if suitable conditions are provided, a diver can stay down a week or a month just as easily as a day. In fact, he might conceivably remain down there until retirement at age 65, and still require no more decompression time than if he came up after twenty-four hours. Obviously then the key to successful prolonged work at considerable depths is to provide suitable living and working conditions.

This idea spurred Captain Cousteau to his "Starfish Village" experiment, and the United States Navy to a long-range "Man-in-the-Sea" program, including "Sealab I" off Bermuda in 1964, and "Sealab II" off La Jolla in 1965. In the former of the two U. S. Navy experiments, four men lived and worked at a depth of 193 feet for eleven days without any noticeable ill effects. In the "Sealab II" project, three teams of divers worked in relays of fifteen days, for a total of forty-five days, ending in October, 1965. Their home base, less picturesque than Captain Cousteau's "Starfish House," was a cylinder fifty-seven feet long, twelve feet in diameter. A medical officer,

Lieutenant Robert Sonnenburg, spent thirty days underwater in two separate shifts. Astronaut Scott Carpenter, doubling as a deep-sea diver, spent thirty consecutive days underwater.

An interesting feature of the Sealab II project was the use of trained porpoises as messengers between divers some hundreds of feet apart. The porpoises had become accustomed to a light harness, and trained to respond to a signal within the hearing range of both the porpoise and the diver (porpoises normally signal to each other with high-frequency sounds scarcely or not at all audible to the human ear). At a given signal the porpoise, swimming freely in the open sea, would go to the diver who had called it, have a message or a small tool such as a crescent wrench attached to its harness, then swim to another diver who had called it. Each time the porpoise performed successfully, it was rewarded with a fish—thus establishing the first underwater C.O.D. delivery service.

A Sealab III project, more complicated and at a greater depth, is programmed for 1966.

To go under the sea and particularly to be able to move about at will, to become a part of the marine environment, is obviously an exciting and fascinating experience. But it is also fraught with danger. Scuba divers regularly work in pairs, so that if one has difficulties, the other can come to his assistance. One of the dangers is from "nitrogen narcosis"; when diving with compressed air, an excess of nitrogen in the blood may cause a feeling of exhilaration. Instead of recognizing this as a danger signal, the diver becomes happy and reckless and takes chances that may result in disaster. In the year 1960, Conrad Limbaugh, a scuba diver of long experience who had trained numerous other divers, became separated from his companion while exploring an underground river near Marseille, France; he swam away from instead of toward the entrance of the cave, and lost his life when his supply of air became exhausted.

On December 3, 1962, the Swiss diver, Hannes Keller, with a British companion, Peter Small, attempted a unique dive off the coast of California to a depth of one thousand feet. The plan was to lower the two men in a diving bell to the proposed depth; then Keller, in a frogman's suit, would leave the diving bell and move around on the bottom. For respiration, Keller tried a mixture of gases that he had successfully used in descending to seven hundred and sixty-eight feet in a Swiss lake. The operation was viewed from the surface by underwater television.

All appeared to go well till the desired depth was reached. The television showed Keller beginning to emerge from the diving bell. Then he dropped the flags he had intended to plant in the bottom in celebration of the achievement, and climbed back into the bell. Something had gone wrong. It was subsequently learned that Keller had discovered from his manometer that the pressure of the respiratory gases was dangerously low. As the surface crew began to draw up the bell, the television screen showed that both men were unconscious. The bell was stopped at two hundred feet down so that the occupants would not be decompressed too rapidly. Two frogmen, Dick Anderson and Christopher Whittacker, went down and discovered that a small piece of rubber had caught under the hatch cover so that the cover was not watertight. They pried the rubber out and tightened down the hatch. Anderson then signalled to Whittacker to ascend and tell the crew of the *Eureka* to haul the bell up. He waited a few minutes; when nothing happened, he himself went up. Whittacker had not arrived! He was never seen again and no one knows what happened to him. The diving bell was brought to the surface. Keller revived, but Peter Small did not.

No doubt men will continue to risk their lives in the effort to penetrate deeper and deeper into the ocean with free-diving equipment. But at present the best way of exploring the vast area beyond the continental shelf is with the use of such devices as the bathyscaphe, Cousteau's diving saucer and "Deep Star," other midget submarines such as the "Alvin" and the "Aluminaut," which gained fame searching for the lost H-bomb in the Mediterranean, or with robots manipulated from above with the help of underwater television.

UNDERWATER ARCHAEOLOGY

Changes in sea level, as already pointed out, are fairly frequent. They may be world-wide and take tens of thousands of years, as when large amounts of water are withdrawn from the sea and frozen into glaciers on land, or when glaciers melt, returning the water to the sea. But changes may also be local, due to earthquakes or the rising or subsidence of the land over longer periods of time.

Helike, a Greek city on the Gulf of Corinth, is said to have been destroyed by an earthquake in the fourth century B.C., causing the land to subside abruptly so that the sea flowed in and submerged the city, leaving not a single rooftop above the water. It is said that visitors would come from great distances to look down with awe at the city beneath the clear blue water and at the great bronze statue of Poseidon, submerged in the element over which he was thought to rule. Explorers have looked for the statue and the city without success; but that does not disprove their existence.

Other cities or areas have gone under the sea, sometimes to the accompaniment of earthquakes. There is evidence of a general subsidence of Mediterranean shores since Roman times, followed by some withdrawal of the sea or re-elevation of the land. The temple at Pozzuoli, an important Roman seaport of the third century A.D., was completely submerged by the fifteenth century; its columns have now emerged again and at low tide even a good deal of the temple floor can be seen.

The famous Blue Grotto on the Island of Capri contains a set of Roman steps extending twenty feet under water, and the evidence is that in Roman times the water in the cave was twenty feet lower than at present. At the ancient level there is a large opening through which light enters from the sea outside, creating the eerie blue glow for which the grotto is famous, but the water level today is perhaps the best possible for bringing out the beauty of the interior. The Romans had some interest in this cave or they would not have built steps in it; but it can hardly have been a "blue grotto" when the steps were built.

Similarly, famous ancient seaports such as those of Pharos, Tyre and Sidon, and Carthage, all provide evidence of breakwaters and other extensive marine installations that are now submerged. From these, archaeologists can reconstruct the grandeur of the harbors.

Colorful tropical fish haunt a weed-shrouded and barnacle-encrusted sunken ship. (Gerhard Lauckner)

Another phase of underwater archaeology that is often rewarding is the search for sunken ships, especially those of classical times. This is not to be confused with the search for sunken treasure, which is exciting, occasionally rewarding, and may even produce results of archaeological or historic interest; but it is hardly archaeology in the best tradition, which is the study of ancient or prehistoric peoples and their modes of life.

Sunken wooden ships are rapidly destroyed by marine wood-boring organisms, unless they are buried in sand or silt; and if they are buried, they are, of course, difficult to find. But even if a ship has entirely disintegrated it may be possible to find metallic objects—an anchor or, with exceptional good fortune, some coins, and perhaps remains of the cargo. The most common objects recovered from sites of ancient wrecks in the Mediterranean are amphorae, that is, earthenware vessels with a handle on each side, used for carrying wine or olive oil. These have been found by the hundreds. Archaeologists can usually identify and date them, and thus learn a great deal about commerce and trade routes of the ancient world. One amphora brought up by Captain Cousteau's Conshelf II expedition in shallow water along the shore of the Red Sea was encrusted with coral and surrounded by the broken fragments of other amphorae. It was found to resemble cargo jars from Rhodes of the third century that had been excavated by Cousteau and his associates in the Mediterranean in 1953. Archaeologists are still trying to determine how amphorae of apparently Greek origin had reached this spot on the shore of the Red Sea.

As the British archaeologist M. C. Flemming has pointed out, it takes so many years to become an established archaeologist that most such men have neither the time nor the athletic ability to become divers as well. As a result, all the diving is being done by amateur archaeologists or by people who are not archaeologists at all. But this may well change in the near future. Meanwhile, it is important that amateurs should seek the advice of professional archaeologists in order that their work may have genuine significance in unravelling the secrets of the past.

75. A 3300-year-old, limestone-encrusted copper ingot, shaped like an ox hide, is recovered from a wreck in the Aegean Sea, southwest of Turkey. It was a form of currency probably of the value of an ox. (Peter Throckmorton, Nancy Palmer Agency)

THE SEARCH FOR SUNKEN SHIPS

Underwater archaeology is a search for underwater treasure, but the search for underwater treasure is not always archaeology.

In the days when Spanish ships were plying the Spanish Main, many ships laden with rich treasure disappeared. The fate of these ships was not always known. They might have fallen victim to pirates or to "respectable" buccaneers like Sir Francis Drake and Sir Henry Morgan, who were licensed to harass Spanish shipping, or they might have grounded on any uncharted reef and sunk without a trace. As a result, there are many legends of treasure ships sunk in the vicinity of the West Indies. With the development of scuba diving, the search for sunken treasure became an exciting pursuit, and many sunken ships have in fact been located. In occasional instances large treasure has been recovered; but generally if the divers find a few Spanish doubloons, or bits of jewelry, or even some tarnished knives or spoons, they consider themselves rewarded for their efforts.

Under the law of the sea, if a ship is abandoned by her captain and crew

76. Above: Florida divers examine a cannon encrusted with barnacles amid the ballast of a ship wrecked in 1733. (Peter Stackpole)

77. Left: Underwater drafting. A scuba diver plots positions of objects of archeological interest on the sea bottom. (Herb Greer, Nancy Palmer Agency)

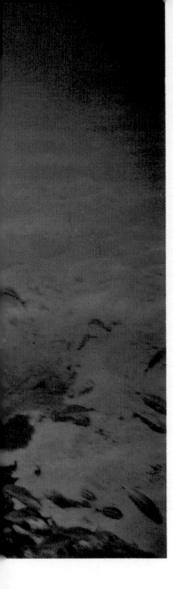

78. Right: Diver exploring a Spanish Loyalist ship sunk around 1933. A good-sized jellyfish is swimming through the rail. (Peter Stackpole)

and is subsequently taken in tow or otherwise brought into port by another vessel, the owners and crew of the latter are entitled to much larger salvage fees than if the ship had not been abandoned—in certain cases amounting even to ownership of the salvaged ship and its cargo. This accounts for the myth that a captain would rather go down with his ship than abandon her. Actually the tradition calls for a captain not to abandon ship before he has seen to the safety of passengers and crew.

Disputes arising under maritime law, generally known as admiralty law, are generally adjudicated by special courts or divisions of courts in the countries involved. Admiralty law with certain exceptions, applies in all navigable waters, not only in the open sea but in territorial and even inland waters. Salvage laws become complicated when a ship is wrecked on shore or sinks in territorial waters (traditionally within the three-mile limit); it is then under the jurisdiction of the government in whose territorial waters it lies. In England, wrecks formerly became the property of the Crown, but in the reign of Queen Victoria laws were passed protecting the rights of the ship's owner on payment of salvage fees. In the United States, jurisdiction over wrecks is given to the individual states, except that the federal government may pre-empt the field when, for example, a sunken ship is a menace to navigation. In Florida, where hunting for undersea treasure has become a favorite outdoor sport, the state issues licenses which permit the treasure-seeker to retain three-fourths of the value of all treasure recovered. Anyone proposing to search for such treasure should acquaint himself with the regulations in the area in which he proposes to work.

Much greater treasure can be salvaged by raising a sunken vessel from the bottom. One of the most famous of such recoveries was that of the Swedish warship *Vasa,* which sank in Stockholm harbor in 1628 in one hundred ten feet of water. The vessel was located by divers in 1956, partially raised and towed to shallower water. By boarding up her gunports and repairing her damaged stern, the salvagers made her reasonably watertight; the water was pumped out, and she was floated to a dry dock.

Thus Sweden has today that incomparable treasure, a complete seventeenth-century warship in a museum building especially erected to house it.

79. Above: Clay pipes and bricks recovered from the sunken ship *Eagle,* an early trader from the Virginia colony. (Peter Stackpole)

80. Far left: Two gold earrings set with crude crystal glass fashioned in the New World recovered from a wreck off Bermuda. (Peter Stackpole)

81. Near left: Spanish coins found in the wreck of the fleet of 1733 off the Florida coast. The coins at left are completely encrusted with a calcareous amalgam; those in the center are partially cleaned; those at right are cleaned and polished. (Robert Stenuit)

15
The Sea and Man's Future

There is abundant testimony from both history and archaeology that man at various times and places has been largely dependent on the sea for his livelihood. With burgeoning populations and dwindling resources on land, it is inevitable that he will become more dependent on it in the future, perhaps to the extent of his very survival on this planet.

If this seems an extravagant statement, let us consider a few facts, some of which have been touched on before. Seventy-five elements have thus far been detected in the sea, and it is assumed that every element naturally occurring on our planet will ultimately be found there. Some of these occur in great abundance and can be extracted readily. A familiar example is common salt, sodium chloride, made up of the two elements sodium and chlorine. Other salts obtained by evaporation of sea water are those of calcium, magnesium, and potassium. Many elements are present in smaller quantities and are more difficult to extract. Some exist only as traces; but since the volume of the oceans is so large, exceeding 330 million cubic miles, a substance present in sea water in an amount of only one part per billion would constitute a total of about 150 billion tons.

At present, elements existing in minute quantities per cubic meter of sea water cannot be extracted economically. But as oceanographic chemistry progresses, methods will improve. Moreover, as demand for various chemical products increases, processes now regarded merely as laboratory experiments may become economically feasible.

About 1850 the French chemist Antoine Jérôme Balard, known as the discoverer of the element bromine, perfected a method for the recovery from sea water of sodium sulphate and potassium chloride along with common salt. His process has been in use for many years at the Giraud solar salt works at the mouth of the Rhone River. Since then, methods have been developed for the commercial extraction of various other chemical substances.

Today millions of people are using products derived either directly or indirectly from the sea without the slightest knowledge of their source. When a housewife buys lobster or fillet of sole at a fishmarket, or a can of tuna or a tube of anchovy paste at a grocery store, she knows of course that she is buying a product of the sea; but if she buys a bottle of milk of

Mountain of salt near San Francisco Bay, where 30,000 acres of ponds produce more than a million tons of sun-evaporated salt in the largest operation of its kind. (Leslie Salt Company)

magnesia at the drug store, she is much less likely to know that this is a suspension of magnesium carbonate, which is today being extracted from sea water in substantial quantities. This is only one of the minor uses of magnesia from sea water. Magnesium hydroxide is also used in pharmaceutical preparations. Magnesium oxide is used in the manufacture of refractory materials, that is, substances that must withstand exceedingly high temperatures, such as refractory clays and firebrick. Magnesium ammonium sulphate is a valuable fertilizer. Metallic magnesium, too, can be extracted from sea water, but the process is not at present economical.

Other elements, including the group of compounds into which they enter, are now being commercially extracted from sea water: potassium, bromine, iodine, and chlorine. Common salt is not only a condiment but a substance necessary to maintain the chemical balance in the fluids of animals; immense quantities of it are used in chemical industries, especially for the production of chlorine, which is used to control the bacterial content of city water systems and as the effective ingredient in innumerable bleaching compounds. As time goes on, more and more elements from the sea will become essential to man to compensate for the exhaustion of the resources on land.

Sea water desalination plant at Eilat, Israel, at the head of the Gulf of Aqaba. (Israeli Information Services)

Off shore oil-drilling platform in the Gulf of Mexico is a barge jacked up on legs that rest on the bottom. The vessel in the background is a tender for carrying men and supplies. (Mobil Photo Library)

FRESH WATER FROM THE SEA

Assuming a marine origin of salt deposits on land, there are two basic commodities he must always obtain from the sea—common salt and fresh water. It may surprise the reader to learn that the ocean is the main supplier of fresh water in the world. The rainfall resulting from evaporation from lakes and streams is relatively minor. Most of the water that falls anywhere on earth, whether as beneficent rain or as devastating floods or as snow on high mountain tops, originates from evaporation at the surface of the ocean.

The shortcoming of natural rainfall is that it is unreliable in terms of human needs. It does not always fall in the right amounts at the right times and places. A sufficient and unfailing source of fresh water has always been essential to man. Nomadic tribes were able to survive by moving from oasis to oasis in the desert or from water hole to water hole in semiarid regions, but the great civilizations of antiquity grew up along major river courses— Babylon by the Euphrates, Egypt along the Nile, India along the Indus and the Ganges, and China and southeast Asia along their several river valleys. If Greece and Rome seem to be exceptions, it may be noted that they were reasonably well watered by numerous smaller streams. The same can be said of the Scandinavian countries.

In northern Europe, cities generally grew up first along the watercourses— the Elbe, the Rhine, the Rhone, the Seine, the Tagus, the Thames. The settlement of North America followed a similar pattern. At this point in the development of civilization, the harbor where a river enters the sea had become essential; the watercourses also provided water transportation to points upstream and, most important of all, a supply of fresh water for a growing population. When habitations spread to areas away from watercourses, there must be a way to convey water to them. This applied as far back as the Roman occupation of Spain: the ancient Roman aqueducts are still impressive sights.

In recent decades the growth of population has placed a strain on the water supply available to many populous areas. It is possible that the human race will outgrow its water supply even faster than it runs out of food. The two problems are, of course, inseparable, because agriculture, at present our main source of food, depends on water. It has been estimated that agricultural production in the United States requires between thirteen thousand and fourteen thousand gallons of water per day per person for every one of 195 million inhabitants. This is in addition to the "domestic water" required for drinking, bathing, washing clothes, watering lawns, and the "industrial water" necessary for the boilers and condensers of manufacturing plants. It is evident that continued growth of population will rapidly overtake the water supply that present sources can provide. There is already a pinch felt in many areas, and the situation promises to grow rapidly worse.

Scientists and engineers are therefore turning increasingly to obtaining fresh water from the sea, whose 300 million cubic miles appear to provide an inexhaustible supply. It is indeed inexhaustible, because all the water vapor, drawn from the ocean to form the clouds that spread rain, return to the ocean through streams, ground water, and in other ways.

Aristotle gave thought to obtaining fresh water from the sea in the fourth century B.C. He noted that if a body of sea water were boiled and a sponge held in the steam until thoroughly saturated, the sponge when squeezed would provide perfectly fresh water. Similarly, some three centuries later Pliny the Elder declared that if fleeces were hung from a ship above the water line, they would absorb the "exhalations" of the sea, and when wrung out would yield fresh water. Pliny was here describing a primitive type of solar still.

The principle of obtaining fresh water from sea water by distillation was lost and rediscovered several times in succeeding centuries: for example, it was rediscovered in 1593 by the English freebooter Sir Richard Hawkins. When Thomas Jefferson was Secretary of State, he recommended that instructions for distilling fresh water from sea water be printed on the back of all clearance papers issued to vessels leaving ports of the United States. Distillation equipment for obtaining fresh water has been fairly standard for years on large seagoing vessels; and during the Second World War various types of solar stills were devised that would enable men on a life raft to distill drinking water by the heat of the sun.

In recent decades quite a few methods, both chemical and physical, have been devised for removing the salt from sea water. But they are generally too expensive to be of practical importance. We shall discuss here three that seem somewhat promising from an economic standpoint.

The first of these removes salt from sea water by refrigeration. When sea water freezes, the ice that forms on top is, under ordinary circumstances, fresh. When Perry traversed the Arctic ice pack on his journey to the North Pole, he was able to get good drinking water by melting any ice at hand. The

The *Glomar Challenger*, a 400 foot research vessel designed for drilling and taking core samples of the sea bottom in all the oceans of the world, is owned by Global Marine, Inc., of Los Angeles. The drilling and sampling, funded by the National Science Foundation, is in charge of the Scripps Institution of Oceanography of the University of California, in cooperation with a number of oceanographic laboratories.
(Scripps Institution)

only exception to this rule is when ice freezes rapidly; then salt crystals may be entrapped in the ice and the melted water will be brackish. It has been found by experiment that the best temperature for "freezing out" the salt from sea water is about 25.7° F.

The practibility of this method of desalting water was borne in on me when I visited a remote desert inn in a subtropical area. The keepers of the inn had sunk a well and reached water, but it was brackish, satisfactory for bathing but not for drinking. Undaunted, they put some water in a deep freeze refrigerator every day, and by melting the ice from the top they obtained good drinking water. This method was economical because the desert inn had its own modest power plant, and it needed good drinking water to stay in business. On a larger scale it might not be feasible. Some competent authorities consider refrigeration the most practicable method of getting fresh water from salt water. It is certainly a method used in nature, generally in areas, such as north of the Arctic Circle and in Antarctica, where nature helps by producing subfreezing temperatures during most months of the year.

An ingenious suggestion has in fact been made that icebergs be towed from Antarctica to coasts where water is at a premium. Large icebergs melt so slowly that they could conceivably be towed several thousand miles and still be large enough to yield considerable water. This may not be as impractical as some say it is, considering the boundless supply of ice in the Antarctic, and the fact that it is relatively close to some of the very dry areas of the world—western Australia, South-West Africa and the west coast of South America. Icebergs from the North Atlantic might be towed to Spain or Morocco, where they might well be welcomed. The future of this idea depends perhaps on a practical experiment and on some further study of the economics of towing icebergs.

Another method of salt-water conversion that has gained favor is the use

of a membrane, sometimes of rather complicated structure, that will allow fresh-water molecules to pass through but keep the salt back. Such membranes are well known, and their properties understood; but the process is still rather expensive. It is not unlike the method by which living organisms maintain their water balance in relation to the medium around them; but since an organism expends a great deal of its energy maintaining this water balance, it is easy to see that on a large scale the cost would be considerable. Substitute man power, for example, for protozoan power, and the magnitude of the problem becomes evident. Barring an unforeseen development, this method appears to be no more economical than any other.

The distillation method, suggested by Aristotle and Pliny, still seems as good as any. But it too is expensive. For distillation in the usual manner, we require heat to boil the water, plus a way of condensing the steam together with a way of getting rid of the concentrated brine in the still. Solar stills would seem to be the answer here, especially in locations with high and fairly constant solar radiation. But it takes either a complicated bank of mirrors to concentrate the solar energy to boil water, or a very large area of glass or other materials to evaporate the water at low temperatures

Upper left: The Floating Instrument Platform (FLIP) is moved into location like a conventional ship; it is then ballasted with water into a vertical position. (Fritz Goro, *Life* Magazine)

Upper right: In this position, FLIP has considerable stability to resist surface waves and provides a four-story laboratory and living quarters for oceanographers. (Scripps Institution of Oceanography)

without boiling, and then to condense and collect it. The use of solar energy has thus far proved useful only in desert areas where high solar radiation is fairly constant and where water is scarce.

A solar distillation plant has recently been installed at Puerto Penasco on the coast of Sonora, Mexico, that can produce water at fifty American cents per thousand gallons. Considering the fact that water was formerly trucked in here at a cost of $6 to $12 per thousand gallons, the new rate appears to be very low.

In pilot operations using other than solar energy, the lowest costs thus far claimed are about sixty cents per thousand gallons. The cost of domestic water from usual sources—lakes, rivers, and watercourses that have been converted to lakes by dams—is in North America from about ten to thirty cents per thousand gallons, including the cost of delivery to the user; and economists have estimated that six cents per thousand gallons is the maximum that can be paid for irrigation water. But, as indicated in the preceding paragraph, the amount that will be paid for water is a matter of supply and demand.

But there are some promising signs on the horizon. One is the possibility of finding some completely new method of getting fresh water from sea water. A second is the good possibility of improving present methods of converting sea water. The derivation of chemicals from the sea has been suggested as one method of offsetting the cost of distillation; at the moment this source of income would appear to meet only a small part of the expense, but the ratio of income to cost may improve with better methods and increased demand for chemicals from the sea. And there are other possibilities for reducing cost or increasing efficiency. The township of Hempstead on Long Island, New York, has devised a plan to use the heat from burning garbage and refuse from a community of eight hundred thousand people to distill sea water to supplement a dwindling water supply. A third, and perhaps the most promising possibility, is the use of atomic energy as a source of power. The most ambitious desalting plant in the United States is being built in Key West, Florida. Using steam to heat the water, it will convert sea water at the rate of 2.62 million gallons every twenty-four hours.

A recent ingenious proposal has been to combine an underground atomic bomb explosion with the heat of the interior of the earth to provide a source of energy for the continuous distillation of sea water. If holes are bored to a depth where the temperature is in excess of 300° F. (a not-too-difficult undertaking: numerous oil wells have been drilled to a depth where the temperature exceeds the boiling point of water) and an atomic bomb exploded at the bottom, a large, very hot chamber would be created. If sea water were then run down into this chamber in a steady stream, a continuous process of distillation would take place. Steam under considerable pressure would emerge at the surface; the sea salts would be left at the bottom; and most of the radioactivity would be trapped there.

The steam could be used to generate electric power sufficient to pay all the costs of the project. Then the steam could be condensed into fresh water at nominal cost. According to one enthusiastic exponent of the project, the water could be given away as a free byproduct! This sounds a little too good to be true, but certainly the idea deserves serious study. In several areas of the world where hot springs and geysers are abundant, the heat and steam are already being used for economic ends.

In New Zealand the hot springs around Rotarua have long been used by the Maoris for cooking food and as a source of hot water. In eastern Siberia, the city of Omsk obtains its domestic hot water from a vast underground source. In Kamchatka, a power plant is being built to operate on steam from thermal waters. It is estimated that the resources of heat and power available in the U.S.S.R. from thermal waters may equal that from one hundred million tons of coal annually. Large resources of underground steam and thermal water are also available in Iceland, Japan, western North America, and elsewhere. It appears that obtaining fresh water from the sea will in the near future be a necessity, and therefore practical.

MINING THE SEA BOTTOM

It is becoming increasingly evident, partly as a byproduct of oceanographic research, that there are vast quantities of minerals, both on the bottom of the sea and beneath the bottom, that are useful to man. Among these are tin, of which large deposits are believed to occur under the Gulf of Siam, and petroleum, reservoirs of which have been discovered beneath the continental shelf in various parts of the world. Diamonds are being obtained from bottom deposits just offshore in South-West Africa; it is not yet known whether they constitute a large or a small resource.

Considerable sums are being spent by private industries in oceanic investigations. The largest investors in such research are the petroleum companies, which are studying the problems of building platforms at greater and greater depths to reach oil resources believed to extend much farther out to sea than those presently known. This research of necessity covers climate, storms, wave action, and better methods of drilling in the sea bottom. It also includes the design of ships that can be used for offshore drilling in areas too deep for platforms. A recent report in *Chemical and Engineering News* claims: "The combined efforts of petroleum companies in such places as the Gulf of Mexico, the North Sea, the Persian Gulf, and many other places probably account for more of the money for ocean research than do all other industries exploiting the seas combined."

The sea bottom is rich in deposits of manganese, nickel, cobalt, copper, and phosphate rock. When manganese nodules were dredged up from the sea bottom on the *Challenger* expedition, they were regarded as interesting curiosities. Dr. John Mero has estimated that there are 1.5 trillion tons of these nodules, and that the supply increases at a rate of ten million tons a year.

Obviously the expense of starting a mining project at the bottom of the sea is huge. It is truly "risk capital" because there is as yet no economical method of exploiting this resource. Several individuals and corporations have investigated the practicability of recovering manganese nodules from the sea. One such entrepreneur, Howard Hughes, has built a ship, the *Glomar Explorer* (not to be confused with the *Glomar Challenger,* p. 70) for exploring manganese deposits on the sea bottom and has devised a barge-like vessel—said to be as large as a nine-story building—for the purpose of mining the nodules. The success of this undertaking will doubtless be determined in the next few years.

The mineral resources of the ocean are, unlike those on land, inexhaustible. Mineral supplies on land become exhausted; many a "ghost town" testifies to prosperous mining operations that went on for years until the gold or silver, copper, coal, or other metal became depleted. The ocean is inexhaustible not simply because it is so large, but because everything that is taken out of it ultimately returns to it. Ocean processes are continuing processes. Just as the water evaporated from the ocean forms clouds that descend as rain and returns by rivers to the sea, everything taken from the ocean finally gets back to it—whether in years, centuries or eons—and thus has the potential of being used over and over again.

Notwithstanding this glowing picture, there are certain danger signs on the horizon. There is the question, for example, of whether man can destroy the sea.

CAN MAN DESTROY THE SEA?

The answer to this is, in one sense, a vigorous no. He cannot physically destroy the ocean. Even if he wanted to get rid of it, there is obviously no place to put three hundred million cubic miles of water. But though he cannot destroy the ocean, he can damage it.

Recently a large chemical company developed a plan for mining phosphate rock, which is abundantly available on the sea bottom in fairly shallow water. The company was ready to proceed when it unexpectedly discovered that the area in which it proposed to operate had been used after the war for dumping live ammunition! The plan was immediately dropped. The ocean has been used as a dumping ground for practically everything that is unwanted on land—sewage, explosives, chemical and atomic wastes. The detergents and insecticides that have come into wide use in recent years, causing large fish kills in fresh-water streams, go on out to sea with unknown but hardly salubrious results. Atomic wastes have been dumped in the sea, and wastes from atomic plants located on fresh-water streams have reached the sea.

Careful and objective studies on the subject tend to show that there is no immediate danger from the radioactivity that has thus far reached the sea. It is present in minimal quantities, well below what is considered the safe level. But some studies have shown that marine organisms tend to concentrate the radioactivity in the water in their body tissues; this of course presents a new potential danger. The use of atomic energy is, moreover, still in its infancy. The problem is likely to grow unless an early solution is found.

We can no longer think of the sea as a vast, illimitable dumping ground for products that man does not know what to do with on land. It must instead be recognized as our greatest natural resource, and one to be conserved in every possible way. So regarded, and wisely used, it can be a permanent source of raw materials, of food, of life-giving water, and of recreation, enjoyment and adventure.

Index

Numbers in parentheses indicate color plates; those in italics indicate pages on which black and white illustrations appear.

This book was planned and produced by Paul Steiner and the staff of Chanticleer Press. Editor: Milton Rugoff. Art Director: Ulrich Ruchti. Production: Gudrun Buettner, assisted by Emma Staffelbach. Printed by Kingsport Press, Kingsport, Tennessee.